WELCOME TO THE JUNGLE

Surviving the Chaos and Building a Roadmap to Digital Transformation Success

ERIC KIMBERLING

Welcome to the Jungle
Surviving the Chaos and Building a Roadmap to Digital Transformation Success

ERIC KIMBERLING

First Edition 2025

Table of Contents

Part I: UNDERSTANDING THE DIGITAL LANDSCAPE

Chapter 1

Introduction: The Digital Jungle

In the modern era, businesses, organizations, and individuals find themselves navigating an increasingly complex digital landscape. Like explorers stepping into an uncharted jungle, we must learn to adapt to shifting terrain, overcome unpredictable challenges, and uncover hidden opportunities. Navigating the Digital Jungle serves as a guide to those embarking on the journey of digital transformation, equipping them with the strategies and tools necessary to thrive in an era where technology is rapidly reshaping the way we work, communicate, and innovate.

The Digital Jungle: Complexity, Opportunity, and Risk

A jungle is an intricate ecosystem—full of life yet unpredictable, teeming with opportunities but fraught with dangers. The digital world mirrors this complexity, with an interconnected network of technologies, platforms, and innovations that continuously evolve. Automation, artificial intelligence, cloud computing, and cybersecurity have become intertwined with business strategy and customer expectations, forcing organizations to adapt or risk being left behind.

Thriving in a jungle requires survival skills, adaptability, and a keen sense of direction. Similarly, success in the digital world demands strategic thinking, data-driven decision-making, and an openness to continuous learning. Businesses that fail to modernize often become entangled in outdated systems, struggling with inefficiencies and rising costs. Others find themselves lost in the overwhelming flood of data, unable to extract meaningful insights. Some are simply outpaced by competitors who embrace digital innovation and respond quickly to emerging trends.

However, for those who understand how to leverage technology effectively, the jungle is not a place of fear—it is a land of opportunity. Digital transformation enables organizations to streamline operations, improve customer experiences, and unlock new sources of revenue. Those who embrace this shift strategically position themselves for sustainable growth, innovation, and long-term success.

Why Digital Transformation Matters Now More Than Ever

Technology is advancing at an unprecedented pace, fundamentally reshaping industries, economies, and everyday life. Organizations that once relied on traditional business models are now facing mounting pressure to adapt. Consumer expectations have shifted, demanding seamless, fast, and highly personalized experiences. Companies that fail to deliver risk losing market share to digital-first competitors.

The rise of disruptive startups has also changed the competitive landscape. These agile, tech-driven businesses leverage automation, data analytics, and AI to drive efficiency, lower costs, and deliver superior products and services. Meanwhile, global connectivity has erased geographical barriers, allowing organizations to reach broader markets, collaborate remotely, and scale operations in ways that were previously impossible.

Data has emerged as one of the most valuable assets in the digital economy. Companies that effectively collect, analyze, and apply data can optimize operations, enhance customer engagement, and gain predictive insights into market trends. However, as businesses become more reliant on digital systems, cybersecurity has become a growing concern. Protecting digital assets is no longer optional—it is a necessity for survival.

For business leaders, entrepreneurs, and decision-makers, understanding these forces is critical. Staying competitive in our current digital-first world requires a proactive approach to technology, strategy, and innovation.

A Roadmap for Digital Success

Just as an explorer would not enter a jungle without a map, a survival kit, and a well-defined strategy, businesses must approach digital transformation with a clear plan. This book aims to demystify the complexities of digital change, offering a structured framework for leveraging technology to drive growth and efficiency.

Understanding the Digital Ecosystem is the foundation of transformation. Technology is no longer just an operational tool; it is the backbone of modern business strategy. We will explore how artificial intelligence and machine learning are revolutionizing business processes, cloud computing is enabling scalable solutions, and cybersecurity is becoming essential in an era of increasing digital threats. Additionally, we will examine the growing role of automation and robotics in reshaping industries and workforce dynamics.

Strategic Digital Leadership is crucial for guiding organizations through transformation. Leaders today must foster a culture of innovation, agility, and adaptability. Cross-functional collaboration between IT, marketing, finance, and operations is essential to bridging the gap between traditional business models and digital-first approaches. Throughout this book, we will discuss the leadership strategies that drive successful digital adoption and long-term sustainability.

Overcoming Challenges in Digital Transformation is a key component of navigating this landscape. Many digital initiatives fail due to resistance to change, lack of strategic clarity, skill gaps, and integration issues. This book will provide insights into best practices for managing change, ensuring smooth implementation, and addressing obstacles before they become major roadblocks.

Harnessing Data and Automation for Decision-Making is central to digital success. Organizations that can extract meaningful insights from vast amounts of data gain a competitive advantage. We will explore data analytics, business intelligence tools, and automation strategies that enable companies to operate proactively rather than reactively.

Creating a Sustainable Digital Future is about more than short-term gains. Digital transformation is an ongoing journey, not a one-time project. Companies must build scalable and adaptable systems that evolve alongside technology. Fostering a culture of continuous learning ensures that teams remain ahead of industry shifts. Balancing profitability with ethical and sustainable business practices is also increasingly important in the contemporary landscape.

By the end of this book, readers will have a comprehensive understanding of how to navigate the digital jungle—anticipating risks, seizing opportunities, and building resilient organizations prepared for the future.

Who This Book is For

Digital transformation affects every industry, from finance and healthcare to retail and manufacturing. This book is designed for business leaders and executives looking to drive innovation, entrepreneurs building digital-first companies, and IT professionals responsible for implementing transformation initiatives. It also serves as a valuable resource for marketers leveraging digital tools to enhance customer engagement, as well as students and professionals eager to understand how technology is shaping the future of business.

Regardless of your role or industry, the principles of digital transformation are universal. Understanding how to navigate technological change is no longer optional—it is essential for long-term success.

Embarking on the Digital Journey

Much like early explorers who braved unknown territories with only a map, survival tools, and a resilient mindset, businesses today must approach digital transformation with strategy, adaptability, and innovation. The digital jungle can be daunting, full of challenges that can disrupt even the most established organizations. However, those who approach it with a willingness to learn and evolve will discover untapped opportunities, new efficiencies, and sustainable competitive advantages.

Technology is not the enemy—it is the key to future success. The question is not whether digital transformation is necessary, but how to navigate it effectively. This book will serve as your guide through the complexities of the digital world, helping you avoid pitfalls, leverage emerging technologies, and carve a path toward digital excellence.

The journey ahead is challenging, but the rewards are vast for those who embrace change.

Welcome to the jungle—let's navigate it together.

Chapter 2

The Evolution of Digital Strategies

The journey of digital transformation is not a recent phenomenon—it has been unfolding for decades, shaped by technological breakthroughs and shifting business landscapes. From the early days of computing to the rise of artificial intelligence, each era has introduced new paradigms that have redefined how organizations operate and compete. Understanding this evolution provides crucial context for navigating today's digital challenges and opportunities.

The first significant wave of digital transformation began in the mid-20th century with the advent of computers and early automation. The mainframe era of the 1950s and 1960s saw large-scale businesses adopting computing power to handle complex calculations and data processing, marking the first steps toward digitization. However, access to these systems was limited to governments and large corporations due to high costs and technical constraints.

During this period, companies like IBM dominated the landscape with room-sized computers that cost millions of dollars and required specialized operators. The famous saying "Nobody gets fired for buying IBM" emerged during this era, reflecting the risk-averse approach many organizations took toward technology adoption. While these early systems provided computational power previously unimaginable, they also introduced the first lessons about the importance of user training, system reliability, and the hidden costs of technology implementation.

The 1970s and 1980s ushered in the age of personal computing and enterprise software, making digital tools more accessible. Companies like IBM, Apple, and Microsoft brought computing power to the masses, while database management and early enterprise resource planning (ERP) systems laid the groundwork for digital business operations. This period marked the beginning of widespread business process automation, as organizations began to recognize that computers could do more than just calculate—they could fundamentally change how work was performed.

However, this era also produced some of the first high-profile digital transformation failures. The introduction of ERP systems, while revolutionary in concept, proved challenging for many organizations to implement successfully. Companies that had operated with manual or semi-automated processes for decades suddenly found themselves trying to adapt to rigid, standardized software systems that required significant changes to established workflows and procedures.

One notable early failure occurred at FoxMeyer Drug, a pharmaceutical distributor that was one of the largest companies in the United States in the 1990s. The company's attempt to implement an ERP system from SAP, combined with warehouse automation, resulted in a series of problems that ultimately contributed to the company's bankruptcy. The implementation was plagued by unrealistic timelines, inadequate testing, insufficient training, and a fundamental misunderstanding of how the new system would integrate with existing business processes. The failure demonstrated that technology implementation without proper change management and realistic planning could destroy even large, established companies.

By the 1990s, the rise of the internet triggered an explosion of connectivity and information sharing. Businesses that embraced web technologies gained unprecedented access to global markets, giving rise to e-commerce giants like Amazon and transforming industries such as finance, retail, and media. The late 1990s also saw the emergence of customer relationship management (CRM) systems, which helped businesses leverage data to understand and engage customers more effectively.

The dot-com boom and subsequent bust provided important lessons about the relationship between technology and business strategy. Companies like Pets.com and Webvan raised hundreds of millions of dollars based on the premise that internet technology alone could disrupt traditional industries. However, these companies failed because they focused primarily on technology without developing sustainable business models or understanding their customers' real needs. The failure of these companies demonstrated that technology is only valuable when it solves genuine business problems and creates real value for customers.

Conversely, companies like Amazon survived the dot-com crash because they combined technological innovation with sound business fundamentals. Amazon's success wasn't just about building a website—it was about reimagining the entire customer experience, from product discovery and ordering to fulfillment and delivery. The company invested heavily in logistics, customer service, and technology infrastructure, creating a platform that could scale efficiently as the business grew.

The early 2000s introduced the social media and mobile revolution, redefining consumer behavior and business interactions. Platforms like Facebook, Twitter, and LinkedIn created new channels for marketing and engagement, while the widespread adoption of smartphones and mobile applications enabled on-the-go digital experiences. Organizations that quickly adapted to this shift leveraged digital marketing, real-time customer engagement, and mobile commerce to stay ahead.

This period also saw the emergence of new categories of digital transformation failures. Many traditional media companies struggled to adapt to the shift from print to digital, underestimating both the speed of change and the fundamental differences between digital and traditional media business models. Newspapers that had dominated local markets for decades found themselves competing against digital-native companies that could deliver news faster, more interactively, and at lower cost.

The music industry provides a particularly instructive example of digital disruption and adaptation challenges. When digital music sharing became popular in the late 1990s and early 2000s, major record labels initially responded with lawsuits and technological barriers rather than embracing new distribution models. This approach allowed companies like Apple to enter the market with iTunes, fundamentally changing how music was sold and consumed. The industry's initial resistance to digital transformation resulted in years of declining revenues and market share losses that could have been avoided with more proactive adaptation strategies.

The last decade has been characterized by the rapid adoption of cloud computing, artificial intelligence, big data, and automation. The ability to store, process, and analyze vast amounts of data has fueled smarter decision-making, predictive analytics, and hyper-personalized customer experiences. The COVID-19 pandemic further accelerated digital transformation, forcing businesses to adopt remote work, e-commerce, and digital collaboration tools at an unprecedented pace.

Several Landmark Developments Shaping Today's Digital Strategies

The digital landscape is evolving at an unprecedented pace, reshaping industries, consumer expectations, and competitive dynamics. Several key developments have driven today's digital strategies, presenting both opportunities and challenges for businesses navigating this digital jungle. Companies that successfully integrate these transformative forces into their strategic roadmaps will not only survive but thrive in the digital economy.

The Shift from Digitization to Digital Transformation

In the past, businesses primarily focused on digitization—converting analog processes into digital formats. This phase was about eliminating paper-based workflows, digitizing records, and using software to improve efficiency. However, the current era of digital transformation extends far beyond simple automation; it requires reimagining business models, processes, and customer experiences using digital-first strategies.

The distinction between digitization and digital transformation is crucial for understanding why many initiatives fail. Digitization projects typically focus on replicating existing processes in digital form, while digital transformation requires fundamental changes to how organizations operate and create value. Companies that approach transformation as merely a technology upgrade often miss the strategic opportunities that digital capabilities can create.

One of the most compelling examples of successful digital transformation is Netflix. Initially a DVD rental company, Netflix recognized the potential of digital streaming and completely overhauled its business model to become a content streaming powerhouse. The transformation wasn't just about technology—it required developing new capabilities in content recommendation, data analytics, and original content production. Today, Netflix invests heavily in AI-driven recommendations, data analytics, and original content production, leveraging technology to stay ahead of the competition.

Netflix's transformation demonstrates several key principles of successful digital strategy. First, the company anticipated technological trends and began investing in streaming capabilities before they became mainstream. Second, Netflix recognized that digital transformation would require new business models, not just new technology. The shift from physical DVD rentals to digital streaming required different pricing strategies, content acquisition approaches, and customer relationship models. Third, the company invested heavily in data analytics and AI to create personalized experiences that would differentiate it from competitors.

However, Netflix's journey also illustrates the ongoing nature of digital transformation. The company has had to continuously evolve its strategy as new competitors like Disney+, HBO Max, and Apple TV+ have entered the market. Success in digital transformation requires not just a one-time change but ongoing adaptation and innovation.

Similarly, Uber revolutionized the transportation industry by using mobile technology, real-time data, and cloud computing to create a seamless ride-hailing experience. By integrating AI-powered pricing algorithms, GPS tracking, and digital payments, Uber transformed personal transportation into an on-demand, data-driven service. The company's success wasn't just about creating a mobile app—it was about reimagining the entire transportation experience and building a platform that could connect drivers and riders efficiently.

Uber's transformation of the transportation industry also demonstrates how digital strategies can create network effects that become increasingly powerful over time. As more drivers joined the platform, wait times decreased for riders. As more riders used the service, income opportunities increased for drivers. This virtuous cycle, enabled by digital technology, created competitive advantages that traditional taxi companies found difficult to match.

However, Uber's journey also highlights some of the challenges and risks associated with digital transformation. The company has faced regulatory challenges in many markets, struggled with profitability despite rapid growth, and dealt with various operational and cultural issues. These challenges remind us that digital transformation involves more than just technology—it requires addressing regulatory, financial, operational, and cultural factors that can impact long-term success.

For businesses today, digital transformation is a necessity. Companies that fail to evolve risk becoming obsolete as competitors leverage technology to innovate and redefine industry norms. The key is to approach transformation strategically, focusing on creating real value for customers rather than simply implementing new technologies.

Cloud Computing and Scalability

The rise of cloud computing has revolutionized digital strategy, enabling businesses to scale operations efficiently without the need for heavy infrastructure investments. Cloud platforms such as Amazon Web Services (AWS), Microsoft Azure, and Google Cloud provide on-demand computing power, storage, and machine learning capabilities, allowing businesses to adapt to changing demands rapidly.

Cloud computing has fundamentally changed the economics of technology investment. In the pre-cloud era, organizations had to make large upfront investments in hardware and software, often overestimating their needs to avoid capacity constraints. This approach tied up capital and made it difficult to adjust technology resources as business needs changed. Cloud computing enables organizations to pay only for the resources they use and scale up or down as needed.

One of the most significant advantages of cloud computing is its ability to level the playing field for startups and smaller businesses. In the past, large enterprises had the upper hand due to their ability to invest in massive IT infrastructure. Today, even small companies can leverage enterprise-grade computing power, enabling them to compete with industry giants. Startups like Airbnb and Dropbox were able to scale rapidly by leveraging cloud infrastructure rather than building their own data centers.

However, cloud adoption has also created new challenges and failure modes. Organizations that migrate to the cloud without properly planning for security, compliance, and cost management often experience significant problems. The 2019 Capital One data breach, which exposed information from over 100 million customers, occurred because of a misconfigured cloud security setting. This incident highlighted the importance of understanding cloud security models and ensuring that organizations have the expertise necessary to manage cloud environments safely.

Cloud computing also enhances business continuity and disaster recovery. Unlike traditional on-premise systems that are vulnerable to outages, cloud-based solutions ensure minimal downtime through redundancy and geographically distributed data centers. This resilience is crucial for businesses that rely on uninterrupted service delivery, such as e-commerce platforms and financial institutions.

The COVID-19 pandemic demonstrated the value of cloud-based business continuity planning. Organizations with cloud-based systems were generally able to transition to remote work more quickly and efficiently than those relying on on-premise infrastructure. Companies that had invested in cloud-based collaboration tools, communication platforms, and remote access capabilities found themselves better prepared for the sudden shift to distributed work models.

Furthermore, the cost-effectiveness and flexibility of cloud solutions empower organizations to scale up or down based on demand. Instead of over-investing in infrastructure that may become obsolete, businesses can subscribe to scalable cloud services, optimizing costs while maintaining agility. This flexibility has become particularly valuable in industries with seasonal demand patterns or rapidly changing market conditions.

However, cloud cost management has become a significant challenge for many organizations. Without proper governance and monitoring, cloud costs can escalate quickly as teams provision resources without considering long-term financial implications. Several high-profile companies have reported unexpected cloud bills that exceeded budgets by substantial margins, highlighting the importance of cloud financial management practices.

Data-Driven Decision-Making and AI

The ability to collect, analyze, and leverage vast amounts of data has become a game-changer for businesses. Big data analytics and AI-driven insights allow companies to make informed decisions based on real-time information rather than intuition or historical trends. However, the implementation of AI and data analytics systems has also produced numerous high-profile failures that offer important lessons for organizations embarking on similar initiatives.

AI-powered data analytics enables businesses to predict customer behavior using advanced machine learning models, optimize supply chains by forecasting demand fluctuations and minimizing waste, enhance marketing campaigns through hyper-personalized recommendations and dynamic content adjustments, and automate business processes, reducing manual effort and increasing efficiency.

Amazon's AI-driven recommendation engine provides an excellent example of successful AI implementation. The system analyzes customer purchase history, browsing behavior, and demographic data to personalize product suggestions, increasing conversion rates and customer satisfaction. Amazon's recommendation system reportedly drives 35% of the company's revenue, demonstrating the significant business impact that well-implemented AI systems can achieve.

However, Amazon's AI journey hasn't been without challenges. The company's attempt to develop an AI-powered recruiting tool had to be abandoned when it was discovered that the system exhibited bias against women. The AI had been trained on historical hiring data that reflected existing gender biases in the tech industry, causing it to systematically downgrade resumes that included words associated with women. This failure highlighted the importance of addressing bias in AI training data and the need for diverse perspectives in AI development teams.

Similarly, AI is transforming the finance industry, where machine learning models detect fraudulent transactions in real-time, reducing financial risks. JPMorgan Chase's COIN (Contract Intelligence) platform uses natural language processing to analyze legal documents and extract important data points, reducing the time required for contract review from hundreds of thousands of hours to seconds. This application of AI has generated significant cost savings while improving accuracy and consistency in contract analysis.

However, the financial services industry has also experienced notable AI failures. Knight Capital Group, a major market maker, lost $440 million in 45 minutes in 2012 due to a malfunctioning algorithmic trading system. The system began executing erroneous trades at high volume, and the company was unable to stop the losses quickly enough to prevent catastrophic damage. Knight Capital was eventually acquired by a competitor, demonstrating how AI and algorithmic failures can threaten the existence of even large, established companies.

Organizations that invest in AI and data-driven decision-making gain a competitive edge by proactively responding to market trends, improving operational efficiency, and offering personalized customer experiences. However, successful AI implementation requires more than just deploying advanced algorithms. Companies must invest in data quality, develop AI governance frameworks, and build organizational capabilities to manage AI systems effectively.

The healthcare industry provides another compelling example of both AI success and failure. IBM's Watson for Oncology was intended to revolutionize cancer treatment by analyzing vast amounts of medical literature and patient data to recommend treatment options. Despite significant investment and high-profile partnerships with major cancer centers, Watson for Oncology failed to deliver meaningful improvements in patient outcomes. The system struggled with incomplete data, biased training sets, and the complexity of oncological decision-making that couldn't be easily reduced to algorithmic rules.

In contrast, Google's DeepMind has achieved remarkable success in medical AI applications, particularly in ophthalmology and protein folding prediction. The key difference lies in the focus on specific, well-defined problems with high-quality training data and clear success metrics. DeepMind's approach demonstrates that AI can achieve breakthrough results when applied to appropriate problems with sufficient data and domain expertise.

The Rise of Digital-First Customer Experiences

Today's consumers expect seamless, personalized experiences across multiple digital touchpoints. Businesses have moved beyond traditional marketing approaches, adopting an omnichannel strategy that integrates social media, mobile apps, chatbots, and e-commerce platforms to create frictionless interactions.

The evolution toward digital-first customer experiences has been driven by changing consumer expectations and the proliferation of digital devices and platforms. Customers now expect to interact with brands across multiple channels and devices while maintaining a consistent experience. This shift has forced companies to rethink their customer engagement strategies and invest in technologies that enable seamless omnichannel experiences.

Brands that excel in digital-first customer experiences focus on personalization using AI to tailor content, recommendations, and offers to individual customers, real-time engagement providing instant customer support via chatbots and AI-powered assistants, mobile-first design ensuring websites and apps are optimized for mobile users, and omnichannel consistency seamlessly integrating online and offline experiences.

Starbucks has mastered digital engagement through its mobile app, which integrates loyalty rewards, mobile payments, and AI-driven product recommendations. Customers can order ahead, customize their drinks, and earn rewards, creating a convenient and personalized customer journey. The Starbucks app has become so successful that mobile orders now represent a significant portion of the company's transactions, demonstrating how digital experiences can drive both customer satisfaction and business results.

The success of Starbucks' digital strategy illustrates several important principles. First, the app solves real customer problems by reducing wait times and enabling customization. Second, it integrates loyalty rewards with the ordering experience, creating incentives for continued use. Third, the system uses data analytics to personalize recommendations and offers, increasing the relevance of marketing communications. Finally, the app creates a seamless bridge between digital and physical experiences, as customers can order digitally but still receive personal service in stores.

Similarly, Nike leverages digital experiences by combining e-commerce, mobile apps, and social media-driven campaigns to build a community-driven brand. Consumers engage with the brand through fitness apps, AR-powered sneaker try-ons, and exclusive online drops, enhancing brand loyalty. Nike's SNKRS app has become a cultural phenomenon among sneaker enthusiasts, creating a sense of community and exclusivity that drives both engagement and sales.

However, creating successful digital-first customer experiences is more challenging than it appears. Many companies have struggled with omnichannel implementation, often creating fragmented experiences that frustrate customers rather than delight them. The key challenges include data integration across multiple systems and touchpoints, consistent branding and messaging across all channels, real-time synchronization of inventory and customer information, and personalization that feels helpful rather than invasive.

Target's early attempts at omnichannel retail provide lessons about the complexity of digital customer experience transformation. The company's initial efforts to integrate online and in-store experiences were hampered by legacy systems that couldn't share data effectively. Customers would see products available online that weren't in stock at local stores, or vice versa. Order fulfillment was inconsistent, with some online orders taking much longer to process than others. These problems created customer frustration and damaged the brand's reputation for reliability.

Target eventually succeeded in its omnichannel transformation, but only after significant investment in system integration, employee training, and process redesign. The company's experience demonstrates that successful digital customer experiences require coordinated changes across technology, operations, and organizational culture.

Businesses that prioritize frictionless, engaging digital experiences will build stronger customer relationships and long-term brand loyalty. However, achieving this requires more than just implementing new technologies—it requires understanding customer needs, designing experiences that solve real problems, and continuously optimizing based on customer feedback and behavior data.

Cybersecurity and Digital Trust

As businesses become more digital, cybersecurity has emerged as a critical pillar of strategy. The growing number of cyber threats, data breaches, and ransomware attacks makes it imperative for organizations to prioritize security, compliance, and digital ethics. The consequences of cybersecurity failures have become increasingly severe, affecting not only the targeted organizations but also their customers, partners, and entire industries.

The evolution of cyber threats has paralleled the advancement of digital technologies. As organizations have become more connected and data-driven, they have also become more vulnerable to sophisticated attacks. Cybercriminals have evolved from individual hackers seeking recognition to organized criminal enterprises and nation-state actors with substantial resources and advanced capabilities.

The 2017 Equifax data breach exemplifies the devastating impact that cybersecurity failures can have on organizations and individuals. The breach exposed personal information of 147 million consumers, including Social Security numbers, birth dates, addresses, and in some cases, driver's license numbers and credit card numbers. The attack exploited a known vulnerability in web application software that Equifax had failed to patch despite being aware of the security flaw for months.

The consequences of the Equifax breach were severe and long-lasting. The company faced over $700 million in fines and settlements, its stock price declined significantly, several executives resigned, and the company's reputation was permanently damaged. More importantly, millions of consumers faced increased risk of identity theft and financial fraud. The incident highlighted how cybersecurity failures at one organization can have cascading effects throughout the economy.

Consumers are increasingly aware of data privacy issues and demand transparency regarding how their information is used. Companies that fail to protect customer data risk losing trust, facing regulatory fines, and suffering reputational damage. The implementation of regulations like the General Data Protection Regulation (GDPR) in Europe and the California Consumer Privacy Act (CCPA) has created legal requirements for data protection and given consumers more control over their personal information.

The Colonial Pipeline ransomware attack in 2021 demonstrated how cybersecurity incidents can affect critical infrastructure and have broader economic impacts. The attack forced the shutdown of the largest fuel pipeline system in the United States for several days, causing gasoline shortages and price increases across the southeastern United States. The incident highlighted the interconnected nature of digital systems and the potential for cyber attacks to affect physical infrastructure and economic stability.

Key cybersecurity strategies include implementing AI-driven threat detection to identify and mitigate cyber threats in real time, encrypting sensitive data to prevent unauthorized access, complying with global data protection regulations such as GDPR and CCPA, and educating employees on cybersecurity best practices to prevent phishing attacks and insider threats.

However, cybersecurity implementation often faces challenges that can undermine its effectiveness. Many organizations treat cybersecurity as a technology problem rather than a business risk management issue. This approach can lead to investments in security tools without adequate attention to processes, training, and governance. Additionally, cybersecurity often competes with other business priorities for resources and attention, leading to underinvestment in security capabilities.

The SolarWinds supply chain attack in 2020 revealed the complexity of modern cybersecurity threats and the limitations of traditional security approaches. The attack compromised SolarWinds' Orion software, which was used by thousands of organizations including government agencies and major corporations. By infiltrating a trusted software supplier, the attackers were able to access the networks of numerous high-value targets without directly attacking them. This incident highlighted the importance of supply chain security and the need for organizations to consider the security practices of their technology vendors and partners.

Companies that prioritize digital trust gain a competitive advantage by demonstrating their commitment to security and privacy. Consumers are more likely to engage with brands that value transparency and ethical data practices. Organizations that invest in robust cybersecurity programs not only protect themselves from threats but also build customer confidence and enable new digital business models that require high levels of trust.

The Future: AI-Driven Automation and Emerging Technologies

Looking ahead, AI-driven automation, blockchain, and immersive technologies are set to define the next frontier of digital strategy. Businesses that anticipate these shifts and invest in emerging technologies will be better positioned for long-term success, while those that ignore these trends risk being disrupted by more agile competitors.

AI-powered automation will continue transforming industries by enabling self-learning systems that optimize operations, predict trends, and enhance customer interactions. AI-driven chatbots, robotic process automation (RPA), and smart assistants will become increasingly prevalent, handling routine tasks and enabling human workers to focus on higher-value activities.

The manufacturing industry provides compelling examples of AI-driven automation success and failure. General Electric's Predix platform was intended to create an industrial internet that would optimize manufacturing processes using AI and IoT sensors. Despite significant investment, the platform failed to gain widespread adoption and was eventually scaled back significantly. The failure was attributed to unclear value propositions, complex implementation requirements, and insufficient customer development.

In contrast, companies like Siemens have successfully implemented AI-driven automation in their manufacturing processes. Siemens' digital factory initiatives use AI to optimize production schedules, predict equipment failures, and improve quality control. The key difference lies in the focused, incremental approach that solves specific problems rather than attempting to transform entire industries simultaneously.

Blockchain technology is revolutionizing industries beyond finance, enabling transparent, decentralized transactions in supply chains, real estate, and digital identity verification. However, blockchain implementation has been marked by both breakthrough successes and notable failures. Many organizations have struggled with blockchain projects that were technically sound but lacked clear business cases or user adoption strategies.

Walmart's use of blockchain for food traceability demonstrates successful blockchain implementation. The system enables the company to trace the source of food products within seconds rather than days, improving food safety and reducing the impact of contamination incidents. The success of this implementation stems from its focus on solving a specific business problem with clear value for both the company and its customers.

The metaverse is emerging as the next iteration of the internet, where businesses create immersive, digital environments for social interaction, work, and commerce. Companies like Meta (formerly Facebook) and Microsoft are already investing heavily in virtual reality (VR) and augmented reality (AR) to reshape how people interact online.

However, metaverse investments have produced mixed results so far. Meta's significant investment in metaverse technologies has yet to generate substantial revenue, and user adoption of VR platforms remains limited. The company's experience highlights the challenges of investing in emerging technologies before markets are ready for widespread adoption.

Organizations that explore AI, blockchain, and immersive technologies now will future-proof their business models, gaining an early-mover advantage in these emerging digital ecosystems. However, success requires balancing innovation with practical business considerations, focusing on specific use cases that create real value rather than implementing technology for its own sake.

Learning from Digital Transformation Failures

The consistent pattern of digital transformation failures across industries and decades reveals several important lessons for organizations embarking on transformation initiatives. Understanding these failure modes is crucial for avoiding common pitfalls and increasing the likelihood of success.

One of the most common causes of failure is the lack of clear strategic vision and objectives. Many organizations begin digital transformation projects without clearly defining what success looks like or how the initiative will create value for customers and the business. This lack of clarity leads to scope creep, conflicting priorities, and ultimately, projects that consume resources without delivering meaningful results.

The German airport Berlin Brandenburg provides a cautionary tale about the importance of clear project management and realistic planning in large-scale digital initiatives. The airport's opening was delayed for nearly a decade due to technical problems with complex digital systems, including fire safety, baggage handling, and building management systems. The project's cost ballooned from an initial estimate of €2 billion to over €6 billion, and the delays had significant economic and reputational consequences for the region.

Another frequent cause of failure is inadequate change management and user adoption strategies. Organizations often focus heavily on technology implementation while underestimating the challenges of getting employees and customers to adopt new systems and processes. Successful digital transformation requires not just new technology but new ways of working, which can create resistance and confusion if not managed carefully.

The implementation of electronic health records (EHR) systems in healthcare provides numerous examples of change management challenges. While EHR systems can improve patient care and operational efficiency, many implementations have struggled with user adoption, workflow disruption, and physician satisfaction. Successful EHR implementations typically involve extensive physician engagement, comprehensive training programs, and careful attention to workflow design that minimizes disruption to patient care.

Technical complexity and integration challenges represent another major source of digital transformation failures. Many organizations underestimate the difficulty of integrating new systems with existing technology infrastructure, leading to cost overruns, delays, and performance problems. Legacy systems that have accumulated over decades can be particularly challenging to integrate with modern digital platforms.

The UK's NHS patient record system provides an example of how technical complexity can derail large-scale digital initiatives. The £12 billion National Programme for IT was intended to create a unified electronic health record system across the entire National Health Service. However, the project encountered significant technical challenges related to system integration, data migration, and performance. The program was ultimately abandoned after consuming billions of pounds without delivering the intended benefits.

Finally, unrealistic expectations about implementation timelines and complexity often contribute to digital transformation failures. Organizations may expect rapid results from complex transformation initiatives, leading to rushed implementations that skip important steps like testing, training, and pilot programs. Digital transformation is typically a multi-year journey that requires patience, persistence, and continuous adjustment based on lessons learned.

Navigating the Continuing Evolution

The evolution of digital strategies reflects a continuous cycle of disruption and adaptation. From early computing to AI-driven decision-making, businesses have had to embrace change to remain competitive. The organizations that have succeeded are those that approached digital transformation strategically, with clear objectives, adequate resources, and realistic expectations about the challenges involved.

As we continue our journey through the digital jungle, understanding these historical shifts and key developments will help us navigate the challenges ahead. The organizations that succeed will be those that remain agile, customer-centric, and ready to harness the next wave of digital innovation while learning from the failures and successes of those who have gone before.

The digital landscape will continue to evolve, presenting new opportunities and challenges for organizations across all industries. Success will require not just technological sophistication but also strategic thinking, effective change management, and a deep understanding of how digital technologies can create value for customers and businesses. Those who master these capabilities will thrive in the digital jungle, while those who ignore these lessons risk being left behind in an increasingly competitive and fast-moving digital economy.

The key to successful navigation lies not in avoiding all risks but in understanding how to manage them effectively while seizing the opportunities that digital transformation can create. This requires a balanced approach that combines technological innovation with sound business fundamentals, strategic planning with agile execution, and ambitious vision with practical implementation. The companies that achieve this balance will be the ones that not only survive but thrive in the digital jungle of the future.

Chapter 3

Core Technologies Driving Change

Now, more than ever, in the fast-paced digital landscape, businesses must leverage a strong technological foundation to remain agile, competitive, and customer-centric. The ability to integrate cutting-edge technologies into core business functions is no longer a luxury—it is a necessity for organizations striving for operational efficiency and strategic growth. However, the path to successful technology implementation is fraught with challenges, and the consequences of failure can be devastating.

The sobering reality is that between 60 and 90 percent of ERP implementations are considered failures or significantly underperform expectations. This staggering failure rate has remained consistent across decades of technological advancement, suggesting that the challenges are not merely technical but fundamentally rooted in organizational, strategic, and change management issues. Understanding both the potential and the pitfalls of core business technologies is essential for executives navigating digital transformation initiatives.

At the heart of digital transformation are Enterprise Resource Planning (ERP) systems and Customer Relationship Management (CRM) platforms, which serve as the backbone of modern businesses. ERP systems streamline core operations by centralizing finance, human resources, supply chain management, and inventory control, ensuring seamless collaboration across departments. Leading ERP solutions like SAP S/4HANA, Oracle NetSuite, and Microsoft Dynamics 365 empower businesses with real-time data visibility, process automation, and predictive analytics when implemented successfully.

However, the history of ERP implementations is littered with cautionary tales that demonstrate how technological sophistication alone cannot guarantee success. Hershey's infamous ERP disaster in 1999 serves as a stark reminder of how implementation failures can threaten even well-established companies. The candy manufacturer's attempt to simultaneously implement SAP, Siebel CRM, and Manugistics supply chain software resulted in a $100 million revenue loss during the critical Halloween candy season. Orders went unfulfilled, distributors couldn't get products, and the company's stock price plummeted. The failure stemmed from an overly aggressive timeline, inadequate testing, insufficient user training, and a fundamental underestimation of the complexity involved in integrating multiple enterprise systems simultaneously.

Similarly, CRM platforms such as Salesforce, HubSpot, and Zoho CRM enable organizations to enhance customer experiences, track interactions, and improve sales performance. By leveraging AI-powered insights, these systems help businesses personalize customer engagement, predict purchasing behavior, and optimize marketing efforts. Yet CRM implementations frequently fail when organizations focus on technology deployment rather than business process transformation and user adoption.

The pharmaceutical giant Pfizer learned this lesson during its global CRM implementation in the early 2000s. The company invested millions in a Siebel CRM system intended to improve sales force effectiveness across multiple countries. However, the implementation struggled with cultural resistance, inadequate change management, and failure to account for regional differences in sales processes and regulatory requirements. Sales representatives found the system cumbersome and irrelevant to their daily work, leading to poor adoption rates and minimal return on investment. The failure highlighted how global technology implementations must account for local variations in business practices and cultural attitudes toward technology.

Beyond ERP and CRM, technologies like Business Intelligence (BI), Artificial Intelligence (AI), Cloud Computing, and Robotic Process Automation (RPA) further enhance efficiency and decision-making when properly implemented. However, each of these technologies presents unique implementation challenges that organizations must navigate carefully. When integrated successfully, these solutions create a connected, data-driven enterprise, allowing organizations to adapt to market changes and drive sustainable growth.

Understanding and implementing these core technologies is crucial for organizations aiming to harness digital tools effectively, optimize operations, and future-proof their business models in an era of rapid technological evolution. However, success requires more than just selecting the right software—it demands a comprehensive approach that addresses organizational readiness, change management, and realistic expectations about implementation complexity and timelines.

Enterprise Resource Planning (ERP) Systems: The Backbone of Business Operations

In the interconnected business environment of today, Enterprise Resource Planning (ERP) systems serve as the central nervous system of organizations, seamlessly integrating essential business functions such as finance, supply chain management, human resources, procurement, and inventory control into a unified platform. By eliminating silos between departments, ERP systems enable real-time data sharing, streamline workflows, and enhance operational efficiency, providing businesses with a strong foundation for growth and scalability.

However, the journey to successful ERP implementation is treacherous, with failure rates that have remained stubbornly high despite decades of technological advancement and implementation methodology improvements. The complexity of modern business operations, combined with the technical challenges of system integration and the human challenges of organizational change, creates a perfect storm for implementation disasters.

Traditionally, ERP systems were monolithic, highly customized, and required significant infrastructure investments, making them rigid and difficult to scale. Companies like SAP and Oracle dominated the market with their on-premise ERP solutions, which demanded heavy upfront costs in hardware, implementation, and maintenance. While these systems provided robust functionalities, their lack of flexibility became a challenge for businesses needing to adapt quickly to market changes.

The automotive industry provides compelling examples of both ERP success and spectacular failure. Ford Motor Company's ambitious attempt to implement a single, global ERP system in the late 1990s and early 2000s resulted in one of the most expensive corporate IT failures in history. The company spent over $400 million on the initiative before ultimately abandoning it. The failure was attributed to the system's inability to handle Ford's complex global manufacturing processes, inadequate customization for regional requirements, and resistance from local operations that had developed their own effective systems over decades.

The Ford failure illustrates a critical lesson about ERP implementations: one size does not fit all, even within a single organization. Different business units, geographic regions, and operational contexts may require different approaches to system design and implementation. Organizations that attempt to force standardization without adequately accounting for legitimate business variations often encounter resistance and operational disruptions that can derail entire projects.

In contrast, Toyota's approach to ERP implementation demonstrates how careful planning and gradual rollout can lead to success. Rather than attempting a single, massive implementation, Toyota implemented its ERP system in phases, starting with less critical operations and gradually expanding to core manufacturing processes. The company invested heavily in change management, user training, and process standardization before technology deployment, ensuring that the organization was ready for the new system before it went live.

As the business landscape evolved, cloud-based ERP solutions emerged as a more agile and scalable alternative. Cloud-based platforms, such as NetSuite, Microsoft Dynamics 365, and Workday, provide companies with modular, software-as-a-service (SaaS) options, allowing organizations to expand or modify their systems based on evolving needs. The adoption of cloud ERP solutions has enabled businesses to scale operations efficiently, reduce infrastructure costs, and support remote workforces. Unlike traditional ERP, cloud-based solutions provide automatic updates, enhanced security, and greater flexibility, ensuring that businesses operate with the latest technological advancements.

However, cloud ERP implementations have introduced new categories of failure. Revlon's bankruptcy in 2022 was partly attributed to problems with its SAP S/4HANA cloud implementation, which disrupted the cosmetics company's ability to fulfill orders and manage inventory effectively. The implementation, which began in 2018, encountered significant data migration issues, system performance problems, and integration challenges with existing systems. These technical problems compounded Revlon's financial difficulties and contributed to operational disruptions that ultimately proved fatal for the company.

The Revlon case demonstrates how ERP implementation failures can create cascading effects that threaten organizational survival. When core business systems fail, the consequences extend far beyond IT departments, affecting customer service, supplier relationships, cash flow, and ultimately, business viability. This reality makes ERP selection and implementation among the highest-stakes decisions that executives face.

The shift toward Composable ERP has further revolutionized how organizations implement and customize their enterprise systems. Instead of being locked into a rigid, all-in-one platform, companies can now select modular ERP components tailored to specific business functions, upgrading or replacing them as needed without disrupting the entire system. This approach allows businesses to remain agile, integrate best-of-breed applications, and adapt their ERP systems to evolving market demands. Companies no longer need to rely on a single vendor for all enterprise functions; instead, they can integrate specialized solutions that best fit their needs.

The composable approach has shown promise in reducing implementation risk by allowing organizations to tackle transformation incrementally. Unilever's adoption of a composable ERP strategy enabled the consumer goods giant to modernize its systems gradually while maintaining operational continuity. Rather than replacing its entire ERP infrastructure at once, Unilever implemented new cloud-based modules for specific functions like financial planning and supply chain management, integrating them with existing systems through APIs and middleware. This approach reduced implementation risk, allowed for better testing and validation, and enabled the organization to learn and adapt throughout the transformation process.

Beyond cloud and modular ERP, organizations are increasingly leveraging low-code and no-code platforms to customize their ERP systems with minimal IT involvement. This trend has empowered businesses to implement digital transformation strategies without requiring extensive programming expertise, further increasing flexibility and efficiency. However, these platforms also introduce new risks related to governance, security, and system integrity that organizations must carefully manage.

The healthcare industry provides sobering examples of how low-code customizations can create unexpected problems. Several hospitals have experienced significant operational disruptions when well-intentioned customizations to their ERP systems created data integrity issues or system performance problems. These incidents highlight the importance of maintaining proper governance and testing protocols even when using seemingly simple customization tools.

With these advancements, modern ERP solutions have evolved into more than just back-office tools; they have become dynamic ecosystems that integrate seamlessly with customer-facing applications, artificial intelligence (AI), and automation tools. The integration of AI into ERP systems has created new opportunities for predictive analytics, automated decision-making, and intelligent process optimization.

AI-powered ERP systems can now predict equipment failures before they occur, optimize inventory levels based on demand forecasting, and automate routine financial processes with unprecedented accuracy. For example, Schneider Electric's implementation of AI-enhanced ERP capabilities has enabled the company to reduce inventory costs by 15% while improving customer service levels through better demand prediction and supply chain optimization.

However, AI integration also introduces new complexities and potential failure modes. Organizations that implement AI-powered ERP features without adequate data quality, proper training data, or clear governance frameworks often experience disappointing results. The AI components may produce inaccurate predictions, automate inappropriate decisions, or create new forms of system complexity that are difficult to troubleshoot and maintain.

ERP systems no longer operate in isolation but rather connect with other business technologies, including Customer Relationship Management (CRM) platforms, business intelligence tools, e-commerce solutions, and AI-driven analytics. Through seamless integration, businesses gain real-time insights into their operations, allowing them to make data-driven decisions that enhance overall performance. A well-implemented ERP system enables companies to anticipate supply chain disruptions, optimize financial planning, and improve inventory management, leading to increased operational resilience.

The COVID-19 pandemic demonstrated both the value of integrated ERP systems and the risks of implementation failure. Companies with robust, well-integrated ERP systems were generally better able to adapt to supply chain disruptions, demand fluctuations, and remote work requirements. However, organizations in the middle of ERP implementations faced particularly severe challenges, as pandemic-related disruptions compounded existing implementation difficulties.

Customer Relationship Management (CRM): Enhancing Customer Engagement

While ERP systems focus on internal business operations, Customer Relationship Management (CRM) platforms play a crucial role in managing external-facing interactions. CRM solutions allow companies to track customer relationships, manage sales pipelines, and optimize marketing efforts, enabling organizations to deliver personalized experiences that enhance customer retention and drive revenue growth. However, like ERP systems, CRM implementations frequently fall short of expectations due to organizational and strategic challenges that extend far beyond technology selection.

The evolution of CRM has transformed it from a simple contact management tool into a comprehensive, AI-driven engagement platform. Companies like Salesforce, HubSpot, Zoho CRM, and Microsoft Dynamics 365 CRM offer sophisticated solutions that centralize customer data across multiple channels, providing sales, marketing, and customer service teams with a unified view of customer interactions. By leveraging AI-powered analytics, businesses can predict customer behavior, automate marketing campaigns, and personalize engagement strategies at scale.

However, the promise of CRM transformation often exceeds the reality of implementation results. A study by Forrester Research found that fewer than 40% of CRM implementations achieve their stated objectives, with user adoption being the primary factor distinguishing successful projects from failures. The telecommunications industry provides particularly instructive examples of both CRM success and failure.

Verizon's early CRM implementation in the 2000s encountered significant challenges when the company attempted to consolidate customer data from multiple legacy systems into a single Siebel CRM platform. The implementation was plagued by data quality issues, as customer information stored in different systems used inconsistent formats, contained duplicates, and reflected different business rules. Sales representatives found that the new system often provided conflicting or outdated customer information, leading them to rely on informal workarounds and personal databases rather than the official CRM system.

The Verizon experience highlights a fundamental challenge in CRM implementations: the quality of customer data is often poor, and consolidating bad data into a new system simply creates a more expensive way to access inaccurate information. Successful CRM implementations require significant investment in data cleansing, standardization, and governance processes that many organizations underestimate or overlook entirely.

In contrast, Amazon's customer-centric approach to CRM demonstrates how technology can be successfully aligned with business strategy to create competitive advantage. Rather than implementing a traditional CRM system, Amazon built its customer relationship capabilities around its core business processes, using data analytics and AI to understand customer behavior and preferences at an unprecedented scale. The company's recommendation engine, which drives approximately 35% of its revenue, represents a form of CRM that is seamlessly integrated into the customer experience rather than confined to back-office operations.

Integrating CRM with other enterprise technologies significantly enhances its effectiveness. When synchronized with ERP, CRM platforms ensure that customer orders, financial data, and supply chain operations are seamlessly aligned, eliminating inefficiencies and improving service delivery. The connection between CRM and marketing automation tools further enhances customer engagement, enabling businesses to create targeted campaigns, automate lead nurturing, and measure marketing performance with precision.

However, integration challenges often undermine CRM implementations. The financial services industry has experienced numerous integration failures where CRM systems could not effectively communicate with core banking systems, loan origination platforms, or compliance databases. These integration problems create data silos that defeat the primary purpose of CRM implementation and often result in customer service representatives having to access multiple systems to serve customers effectively.

Wells Fargo's customer account fraud scandal, which emerged in 2016, was partly enabled by disconnected systems that made it difficult to track customer interactions and identify inappropriate sales practices. While the scandal was primarily a result of cultural and incentive problems, the bank's fragmented technology systems made it harder to detect patterns of misconduct and ensured that customers couldn't easily see all their accounts in a single view. This case demonstrates how CRM and system integration failures can contribute to compliance and reputational risks.

AI and automation have revolutionized CRM functionality, making it an indispensable asset for modern businesses when implemented correctly. AI-driven chatbots and virtual assistants provide real-time customer support, reducing response times and improving customer satisfaction. Predictive analytics enable sales teams to identify high-value leads, optimize pricing strategies, and anticipate customer needs, ultimately increasing conversion rates. Companies that harness AI within their CRM systems can gain a significant competitive advantage through more proactive and personalized customer interactions.

The insurance industry provides compelling examples of AI-powered CRM success and failure. Progressive Insurance's use of AI-driven analytics to personalize customer interactions and pricing has contributed to the company's strong growth and customer satisfaction ratings. The company's CRM system uses machine learning algorithms to analyze customer behavior, predict risk factors, and customize insurance offerings for individual customers.

However, AI-powered CRM implementations can also create new forms of failure. Several financial services companies have experienced problems with AI-driven customer service chatbots that provided inaccurate information, failed to understand customer queries, or escalated issues inappropriately. These failures often result from inadequate training data, insufficient testing, or unrealistic expectations about AI capabilities.

The pharmaceutical industry has seen mixed results from AI-enhanced CRM implementations. While some companies have successfully used AI to identify potential research collaboration partners and optimize physician engagement strategies, others have struggled with AI systems that made inappropriate recommendations or failed to account for regulatory constraints on pharmaceutical marketing.

Far from being just a tool for sales teams, CRM has evolved into a strategic asset that informs business decisions across multiple departments. Marketing teams rely on CRM to execute data-driven campaigns, while customer service teams use it to track customer history and resolve issues efficiently. By integrating CRM with ERP, AI, and other digital tools, organizations can create a seamless, customer-centric approach that enhances loyalty and long-term engagement.

However, this evolution has also increased the complexity and risk associated with CRM implementations. As CRM systems become more central to business operations, the consequences of implementation failure become more severe. Organizations that experience CRM failures may find themselves unable to serve customers effectively, comply with regulatory requirements, or execute basic sales and marketing functions.

The retail industry provides numerous examples of how CRM failures can disrupt customer relationships. Target's early attempts at personalized marketing based on customer purchase data famously resulted in the company sending pregnancy-related promotions to customers before they had announced their pregnancies, creating privacy concerns and customer discomfort. While this incident was not technically a system failure, it illustrates how powerful CRM capabilities can create unintended consequences when not carefully managed.

The Future of Business Technology: A Unified Approach

As digital transformation accelerates, businesses are moving toward a fully integrated technology ecosystem where ERP, CRM, AI, business intelligence, and automation tools work in harmony. The ability to connect these systems ensures that data flows seamlessly across the organization, enabling leaders to make informed, strategic decisions. Companies that embrace cloud-based, modular ERP solutions and AI-powered CRM platforms will be better positioned to adapt to market changes, enhance operational efficiency, and deliver superior customer experiences.

However, achieving this integrated vision requires overcoming significant technical and organizational challenges. System integration projects are inherently complex and risky, often involving multiple vendors, disparate data formats, and conflicting business rules. The failure rate for large-scale integration projects remains high, with many organizations underestimating the time, cost, and expertise required to connect different systems effectively.

The automotive industry's experience with digital transformation illustrates both the potential and the pitfalls of integrated technology approaches. Tesla's integrated approach to manufacturing, sales, and service systems has enabled the company to operate with unprecedented efficiency and customer responsiveness. The company's systems are designed to work together from the beginning, enabling seamless data flow from customer orders through manufacturing and delivery.

In contrast, traditional automotive manufacturers have struggled with integration challenges as they attempt to modernize legacy systems that were never designed to work together. General Motors' attempt to integrate its various systems during the 2000s encountered significant problems when different systems used incompatible data formats and business rules. The integration project required extensive custom development work and took several years longer than originally planned.

The shift toward digital-first business models has highlighted the importance of real-time data, automation, and predictive analytics. Organizations that fail to modernize their ERP and CRM systems risk falling behind competitors that leverage AI-driven insights and agile technology solutions. In this era of rapid technological advancement, investing in integrated business platforms is essential for sustained growth and success.

However, the pressure to modernize quickly can lead to premature technology adoption and implementation shortcuts that increase the risk of failure. Organizations that rush into digital transformation without adequate planning, preparation, and change management often experience disappointing results that can set back their modernization efforts by years.

The healthcare industry provides sobering examples of how digital transformation pressure can lead to poor decision-making. Several hospital systems have experienced significant operational disruptions after rushing to implement new ERP systems in response to regulatory requirements or competitive pressure. These failures often result from inadequate planning, insufficient testing, and unrealistic implementation timelines driven by external pressures rather than organizational readiness.

By adopting cloud-based, composable ERP solutions and AI-driven CRM platforms, businesses can streamline internal operations while simultaneously enhancing customer engagement. These systems, when integrated effectively, provide a comprehensive digital infrastructure that supports both operational efficiency and customer-centric strategies. Organizations that invest in these technologies today will be well-positioned to thrive in the evolving digital economy, ensuring resilience and sustained competitive advantage in the years to come.

Other Critical Business Technologies Transforming Organizations

Beyond ERP and CRM, a variety of other technologies are driving digital transformation across industries. However, each of these technologies presents unique implementation challenges and failure modes that organizations must understand and prepare for.

Artificial Intelligence (AI) and Machine Learning (ML) are at the forefront of this revolution, enabling businesses to harness data for predictive analytics, automation, and enhanced decision-making. AI-powered tools analyze vast datasets to uncover insights, optimize workflows, and drive efficiencies. In marketing, AI-driven platforms such as HubSpot and Salesforce Einstein personalize customer interactions by predicting behaviors and recommending targeted campaigns. In finance, AI-powered algorithms assist in fraud detection, risk assessment, and algorithmic trading, empowering organizations to mitigate risks and maximize profitability.

However, AI implementations are particularly prone to failure due to the complexity of the technology and unrealistic expectations about its capabilities. The financial services industry has experienced numerous AI implementation failures where sophisticated machine learning models failed to perform as expected in real-world conditions.

JPMorgan Chase's LOXM algorithm, designed for automated equity trading, had to be discontinued after it began making trading decisions that human traders couldn't understand or explain. While the algorithm was technically functional, its "black box" nature created regulatory and risk management concerns that ultimately made it unsuitable for production use. This failure highlights the importance of AI explainability and the need for human oversight in AI-powered systems.

The healthcare industry has seen mixed results from AI implementations, with some spectacular successes and notable failures. While AI has shown promise in medical imaging and drug discovery, implementations in clinical decision support have been more challenging. IBM's Watson for Oncology, which was intended to assist doctors in cancer treatment decisions, was criticized for providing biased and sometimes unsafe treatment recommendations. The system was trained primarily on data from a single cancer center, limiting its generalizability to other patient populations and treatment protocols.

Business Intelligence (BI) and Data Analytics platforms have become indispensable for organizations seeking to interpret complex data and make informed decisions. Tools like Tableau, Power BI, and Looker enable businesses to visualize data trends, forecast customer behavior, and enhance financial planning through real-time analytics. AI enhances BI by automating data processing, identifying patterns, and generating predictive models that allow companies to anticipate market shifts and operational bottlenecks before they occur.

However, BI implementations frequently fail when organizations lack adequate data governance, quality control, or analytical skills. The retail industry has experienced numerous BI project failures where companies invested heavily in analytics platforms but failed to achieve meaningful insights due to poor data quality or lack of analytical expertise.

JCPenney's data-driven pricing strategy under former CEO Ron Johnson provides a cautionary tale about the limitations of analytics when not properly grounded in customer understanding. The company used sophisticated analytics to eliminate sales and coupons in favor of "everyday low prices," but the strategy failed catastrophically because it ignored customers' psychological attachment to sales and discounts.

The analytics were technically correct but strategically misapplied, resulting in massive customer losses and Johnson's eventual departure.

Supply Chain Management (SCM) Software has become a critical component of digital business operations. Platforms like SAP SCM and Oracle SCM Cloud optimize logistics, procurement, and inventory control by automating processes, predicting demand fluctuations, and improving supplier collaboration. When integrated with AI, SCM solutions enhance supply chain resilience and efficiency by providing real-time tracking, dynamic route optimization, and predictive maintenance for logistics operations.

The COVID-19 pandemic exposed the weaknesses in many companies' supply chain systems, as organizations with inadequate SCM capabilities struggled to adapt to rapidly changing conditions. Companies that had invested in robust, integrated SCM systems were generally better able to navigate supply chain disruptions, while those with fragmented or outdated systems faced significant operational challenges.

Target's early investment in supply chain technology enabled the company to adapt quickly to pandemic-related changes in customer behavior and supply chain conditions. The company's integrated systems allowed it to rapidly expand its curbside pickup and same-day delivery capabilities, helping it gain market share during a challenging period for retail.

However, SCM implementations can also fail spectacularly when not properly managed. Nike's demand planning system failure in 2001 resulted in a $100 million inventory write-down when the company's new forecasting system significantly overestimated demand for certain products while underestimating demand for others. The failure was attributed to inadequate testing, poor data quality, and insufficient user training on the new system.

Human Capital Management (HCM) and HR Technology are transforming workforce planning, talent acquisition, and payroll processing. AI-driven HR systems, such as Workday, BambooHR, and ADP, streamline recruitment by using natural language processing (NLP) to scan resumes, match candidates with job descriptions, and assess skills. AI-powered chatbots assist HR teams by automating employee inquiries and onboarding processes. Furthermore, predictive workforce analytics enable companies to anticipate employee attrition, measure engagement, and develop proactive retention strategies.

However, AI-powered HR systems have created new categories of failure related to bias, privacy, and regulatory compliance. Amazon's AI-powered recruiting tool had to be abandoned when it was discovered that the system exhibited significant bias against women, systematically downgrading resumes that included words associated with female candidates. The system had learned these biases from historical hiring data that reflected existing workplace inequalities.

The use of AI in HR also raises privacy and regulatory concerns that many organizations are not adequately prepared to address. Several companies have faced legal challenges related to AI-powered hiring systems that may discriminate against protected classes or violate privacy regulations.

Robotic Process Automation (RPA) and AI-driven automation are redefining how businesses handle routine tasks. Platforms like UiPath, Automation Anywhere, and Blue Prism automate repetitive processes such as invoice processing, financial reconciliation, customer inquiries, and data entry. AI enhances RPA by enabling bots to make decisions based on real-time data, learn from user behavior, and adapt workflows dynamically. This convergence of AI and automation reduces operational costs, enhances accuracy, and allows employees to focus on strategic initiatives rather than mundane administrative tasks.

However, RPA implementations frequently fail when organizations underestimate the complexity of their existing processes or lack adequate governance frameworks. The insurance industry has experienced numerous RPA failures where automation projects created new problems rather than solving existing ones.

A major insurance company's attempt to automate claims processing resulted in significant customer service problems when the RPA system began processing claims that should have required human review. The system was technically functioning as designed, but the business rules programmed into the system were inadequate for handling the full complexity of insurance claims processing.

The rise of e-commerce and digital payment solutions has further accelerated digital transformation. Platforms like Shopify, Magento, and BigCommerce integrate with ERP and CRM systems to facilitate seamless online transactions, while AI-driven recommendation engines enhance the customer experience by providing personalized product suggestions. Payment solutions such as Stripe, PayPal, and Apple Pay are revolutionizing the way customers purchase goods and services by offering secure, AI-powered fraud detection, real-time payment processing, and seamless checkout experiences.

However, e-commerce platform implementations can fail when organizations underestimate the complexity of integrating online and offline operations. Several major retailers have experienced significant problems during e-commerce platform migrations, resulting in lost sales, customer frustration, and operational disruptions.

Cybersecurity and AI-Driven Threat Detection have become essential for safeguarding business operations in the digital age. AI-powered security platforms such as Darktrace and CrowdStrike leverage machine learning algorithms to detect anomalies, identify potential cyber threats, and respond to attacks in real time. These technologies help businesses prevent data breaches, secure sensitive information, and comply with regulatory requirements. As cyber threats become more sophisticated, AI is playing a crucial role in ensuring proactive threat mitigation and business continuity.

However, AI-powered cybersecurity systems can also create new vulnerabilities and failure modes. Some organizations have experienced problems with AI security systems that generated too many false alarms, overwhelming security teams and potentially masking real threats. Other companies have struggled with AI systems that were inadequately trained or failed to adapt to evolving threat patterns.

AI is not just another tool in the business technology stack—it is a transformative force reshaping industries, streamlining processes, and unlocking new opportunities for innovation. Organizations that effectively leverage AI-driven solutions gain a competitive edge by enhancing operational efficiency, improving decision-making, and delivering exceptional customer experiences. However, successful AI implementation requires careful planning, realistic expectations, and ongoing management to avoid the pitfalls that have derailed many AI initiatives.

Navigating the Digital Landscape Through Technology Integration

The digital transformation journey is complex, requiring companies to carefully align their technology strategies with business objectives. Organizations that effectively integrate ERP and CRM systems ensure that workflows and business processes are synchronized across departments, leading to greater efficiency and improved decision-making. These integrated systems provide a centralized hub for managing customer interactions, tracking financial performance, overseeing supply chain logistics, and optimizing human capital management. However, simply implementing these tools is not enough—businesses must ensure seamless interoperability between platforms to maximize their benefits.

The challenge of system integration has become more complex as organizations adopt best-of-breed solutions that may not naturally work together. While this approach can provide superior functionality in specific areas, it also creates integration challenges that can undermine the overall benefits of digital transformation.

The pharmaceutical industry provides instructive examples of both successful and failed integration efforts. Merck's global ERP integration project successfully connected operations across multiple countries and business units, enabling the company to operate more efficiently and respond more quickly to market opportunities. The success was attributed to strong executive sponsorship, comprehensive planning, and significant investment in change management and user training.

In contrast, a major pharmaceutical company's attempt to integrate its research and development systems with its commercial operations encountered significant problems when the different systems couldn't effectively share data about drug development progress and regulatory status. The integration failure slowed product development timelines and created compliance risks that ultimately required expensive remediation efforts.

The Power of Technology Integration in Business Operations

With our rapidly evolving digital landscape, businesses must go beyond simply adopting new technologies; they must ensure these technologies work seamlessly together to drive efficiency, innovation, and competitiveness. A strategic approach to technology integration enables organizations to enhance operational efficiency, improve decision-making, future-proof their operations, optimize supply chains, and bolster cybersecurity. By aligning enterprise technologies such as ERP, CRM, AI, Business Intelligence (BI), automation, and cloud computing, businesses can unlock new levels of agility and resilience.

However, achieving successful integration requires overcoming significant technical, organizational, and cultural challenges. Many integration projects fail not because of technical limitations but because of inadequate planning, unrealistic expectations, or insufficient attention to change management.

The manufacturing industry provides numerous examples of both integration success and failure. General Electric's attempt to create an integrated industrial internet platform (Predix) represented one of the most ambitious technology integration projects in recent history. Despite significant investment and technical sophistication, the project ultimately failed to achieve its objectives and was scaled back dramatically. The failure was attributed to overly complex technology architecture, unclear value propositions, and insufficient customer validation.

Enhancing Operational Efficiency with AI and Automation

Artificial Intelligence (AI) and automation are transforming how businesses function by streamlining workflows, reducing manual effort, and improving the accuracy of routine tasks. The integration of AI-powered predictive analytics enables businesses to anticipate market trends, customer demands, and potential operational disruptions, allowing them to be proactive rather than reactive. AI-driven chatbots and virtual assistants are revolutionizing customer service by providing real-time responses, handling inquiries, and resolving issues without human intervention, significantly enhancing customer satisfaction when implemented correctly.

However, the implementation of AI and automation systems is fraught with challenges that many organizations underestimate. The complexity of AI systems, combined with the need for high-quality training data and ongoing maintenance, creates numerous opportunities for failure.

The automotive industry's experience with AI-powered quality control systems illustrates both the potential and the pitfalls of AI implementation. While some manufacturers have successfully used computer vision systems to detect defects in painted surfaces or assembled components, others have experienced problems with AI systems that generated too many false positives or failed to detect certain types of defects.

Ford's implementation of AI-powered predictive maintenance systems has shown mixed results, with some applications successfully reducing equipment downtime while others have struggled with data quality issues and integration challenges. The company's experience highlights the importance of starting with high-quality data and clear use cases when implementing AI systems.

Beyond customer engagement, Robotic Process Automation (RPA) is making business processes more efficient by automating repetitive and time-consuming tasks. Solutions such as UiPath, Automation Anywhere, and Blue Prism allow organizations to automate workflows like invoice processing, data entry, financial reconciliation, HR onboarding, and compliance monitoring. When integrated with ERP and CRM systems, RPA ensures that critical business processes such as order management, supply chain tracking, and payroll processing are executed seamlessly, reducing human error and operational bottlenecks.

However, RPA implementations frequently encounter problems that organizations don't anticipate. Many RPA projects fail because organizations attempt to automate processes that are poorly designed or overly complex. The automation simply makes bad processes faster rather than better, often creating new problems or inefficiencies.

A major financial services company's attempt to automate its mortgage application processing encountered significant problems when the RPA system began processing applications that contained errors or incomplete information. The system was designed to handle standard applications efficiently, but it couldn't adapt to the variations and exceptions that are common in mortgage processing. The result was increased processing errors and customer complaints rather than the improved efficiency that the company had expected.

A well-integrated AI and automation ecosystem frees up employees to focus on higher-value strategic initiatives rather than mundane administrative tasks. This shift increases workforce productivity, lowers operational costs, and accelerates decision-making by eliminating inefficiencies and redundancies in business processes. However, achieving these benefits requires careful attention to change management and employee training to ensure that workers can adapt to new roles and responsibilities.

Leveraging Business Intelligence for Data-Driven Decision-Making

In the current digital economy, data is one of the most valuable assets a business can leverage. Organizations that harness the power of Business Intelligence (BI) platforms gain a competitive edge by extracting meaningful insights from vast amounts of data. Platforms such as Tableau, Power BI, and Looker provide businesses with data visualization, interactive dashboards, and predictive analytics, helping them make more informed decisions.

However, BI implementations frequently fail when organizations lack adequate data governance, analytical skills, or clear business objectives. The retail industry has experienced numerous BI project failures where sophisticated analytics platforms were implemented but failed to deliver meaningful business value.

Sears' investment in data analytics and BI tools during its decline illustrates how technology alone cannot solve fundamental business problems. The company implemented sophisticated analytics platforms and hired data scientists to analyze customer behavior and optimize operations. However, these investments failed to reverse the company's decline because the underlying business model was fundamentally flawed, and the organization lacked the agility to act on analytical insights effectively.

When BI tools are integrated with ERP and CRM platforms, businesses gain a 360-degree view of their operations, allowing leadership teams to analyze performance metrics, identify inefficiencies, and develop data-driven strategies. By utilizing real-time dashboards, companies can track customer behavior, sales trends, financial performance, inventory levels, and workforce productivity, ensuring that all key business functions are optimized for efficiency.

However, achieving this integrated view requires overcoming significant data quality and integration challenges. Many organizations discover that their data is inconsistent, incomplete, or stored in incompatible formats across different systems. The process of cleaning and standardizing data for BI purposes often takes much longer and costs more than organizations initially expect.

The healthcare industry provides compelling examples of both BI success and failure. Mayo Clinic's use of integrated BI platforms to analyze patient outcomes and optimize treatment protocols has contributed to the organization's reputation for clinical excellence. The clinic's BI systems integrate data from electronic health records, laboratory systems, and medical devices to provide clinicians with comprehensive insights into patient care.

In contrast, several healthcare organizations have struggled with BI implementations that failed to account for the complexity of medical data and clinical workflows. These failures often result from unrealistic expectations about data quality, insufficient involvement of clinical staff in system design, or inadequate attention to regulatory requirements for medical data handling.

With AI-powered BI analytics, businesses can go beyond traditional reporting and uncover hidden patterns in data. For example, AI can predict customer churn, suggest pricing strategies based on historical trends, and recommend supply chain optimizations to minimize operational disruptions. Data-driven organizations can make agile decisions based on concrete evidence rather than intuition, reducing risks and increasing profitability.

However, AI-enhanced BI systems introduce new complexities and potential failure modes. Organizations may struggle with AI models that produce results they cannot explain or validate, creating compliance and risk management challenges. The financial services industry has experienced problems with AI-powered analytics that generated trading recommendations or credit decisions that regulators could not adequately review or understand.

Future-Proofing Operations with Scalable, Cloud-Based Solutions

As businesses continue to expand and adapt to a fast-changing global economy, they require scalable, cloud-based solutions that support agility, remote work, and integration with third-party applications. Cloud-based ERP and CRM platforms, such as Salesforce, Oracle Cloud, and Microsoft Dynamics 365, provide organizations with the flexibility to scale their operations, enhance collaboration, and access real-time data from anywhere in the world.

However, cloud migrations are complex undertakings that can disrupt business operations if not properly managed. The financial services industry has experienced several high-profile cloud migration failures where organizations underestimated the complexity of moving critical systems to cloud environments.

TSB Bank's disastrous IT migration in 2018 serves as a cautionary tale about the risks of large-scale system migrations. The bank's attempt to migrate customer accounts from a legacy system to a new cloud-based platform resulted in widespread service outages that lasted for weeks. Customers were unable to access their accounts, payments were processed incorrectly, and the bank's reputation was severely damaged. The failure was attributed to inadequate testing, poor project management, and unrealistic timelines that didn't account for the complexity of migrating financial data and systems.

The benefits of cloud-based platforms extend far beyond scalability. Cost efficiency is a major advantage, as organizations no longer need to invest in expensive on-premise servers, software maintenance, or IT infrastructure upgrades. Instead, businesses can subscribe to cloud-based services on a pay-as-you-go basis, ensuring that technology investments align with business needs.

However, cloud cost management has become a significant challenge for many organizations. Without proper governance and monitoring, cloud costs can escalate quickly as different teams provision resources without considering long-term financial implications.

Several companies have reported cloud bills that exceeded their traditional IT costs, highlighting the importance of cloud financial management practices.

Security and reliability are also key reasons why businesses are shifting to the cloud. Leading cloud service providers offer built-in security features such as encryption, access controls, and continuous system monitoring, ensuring that data is protected from cyber threats. Additionally, automated software updates and system patches help organizations stay compliant with evolving regulatory standards.

However, cloud security is a shared responsibility model, and many organizations struggle to understand and implement their security obligations properly. The 2019 Capital One data breach, which exposed information from over 100 million customers, occurred because of a misconfigured cloud security setting. This incident highlighted the importance of understanding cloud security models and ensuring that organizations have the expertise necessary to manage cloud environments safely.

By moving core business applications to the cloud, organizations gain the ability to integrate with AI-powered analytics, automation tools, and third-party business applications, creating an interconnected digital ecosystem that supports real-time collaboration, improved operational efficiency, and seamless digital transformation.

Optimizing the Supply Chain with AI and Predictive Analytics

Supply Chain Management (SCM) is another critical area where AI-driven technology integration is making a profound impact. The ability to predict demand fluctuations, track inventory in real time, and optimize logistics operations has become essential for businesses looking to enhance supply chain efficiency and reduce costs. AI-powered SCM platforms like SAP SCM and Oracle SCM Cloud provide real-time supply chain visibility, helping companies respond proactively to disruptions.

However, supply chain AI implementations face unique challenges related to data quality, system integration, and the complexity of global supply networks. The COVID-19 pandemic exposed weaknesses in many AI-powered supply chain systems that had been trained on historical data that no longer reflected current market conditions.

By integrating AI-powered analytics with ERP and logistics platforms, businesses achieve greater accuracy in demand forecasting, ensuring just-in-time inventory replenishment that minimizes stockouts and reduces excess inventory costs. Predictive maintenance, another AI-driven solution, helps manufacturers and logistics providers minimize equipment downtime by identifying potential failures before they occur, preventing costly delays and disruptions.

However, predictive maintenance systems require high-quality sensor data and sophisticated analytical models that many organizations struggle to implement effectively. Several manufacturing companies have experienced problems with predictive maintenance systems that generated too many false alarms or failed to predict actual equipment failures.

AI-enabled supply chain solutions also optimize route planning, delivery schedules, and procurement strategies. For example, AI algorithms analyze historical sales data and external factors such as weather patterns, economic trends, and geopolitical risks to anticipate disruptions and recommend alternative sourcing strategies. Organizations that embrace AI-driven supply chain integration experience improved operational resilience, reduced waste, and enhanced supplier collaboration.

The logistics industry provides compelling examples of both AI success and failure in supply chain optimization. UPS's ORION (On-Road Integrated Optimization and Navigation) system uses AI algorithms to optimize delivery routes, reducing fuel consumption and improving delivery efficiency. The system analyzes multiple variables including traffic patterns, delivery time windows, and package characteristics to determine optimal routes for delivery drivers.

However, AI-powered logistics systems can also fail when they don't adequately account for real-world complexities. Several delivery companies have experienced problems with AI routing systems that generated theoretically optimal routes that were impractical for drivers to follow due to traffic conditions, customer preferences, or physical constraints.

Strengthening Cybersecurity with AI-Driven Threat Detection

As businesses accelerate their digital transformation efforts, cybersecurity has become a top priority. The rise of cyber threats such as ransomware attacks, data breaches, and insider threats has forced organizations to adopt AI-driven cybersecurity solutions that provide real-time threat detection and response capabilities. Platforms such as Darktrace,

CrowdStrike, and Palo Alto Networks use machine learning algorithms to detect anomalies, identify potential cyber threats, and neutralize attacks before they escalate.

However, AI-powered cybersecurity systems introduce new complexities and potential failure modes. Some organizations have experienced problems with AI security systems that generated excessive false alarms, overwhelming security teams and potentially masking real threats. The challenge lies in tuning AI systems to detect genuine threats while minimizing false positives.

By integrating AI-powered security tools with ERP, CRM, and cloud-based infrastructures, businesses can proactively defend against cyber threats while ensuring compliance with regulatory requirements such as GDPR, CCPA, and HIPAA. AI-driven security systems continuously monitor network activity, analyze user behavior, and identify suspicious patterns, allowing organizations to take preemptive action against potential security breaches.

The financial services industry has seen both successful AI cybersecurity implementations and notable failures. JPMorgan Chase's investment in AI-powered fraud detection has helped the bank identify and prevent billions of dollars in fraudulent transactions. The bank's AI systems analyze transaction patterns, customer behavior, and external data sources to identify potentially fraudulent activity in real time.

However, other financial institutions have struggled with AI cybersecurity systems that created new vulnerabilities or failed to detect sophisticated attacks.

The challenge lies in ensuring that AI systems are properly trained, regularly updated, and integrated with human oversight processes.

In addition to AI-driven threat detection, businesses are leveraging blockchain technology to enhance cybersecurity. Blockchain's decentralized nature ensures that data integrity is maintained, reducing the risk of unauthorized alterations or fraudulent transactions. Companies that invest in AI-powered security frameworks and blockchain-driven data protection will gain a competitive edge in maintaining digital trust and compliance.

However, blockchain implementations in cybersecurity have faced their own challenges. Several organizations have experienced problems with blockchain systems that were too slow for real-time security applications or created new complexities in system management and maintenance.

Building Resilient, Intelligent, and Future-Ready Operations

To compete in a digital-first world, businesses must do more than just adopt new technologies—they must build resilient, intelligent, and future-ready operations that can withstand disruptions while seizing emerging opportunities. Digital transformation is not simply about keeping pace with competitors; it is about leveraging technology to drive sustainable growth, enhance efficiency, and future-proof the business against unforeseen challenges. Organizations that embrace a strategic, well-integrated technology approach will position themselves for long-term success in an increasingly complex and competitive marketplace.

However, building resilient operations requires learning from the failures of organizations that have attempted digital transformation without adequate preparation or realistic expectations. The retail industry provides numerous examples of companies that invested heavily in digital technologies but failed to achieve sustainable competitive advantages.

Toys"R"Us invested significantly in e-commerce and digital marketing technologies in its final years, but these investments couldn't overcome fundamental problems with the company's cost structure, store locations, and competitive positioning. The company's digital transformation efforts were too little, too late, highlighting the importance of timing and strategic alignment in technology investments.

Resilience in the digital age requires more than just technological upgrades—it demands a fundamental shift in how businesses operate, innovate, and adapt to rapidly changing environments. A truly future-ready enterprise is one that is agile, data-driven, and capable of scaling operations without disruption. Achieving this level of resilience requires companies to adopt a holistic approach to technology, ensuring that their core digital systems—ERP, CRM, business intelligence (BI), artificial intelligence (AI), and automation solutions—work seamlessly together to drive efficiency and innovation.

The automotive industry's ongoing transformation illustrates both the opportunities and challenges of building resilient, technology-enabled operations. Tesla's integrated approach to manufacturing, sales, and service has enabled the company to operate with unprecedented efficiency and responsiveness to customer needs. However, traditional automotive manufacturers have struggled to achieve similar integration while maintaining their existing operations and dealer networks.

General Motors' experience with digital transformation demonstrates both the potential and the challenges of building resilient operations. The company's investment in electric vehicle technology, autonomous driving capabilities, and digital customer experiences represents a comprehensive transformation of its business model. However, the transformation has required significant investment, cultural change, and operational reorganization that has taken years to implement.

Adopting an Integrated, Holistic Technology Strategy

One of the biggest challenges businesses face today is technology fragmentation—using disparate systems that do not communicate with each other effectively. Many organizations have separate platforms for enterprise resource planning (ERP), customer relationship management (CRM), and analytics, leading to data silos, inefficiencies, and misalignment across departments. To build a resilient and future-ready enterprise, businesses must adopt an integrated, holistic technology strategy that aligns these systems into a single, cohesive digital ecosystem.

However, achieving integration is more challenging than many organizations anticipate. The complexity of modern business systems, combined with legacy technical debt and organizational silos, creates numerous obstacles to successful integration. Many integration projects fail because organizations underestimate the time, cost, and expertise required to connect different systems effectively.

An integrated approach allows businesses to streamline workflows and improve operational efficiency by ensuring that all departments—from finance and HR to sales and supply chain—operate with a unified data set. This integration provides real-time visibility into key performance indicators, allowing decision-makers to act swiftly and confidently. It enhances collaboration across teams, enabling seamless data sharing and communication between different business units, and optimizes customer interactions, ensuring that data from CRM platforms informs marketing strategies, sales initiatives, and customer service responses.

The healthcare industry provides instructive examples of both successful and failed integration efforts. Kaiser Permanente's integrated approach to healthcare technology has enabled the organization to provide coordinated care across multiple specialties and locations. The company's integrated electronic health record system allows clinicians to access comprehensive patient information regardless of where patients receive care within the Kaiser system.

However, many healthcare organizations have struggled with integration projects that attempted to connect systems from different vendors with incompatible data formats and business rules. These integration failures often result in clinicians having to access multiple systems to serve patients effectively, defeating the purpose of the integration effort.

By breaking down barriers between critical business systems, organizations can operate with greater agility, respond faster to market changes, and create a more intelligent, data-driven enterprise. However, successful integration requires more than just technical connectivity—it requires organizational alignment, process standardization, and cultural change that many organizations find challenging to achieve.

The Long-Term Impact of a Well-Executed Digital Strategy

Organizations that commit to a strategic, well-integrated technology approach will not only thrive in the present but also position themselves for long-term, sustainable success. The rapid evolution of technology continues to redefine industries, reshaping the way businesses operate, compete, and engage with customers. Companies that invest in cloud computing, artificial intelligence (AI), automation, and cybersecurity will remain agile, innovative, and well-prepared to navigate the complexities of an increasingly digital world.

However, the long-term success of digital strategies depends on organizations' ability to learn from failures and adapt their approaches based on experience. The technology industry itself provides compelling examples of companies that achieved long-term success through iterative learning and adaptation rather than perfect initial implementations.

The long-term success of any organization depends on its ability to adapt and innovate in response to emerging technological advancements. Businesses that embrace digital transformation are not just improving operational efficiency;

they are future-proofing their enterprises against disruptions and unforeseen challenges. Digital transformation is not a one-time project but a continuous journey that requires companies to stay ahead of trends, optimize technology adoption, and foster a culture of innovation.

Microsoft's transformation under CEO Satya Nadella demonstrates how established technology companies can reinvent themselves through strategic digital transformation. The company's shift from a software licensing model to a cloud-based subscription model required fundamental changes in technology architecture, sales processes, and organizational culture. The transformation was successful because it was comprehensive, well-planned, and executed over multiple years with strong leadership commitment.

Sustained Competitiveness Through Innovation and Technology Adoption

The future of business belongs to organizations that are willing to evolve, experiment, and invest in the right digital solutions. Companies that successfully integrate AI, cloud computing, data analytics, and automation into their operations gain a significant advantage over those that remain reliant on outdated systems and manual processes. The ability to harness real-time data, automate decision-making, and enhance scalability enables businesses to optimize processes and respond swiftly to market demands.

However, sustained competitiveness requires more than just technology adoption—it requires building organizational capabilities that enable effective technology use. This includes developing analytical skills, fostering data-driven decision-making cultures, and creating governance frameworks that ensure technology investments align with business objectives.

For example, AI-driven analytics allow businesses to predict customer behavior, identify emerging trends, and personalize customer interactions with unprecedented accuracy. Machine learning algorithms can analyze vast amounts of data to forecast sales patterns, detect inefficiencies, and optimize pricing strategies, giving businesses a competitive edge in their respective markets. Companies that invest in AI-powered solutions will be able to anticipate industry shifts and proactively adjust their business models to remain ahead of the curve.

However, achieving these benefits requires overcoming significant implementation challenges. Many AI projects fail because organizations lack adequate data quality, analytical expertise, or realistic expectations about AI capabilities. Successful AI implementation requires a systematic approach that starts with clear business objectives and gradually builds capabilities over time.

Cloud computing is another game-changing technology that ensures long-term business resilience. Organizations that transition to cloud-based infrastructures gain the flexibility to scale operations, reduce costs, and enhance data security. Cloud platforms provide on-demand computing power, seamless integrations, and global accessibility, enabling businesses to expand into new markets without the burden of heavy infrastructure investments. Moreover, cloud-based collaboration tools facilitate remote work and cross-border partnerships, further enhancing business agility.

The financial services industry provides compelling examples of both successful and failed cloud transformations. Capital One's early adoption of cloud computing enabled the bank to operate more efficiently and develop innovative financial products more quickly than competitors with traditional IT infrastructures. The bank's cloud-first strategy required significant investment in new skills and capabilities, but it ultimately provided substantial competitive advantages.

Automation is revolutionizing operational efficiency by eliminating repetitive tasks, reducing errors, and optimizing resource allocation. Businesses that implement robotic process automation (RPA) in areas such as finance, HR, and supply chain management can reallocate human capital toward more strategic initiatives. Automated workflows not only improve accuracy and productivity but also enhance compliance and regulatory adherence.

However, automation implementations must be carefully managed to avoid creating new problems or disrupting essential business processes. Organizations that rush into automation without adequate planning often experience disappointing results or unintended consequences.

Technology as a Core Enabler of Transformation and Innovation

The key to building a resilient, intelligent, and future-ready enterprise lies in viewing technology not just as a tool, but as a core enabler of transformation and innovation. Businesses that recognize the strategic importance of digital investments will lead the next wave of industry advancements.

However, this recognition must be coupled with realistic expectations and careful implementation planning. The history of digital transformation is filled with examples of organizations that understood the strategic importance of technology but failed in execution due to inadequate planning, unrealistic timelines, or insufficient attention to organizational change management.

One of the most important aspects of long-term digital strategy is cultivating a culture of continuous learning and adaptability. Digital transformation is not only about implementing new technologies—it requires shifting mindsets, upskilling employees, and fostering innovation at all levels of the organization. Companies that encourage digital literacy and innovation will empower their workforce to adopt new tools, improve efficiency, and drive business growth.

The pharmaceutical industry's experience with digital transformation illustrates the importance of organizational culture in technology adoption. Companies that have successfully implemented digital R&D platforms and data analytics capabilities have typically invested heavily in training scientists and researchers to use new tools effectively. Organizations that have struggled with digital transformation often underestimated the cultural and skill changes required to realize the benefits of new technologies.

Moreover, digital transformation should align with customer expectations. Modern consumers demand seamless, personalized, and connected experiences across all touchpoints. Businesses that integrate AI-powered chatbots, predictive analytics, and omnichannel engagement into their customer experience strategies will strengthen brand loyalty and increase customer retention. Companies like Amazon, Apple, and Google continue to set industry benchmarks by leveraging technology to enhance customer interactions and drive innovation.

However, meeting customer expectations requires more than just implementing customer-facing technologies. It requires integrating back-office systems with customer-facing platforms to ensure that customer interactions are supported by accurate, real-time information and efficient business processes.

Long-Term Business Resilience and Sustainable Growth

The digital economy rewards businesses that are forward-thinking, adaptable, and committed to technological excellence. Companies that embrace AI, cloud computing, automation, and cybersecurity will create long-term business resilience by future-proofing their operations, enhancing customer engagement, and driving efficiency.

However, resilience also requires learning from failures and building organizational capabilities that enable effective technology management. Organizations that achieve long-term success in digital transformation typically develop strong project management capabilities, invest in change management, and maintain realistic expectations about implementation timelines and complexity.

Sustainability is also becoming a key factor in long-term digital strategy. Businesses that leverage green technology, energy-efficient cloud solutions, and data-driven sustainability practices will not only reduce costs but also align with environmental, social, and governance (ESG) goals. Companies that integrate sustainability into their digital transformation initiatives will gain a competitive edge while contributing to a more responsible digital economy.

The manufacturing industry provides examples of how digital transformation can support sustainability objectives. Companies that implement IoT sensors and AI-powered analytics to optimize energy consumption and reduce waste have achieved both cost savings and environmental benefits. However, these implementations require careful planning and ongoing management to ensure that sustainability objectives are actually achieved.

Ultimately, organizations that commit to a well-executed digital strategy will shape the future of their industries. By prioritizing innovation, integration, and scalability, businesses can unlock new opportunities, drive long-term profitability, and stay ahead of the competition. Companies that fail to invest in technology will struggle to keep pace with market leaders who use digital transformation as a catalyst for growth and disruption.

The Path Forward

To remain at the forefront of the digital revolution, organizations must continuously evolve, experiment, and embrace technological advancements. Success in the digital era requires a proactive mindset, strategic investments, and a commitment to leveraging technology as a driver of business value.

However, success also requires learning from the failures of others and approaching digital transformation with realistic expectations and adequate preparation. The organizations that will thrive in the digital future are those that combine technological sophistication with strong execution capabilities, effective change management, and a deep understanding of their customers and markets.

The future of business belongs to those that navigate the digital jungle with confidence, embrace AI-driven automation, invest in cloud-based scalability, and prioritize cybersecurity. Those that take bold steps today will not only survive but thrive in the digital age, setting new standards for excellence and innovation.

By treating technology as a core enabler of business transformation, companies can ensure long-term success, maximize efficiency, and foster innovation. In doing so, they will be well-positioned to lead their industries, shape market trends, and define the future of the global economy. The key lies not just in adopting new technologies, but in implementing them thoughtfully, learning from both successes and failures, and maintaining the organizational capabilities necessary to adapt and evolve in an ever-changing digital landscape.

Chapter 4

The Human Element

In the modern business landscape, digital transformation is often viewed through a technological lens—a process defined by the adoption of artificial intelligence (AI), cloud computing, automation, and data analytics. While these innovations are essential drivers of efficiency, agility, and competitiveness, technology alone does not determine the success of digital transformation. The human element—employees, leadership, organizational culture, and customer experience—plays an equally, if not more, critical role in ensuring that technology delivers meaningful and sustainable outcomes.

The sobering reality is that despite unprecedented investment in digital technologies, failure rates remain alarmingly high. Consider the case of J.C. Penney's disastrous ERP implementation in the early 2000s, which resulted in empty shelves, inventory nightmares, and contributed to the retailer's eventual bankruptcy. The technology worked perfectly—the problem was that leadership failed to prepare their workforce for the massive operational changes the system required. Employees couldn't adapt to new processes, vendors weren't properly onboarded to the new system, and customer service deteriorated rapidly as staff struggled with unfamiliar interfaces.

This pattern repeats across industries with disturbing regularity. Nike's infamous "i2" demand planning system implementation in the early 2000s cost the company over $100 million and resulted in a $200 million loss in sales when the AI-driven forecasting system made catastrophic inventory predictions. The technology was sophisticated, even revolutionary for its time, but Nike's leadership failed to account for the human elements: employees didn't trust the AI recommendations, regional managers continued using their old manual processes, and the cultural resistance to algorithmic decision-making was never addressed.

At its core, digital transformation is not simply about integrating new software, automating workflows, or migrating to the cloud. It is about people—how they engage with technology, adapt to change, and contribute to a digitally empowered organization. Employees must not only understand how to use new tools but also embrace the mindset required for continuous learning, innovation, and collaboration. Leadership must guide organizations through digital shifts with vision, strategy, and empathy, ensuring that technological advancements align with business goals and human needs.

The emergence of artificial intelligence has amplified these human challenges exponentially. While AI promises to revolutionize everything from customer service to supply chain optimization, its implementation often triggers profound psychological responses among employees. The fear of job displacement, the anxiety of working alongside intelligent systems, and the challenge of maintaining human relevance in an increasingly automated world create resistance that no amount of technical sophistication can overcome.

Organizations that underestimate the human factor in digital transformation risk facing resistance, disengagement, and implementation failures. A technology-first approach that neglects employees' needs, skills, and concerns often results in low adoption rates, inefficient processes, and cultural friction. Studies have consistently shown that 70% of digital transformation initiatives fail, not due to technological shortcomings but because of people-related challenges such as lack of employee buy-in, inadequate training, and cultural inertia. To succeed, businesses must prioritize change management, employee engagement, and leadership alignment, ensuring that digital adoption enhances both productivity and workplace satisfaction.

The case of Hertz's recent AI-driven dynamic pricing debacle illustrates how even well-intentioned AI implementations can backfire when human factors are ignored. The rental car company implemented sophisticated algorithms to optimize pricing in real-time, but failed to train customer service representatives on how to explain the system to confused customers. When rental prices fluctuated dramatically within minutes, customers felt deceived, and frontline employees couldn't provide satisfactory explanations for pricing decisions they didn't understand themselves. The result was a public relations nightmare that ultimately led to the suspension of the AI pricing system and significant revenue losses.

Moreover, digital transformation is not an isolated IT initiative—it is a fundamental reimagining of how organizations operate and deliver value. This shift requires businesses to build digital fluency among employees at all levels, empowering them to use technology effectively while also fostering critical thinking, problem-solving, and adaptability. In the age of AI, this challenge becomes even more complex. Employees must learn not just to use AI tools, but to collaborate with them, understand their limitations, and maintain the human judgment necessary to interpret AI recommendations within proper business context.

Digital tools should enhance human potential, not replace it, and organizations must create an environment where employees feel empowered rather than threatened by technological advancements. This is particularly crucial as AI becomes more prevalent in business processes. The most successful AI implementations are those where human workers become AI-enhanced rather than AI-replaced, developing new skills that complement machine capabilities rather than compete with them.

Beyond internal stakeholders, the human element extends to customers, partners, and broader communities. Digital transformation must ultimately serve people—enhancing customer experiences, simplifying interactions, and delivering greater value. A seamless digital experience is only possible when organizations understand customer expectations, leverage data responsibly, and personalize engagement strategies. Businesses that integrate customer-centric design, ethical AI practices, and data transparency into their digital strategies will build trust, loyalty, and long-term success.

The recent challenges faced by several major banks implementing AI-powered chatbots demonstrate this principle clearly. While the technology could handle routine inquiries efficiently, customers became frustrated when complex issues were routed through multiple AI systems without human intervention. Banks that achieved success with AI customer service were those that designed hybrid systems where AI handled routine tasks while seamlessly escalating complex issues to human agents who were properly trained to work with AI-generated customer insights.

Leadership as the Catalyst for Change

Digital transformation is more than just the adoption of new technologies—it represents a fundamental shift in how organizations operate, compete, and deliver value. While technological advancements such as cloud computing, artificial intelligence, and automation play a significant role, their success depends largely on the people who implement, manage, and use them. At the heart of this transformation is leadership, the driving force that ensures digital initiatives are not just adopted but effectively integrated into an organization's culture and strategy.

The spectacular failure of Target's multi-billion-dollar Canadian expansion offers a masterclass in how poor leadership can derail even the most technologically advanced initiatives. Target invested heavily in sophisticated supply chain management systems, inventory optimization software, and point-of-sale technologies. However, leadership failed to adequately prepare for the cultural and operational differences between the U.S. and Canadian markets. The company's executives assumed that their proven American systems would translate seamlessly across the border, ignoring the need for localized change management, employee training, and cultural adaptation. The result was empty shelves, frustrated customers, and a complete market exit that cost the company over $2 billion.

Successful digital transformation requires visionary leaders who can set the tone, create urgency, and align teams around a shared vision. It is not simply about rolling out new software or automating processes but about inspiring confidence, overcoming resistance, and fostering a culture of innovation. Leaders must communicate the purpose of transformation clearly, making sure employees understand how these changes will benefit both the organization and their individual roles. Without strong leadership, digital transformation efforts often fail—not because of technological shortcomings, but due to a lack of strategic direction and employee engagement.

The integration of AI into business processes presents unique leadership challenges that traditional change management approaches often inadequately address. When PwC surveyed 500 executives about their AI initiatives, they found that 76% identified "lack of AI expertise among leadership" as the primary barrier to successful implementation. Leaders who don't understand AI capabilities and limitations cannot effectively guide their organizations through AI-driven transformation, often setting unrealistic expectations or failing to prepare their workforce for the changes ahead.

One of the biggest obstacles to successful digital transformation is organizational resistance to change. Employees who are accustomed to traditional processes may feel threatened by automation or overwhelmed by the learning curve associated with new technologies. This resistance becomes particularly acute with AI implementations, where employees may fear not just job displacement but the existential threat of being replaced by intelligent machines. Leaders must take proactive steps to address these concerns, ensuring that teams are well-prepared, trained, and motivated to embrace digital initiatives. This includes providing ongoing education, fostering open dialogue, and demonstrating how technology enhances rather than replaces human capabilities.

Consider the contrasting approaches of two major retailers implementing AI-powered inventory management systems. Company A's leadership communicated the change as a cost-cutting measure that would "optimize workforce efficiency"—corporate speak that employees correctly interpreted as potential layoffs. The implementation faced massive resistance, with warehouse workers finding creative ways to circumvent the new system and managers providing minimal support for training initiatives. Company B's leadership, by contrast, framed the same technology as an opportunity for employees to focus on higher-value activities like customer service and strategic planning, while the AI handled routine inventory tracking. They invested heavily in retraining programs and created new career paths that incorporated AI collaboration skills. The difference in outcomes was dramatic: Company A's system was eventually abandoned after two years of poor performance, while Company B saw significant improvements in both efficiency and employee satisfaction.

When transformation efforts fail, it is rarely due to flaws in the technology itself. Instead, failure often stems from a lack of strong leadership, clear communication, and a commitment to change management. Without effective leadership, organizations risk fragmented implementation, employee pushback, and disjointed digital strategies that fail to deliver measurable value. Leaders play a critical role in bridging the gap between traditional business models and digital-first strategies, ensuring that transformation is not just embraced but successfully executed across all levels of the organization.

The bankruptcy of Toys"R"Us provides a cautionary tale about how leadership failures can compound technological shortcomings. While the toy retailer invested millions in e-commerce platforms and digital marketing tools, leadership never developed a coherent strategy for competing with Amazon and other digital-native retailers. Executives continued to focus on traditional retail metrics while their digital initiatives remained siloed from core business operations. The company's leadership failed to recognize that digital transformation required fundamental changes to business models, not just the addition of digital channels. When customer preferences shifted decisively toward online shopping, Toys"R"Us found itself with expensive digital tools that weren't integrated into a viable business strategy.

Digital transformation demands more than executive mandates—it requires commitment, transparency, and a willingness to rethink how work gets done. Leaders must ensure that employees feel empowered rather than displaced, and that digital adoption is framed as an opportunity rather than a disruption. By fostering a people-centric approach to digital transformation, leaders can drive meaningful change, enhance workforce engagement, and position their organizations for long-term success in an increasingly digital world.

The rise of AI adds another layer of complexity to leadership challenges. AI systems can make thousands of decisions per second, but they cannot provide the strategic vision, emotional intelligence, and ethical judgment that effective leadership requires. Leaders must learn to work with AI as a powerful tool while maintaining their essential human role in setting direction, inspiring teams, and making complex judgments that algorithms cannot handle.

The Role of Leadership in Driving Digital Change

Although digital transformation requires an organization-wide effort, it must begin at the top. Leaders serve as the driving force behind change, ensuring that transformation efforts are aligned with long-term business objectives and properly communicated across teams. Without clear leadership, digital initiatives risk becoming fragmented and ineffective, leading to confusion, inefficiencies, and widespread resistance among employees.

The collapse of Blockbuster Video stands as perhaps the most famous example of leadership failure in the digital age. While Netflix was investing in streaming technology and algorithmic recommendation systems, Blockbuster's leadership remained focused on optimizing their physical rental model. The company actually developed early digital capabilities, including an online rental service and streaming technology, but leadership never committed to cannibalizing their profitable physical stores. CEO John Antioco was reportedly forced out in 2007 partly because he pushed too aggressively for digital transformation, illustrating how even well-intentioned leaders can fail when they don't have organizational support for fundamental change.

One of the biggest challenges organizations face in digital transformation is navigating uncertainty. Employees often feel uncertain about how new technologies will impact their job roles, while customers may struggle with inconsistencies in digital service delivery. If leadership fails to address these uncertainties, businesses risk implementing technology for its own sake rather than leveraging it for true innovation and competitive advantage.

The uncertainty becomes exponentially greater with AI implementations. Unlike traditional software that follows predetermined rules, AI systems learn and evolve, sometimes producing unexpected results that even their creators cannot fully explain. This "black box" nature of AI creates unique leadership challenges. When JPMorgan Chase implemented AI for fraud detection, the system initially flagged thousands of legitimate transactions as suspicious, creating customer service nightmares. Leadership had to quickly develop new protocols for human oversight of AI decisions and create clear escalation procedures for when AI recommendations seemed questionable.

To ensure a successful digital transition, leaders must embody key qualities that define effective digital leadership. These include the ability to think strategically, embrace adaptability, communicate effectively, and foster collaboration. A well-structured digital strategy is not just about deploying technology—it is about aligning people, processes, and organizational culture to achieve digital maturity.

Organizations that lack strong digital leadership often encounter significant barriers to transformation. Employees may be resistant to adopting new tools, departments may operate in silos, and digital projects may stall due to unclear objectives. Without a guiding force, transformation efforts can become reactionary rather than proactive, leading to inefficiencies and missed opportunities.

The case of General Electric's attempted digital transformation under Jeff Immelt illustrates how even experienced leaders can struggle with digital initiatives. GE invested billions in creating GE Digital, hiring thousands of software engineers and attempting to transform itself into a "digital industrial company." However, leadership never successfully integrated digital capabilities with the company's traditional manufacturing strengths. The digital initiatives remained largely separate from core business operations, and when financial pressures mounted, the digital division was quickly dismantled with massive layoffs. The failure wasn't technological—GE developed impressive industrial AI applications—but leadership couldn't create a coherent strategy that leveraged digital capabilities to enhance rather than replace traditional competencies.

Leadership must also ensure that digital transformation is not just a short-term initiative but a continuous process. The digital landscape is constantly evolving, and organizations must be prepared to adapt, iterate, and innovate over time. Leaders who recognize digital transformation as an ongoing journey rather than a one-time implementation are better positioned to drive sustained growth and agility.

This continuous adaptation is particularly crucial in the AI era, where capabilities advance rapidly and new applications emerge constantly. Leaders must create organizational structures that can quickly evaluate and implement new AI tools while maintaining focus on core business objectives. Microsoft's approach under Satya Nadella exemplifies this balance—the company continuously integrates new AI capabilities into existing products while maintaining clear strategic priorities around cloud computing and productivity software.

Ultimately, the success of digital transformation depends on how well leaders can align their teams, address concerns, and create a unified vision for change. By fostering a culture of collaboration, experimentation, and learning, leaders can ensure that digital transformation is embraced at all levels of the organization, driving long-term success and resilience.

Vision and Strategic Thinking

A successful digital transformation begins with a clear and compelling vision. Leaders must define why transformation is necessary, identifying the business challenges it addresses and the opportunities it unlocks. Without a well-articulated purpose, digital initiatives risk lacking direction, leading to wasted investments and missed potential.

The failure of Quibi, the short-form video streaming service, demonstrates how technological sophistication cannot compensate for strategic confusion. Despite raising $1.75 billion and employing cutting-edge video technology optimized for mobile viewing, Quibi collapsed within months of its launch. The platform's leadership had a clear vision of the technology they wanted to build but failed to develop a coherent strategy for why consumers would choose their service over existing alternatives. The technology worked flawlessly, but without a compelling strategic rationale, even the most advanced digital capabilities became irrelevant.

Strategic thinking ensures that digital investments are not random but aligned with broader business objectives such as enhancing customer experience, streamlining operations, or creating new revenue streams. Rather than simply following trends, effective leaders make informed, data-driven decisions that maximize the value of digital initiatives.

In the AI domain, strategic thinking becomes even more critical because AI capabilities can be seductive in their potential while being devastating in their misapplication. Lowe's learned this lesson painfully when they deployed AI-powered robots in stores to help customers find products. While the technology was impressive, the robots struggled with the complex, dynamic environment of retail stores and often provided incorrect directions or became stuck navigating around displays and customers. The strategic flaw wasn't in the AI technology itself, but in the assumption that customer service was primarily an information problem rather than a relationship and problem-solving challenge that required human judgment and empathy.

Defining what success looks like is crucial in any transformation effort. Establishing clear metrics and key performance indicators (KPIs) allows organizations to track progress, measure impact, and refine strategies over time. Leaders who emphasize measurable outcomes ensure that digital efforts remain results-driven rather than merely reactive to technological advancements.

However, measuring success in AI implementations requires more sophisticated metrics than traditional technology projects. ROI calculations must account for learning curves, false positives, and the time required for AI systems to accumulate enough data to perform optimally. Leaders must also establish metrics for human-AI collaboration effectiveness, not just system performance in isolation.

Successful leaders also ensure that digital transformation aligns with customer expectations. Businesses today must focus on customer-centric innovation, using technology to enhance engagement, personalize interactions, and improve overall satisfaction. By keeping customer needs at the center of digital strategies, organizations can drive loyalty, retention, and long-term growth.

The contrasting fates of Kodak and Fujifilm illustrate the critical importance of customer-centric strategic thinking in digital transformation. Both companies faced the same technological disruption when digital photography emerged, but their strategic responses couldn't have been more different. Kodak's leadership, despite actually inventing the digital camera, couldn't envision a strategy where digital technology enhanced rather than replaced their film business. They viewed digital as a threat to be minimized rather than an opportunity to better serve evolving customer needs. Fujifilm, by contrast, leveraged their chemical expertise and customer relationships to diversify into cosmetics, pharmaceuticals, and advanced materials, using digital technologies to enhance their capabilities in these new markets. Today, Fujifilm thrives while Kodak exists primarily as a brand licensing entity.

A strong vision not only guides transformation efforts but also inspires employees to embrace change. When employees understand the purpose behind digital initiatives, they are more likely to adopt new tools, experiment with innovative solutions, and contribute to a culture of digital innovation. Leaders who effectively communicate why digital transformation matters ensure that their teams are motivated, engaged, and committed to success.

The importance of vision becomes even more critical with AI implementations because of the profound psychological impact these technologies can have on employees. When IBM Watson was first deployed in healthcare settings to assist with cancer diagnosis, many oncologists initially resisted the system because they perceived it as questioning their professional judgment. IBM's leadership eventually reframed Watson not as a replacement for medical expertise but as a tool that could help doctors access and analyze vast amounts of medical literature more efficiently. This strategic repositioning—from AI as competitor to AI as collaborator—was essential to gaining physician acceptance and ultimately improving patient outcomes.

Agility and Adaptability

The digital landscape is constantly evolving, presenting organizations with new technological advancements, shifting consumer behaviors, and unexpected market disruptions. Businesses that once thrived on structured, long-term planning now find themselves needing to adopt a more dynamic and flexible approach to stay competitive. The ability to adapt quickly and pivot strategically is no longer a luxury—it is a necessity.

The COVID-19 pandemic provided perhaps the most dramatic real-world test of organizational agility in modern business history. Companies that had invested in digital infrastructure and cultivated adaptive cultures were able to pivot rapidly to remote work, e-commerce, and digital customer engagement. Meanwhile, organizations with rigid systems and hierarchical decision-making structures struggled to respond to rapidly changing conditions.

Traditional leadership models, which emphasize hierarchical decision-making and rigid strategic frameworks, often fail to keep pace with rapid technological change. In contrast, agile leadership embraces transformation as an ongoing and iterative process rather than a one-time initiative. Agile leaders understand that the digital economy demands continuous learning, experimentation, and innovation, and they create an organizational culture that encourages adaptability at all levels.

The rise of AI has accelerated the need for organizational agility because AI capabilities evolve at unprecedented speeds. OpenAI's release of ChatGPT in late 2022 fundamentally disrupted entire industries within months, forcing organizations to rapidly reassess their strategies for content creation, customer service, and knowledge work. Companies that had established agile decision-making processes were able to quickly experiment with AI applications and develop new capabilities, while those with rigid approval processes and slow adaptation cycles found themselves scrambling to catch up.

A key characteristic of agile leaders is their willingness to embrace uncertainty and navigate ambiguity. Rather than seeing change as a disruption, they view it as an opportunity to evolve, improve, and gain a competitive edge. These leaders cultivate a growth mindset, where failure is not seen as a setback but as a learning experience that informs future strategies. By fostering an environment that supports experimentation, they ensure that employees feel safe to take calculated risks and contribute to innovation.

The contrasting approaches of Netflix and Blockbuster during the streaming revolution perfectly illustrate the difference between agile and rigid leadership mindsets. Netflix's leadership continuously experimented with new technologies and business models, from DVD-by-mail to streaming to original content production. They were willing to cannibalize their own profitable services to stay ahead of changing customer preferences. Blockbuster's leadership, meanwhile, remained committed to optimizing their existing store-based model, viewing each new technology as a potential threat rather than an opportunity for evolution.

One of the most critical aspects of agility in leadership is the ability to analyze real-world data and adjust strategies in real time. Businesses that base decisions on static plans rather than data-driven insights risk falling behind their competitors. Agile organizations leverage AI, predictive analytics, and real-time market feedback to refine their approaches, ensuring that they remain relevant and customer-centric.

However, the increasing reliance on AI for real-time decision-making creates new challenges for agile leadership. AI systems can process data and identify patterns far faster than humans, but they can also amplify biases and make errors at scale. Agile leaders must develop the capability to quickly identify when AI-driven decisions are producing suboptimal results and have the courage to override algorithmic recommendations when human judgment suggests a different course of action.

Adaptability also extends to organizational structures. Companies that succeed in digital transformation often flatten hierarchies, encourage decentralized decision-making, and empower teams to act autonomously. This shift allows organizations to respond faster to changes in the market while fostering a sense of ownership and accountability among employees.

Amazon's approach to organizational agility exemplifies these principles in action. The company's "two-pizza team" rule—teams should be small enough to be fed with two pizzas—enables rapid decision-making and experimentation. Each team has the autonomy to develop and test new features without navigating complex approval processes. This structure allowed Amazon to quickly adapt AI capabilities across their entire ecosystem, from recommendation engines to logistics optimization to voice assistants, while traditional retailers struggled with siloed decision-making processes.

The failure of Yahoo to adapt to changing digital landscapes provides a sobering counterexample. Despite being an early internet pioneer with significant technological capabilities, Yahoo's leadership failed to develop the organizational agility necessary to compete with Google in search or Facebook in social media. The company's hierarchical structure and bureaucratic decision-making processes prevented rapid experimentation and adaptation. When they finally attempted to implement AI-driven personalization and search improvements, they were years behind competitors who had been iterating rapidly on these technologies.

Ultimately, agility and adaptability define which businesses will lead and which will struggle in the digital era. Leaders who embrace continuous learning, iterative improvements, and real-time decision-making create resilient and future-ready organizations that can thrive in the face of technological disruption and evolving customer expectations.

Empathy and Communication

Digital transformation is not just about technology—it is about people. Whenever new systems, tools, or workflows are introduced, employees often face uncertainty, fear, and resistance. Many worry about job displacement due to automation, while others struggle with the steep learning curve associated with digital adoption. If these concerns are not acknowledged and addressed, transformation efforts can fail due to disengagement and lack of trust.

The introduction of AI into workplace environments has intensified these human concerns exponentially. Unlike previous technological changes that primarily affected specific job functions, AI has the potential to impact knowledge work across all organizational levels. The psychological impact cannot be underestimated—employees often experience what researchers term "algorithmic anxiety," a complex mix of fear about job security, concerns about surveillance, and uncertainty about their future role in an AI-augmented workplace.

Effective leaders prioritize empathy and communication, ensuring that employees feel heard, valued, and supported throughout the transition. Empathy allows leaders to understand employee concerns and proactively address challenges, making the process smoother for everyone involved. Transformation efforts must be framed as opportunities for growth and efficiency, rather than a top-down mandate imposed without consultation.

The case of a major insurance company's AI implementation illustrates both the pitfalls and potential of empathetic leadership during digital transformation. Initially, the company's executives announced that AI would be used to automate claims processing, resulting in immediate panic among claims adjusters who feared mass layoffs. Productivity plummeted as employees spent more time updating their resumes than learning new systems. However, after six months of poor results, new leadership took a dramatically different approach. They reframed the AI implementation as an opportunity for claims adjusters to become "claims consultants," using AI to handle routine cases while they focused on complex claims requiring human judgment and customer interaction. They provided extensive retraining, created new career advancement paths, and guaranteed that no employees would be laid off due to AI implementation. The transformation in employee attitudes was dramatic—what had been seen as a threat became viewed as an enhancement to their professional capabilities.

One of the most powerful tools in managing change is transparent communication. Leaders who provide a clear, consistent narrative about why digital transformation is happening and how it benefits employees foster trust and engagement. When employees understand the purpose behind the change, they are more likely to support and participate in transformation efforts rather than resist them.

However, communication around AI implementations requires particular sophistication because the technology itself can seem mysterious or threatening. Leaders must be able to explain AI capabilities and limitations in accessible terms while addressing both rational concerns about job security and emotional concerns about human relevance in an increasingly automated world.

Listening to employee feedback is also essential in easing fears and building an inclusive digital culture. Leaders who actively seek input from employees, address concerns, and involve them in shaping digital strategies can significantly reduce resistance. Open discussions, town hall meetings, and internal surveys can provide valuable insights into employee sentiment, helping leadership fine-tune their approach.

A global consulting firm's approach to implementing AI-powered research tools demonstrates the power of inclusive communication. Rather than simply rolling out new AI systems, leadership created "AI councils" that included representatives from every department and seniority level. These councils were responsible for identifying use cases, testing new tools, and providing feedback on implementation approaches. Employees who initially felt threatened by AI research capabilities became champions of the technology because they had a voice in shaping how it was deployed. The firm found that this inclusive approach not only reduced resistance but actually led to more innovative AI applications because frontline employees identified use cases that management had overlooked.

Additionally, ongoing training and support are crucial for helping employees navigate digital transformation with confidence. Leaders who provide structured learning programs, mentorship, and hands-on training opportunities ensure that employees are equipped with the skills they need to thrive in a digital-first environment. Training should not be a one-time event but a continuous process that enables employees to stay up to date with new tools and technologies.

The challenge of training becomes more complex with AI because the technology continues to evolve rapidly, and the skills required to work effectively with AI are still being defined. Progressive organizations are developing "AI literacy" programs that teach employees not just how to use specific AI tools, but how to think critically about AI recommendations, understand basic concepts of machine learning, and collaborate effectively with intelligent systems.

A culture of open dialogue ensures that change is not feared but embraced. When employees feel that they have a voice in the transformation process, they are more likely to engage actively rather than resist. Leaders who foster a sense of inclusion, reassurance, and shared vision will strengthen employee commitment, making digital transformation a collaborative and successful endeavor.

The pharmaceutical company Merck provides an excellent example of how empathetic communication can transform AI adoption. When the company began implementing AI for drug discovery, many research scientists initially viewed the technology as a threat to the creative and intellectual aspects of their work. Leadership addressed these concerns through a series of "AI and the Future of Science" dialogues where scientists could voice their concerns and learn about how AI could enhance rather than replace human creativity in research. They brought in AI researchers who had scientific backgrounds to explain how machine learning could accelerate hypothesis testing and pattern recognition while leaving the essential work of creative problem-solving and ethical decision-making to human scientists. This approach transformed skeptical scientists into enthusiastic AI adopters who found that the technology freed them to focus on the most intellectually stimulating aspects of their work.

Collaboration and Empowerment

Digital transformation cannot be achieved in isolation—it requires collaboration across departments, roles, and expertise levels. A siloed approach to digital initiatives leads to inefficiencies, misalignment, and slow adoption rates. Instead, leaders must create an inclusive, team-oriented culture where employees feel empowered to contribute to transformation efforts.

The failure of many enterprise AI implementations can be traced directly to lack of cross-functional collaboration. Technical teams develop sophisticated algorithms in isolation, business units create requirements without understanding AI capabilities, and end users receive finished systems that don't match their actual workflow needs. This disconnect has led to what researchers call the "AI deployment gap"—the significant difference between AI's potential and its actual business impact in most organizations.

Cross-functional collaboration is critical in digital transformation. Since digital initiatives impact multiple areas—including IT, marketing, finance, operations, and customer service—teams must work together seamlessly to ensure that digital strategies are effectively implemented. For example, a new AI-powered customer service chatbot should not be developed by IT alone—it must involve input from customer experience teams, data analysts, and frontline employees to ensure that it aligns with customer expectations.

The success of JPMorgan Chase's AI implementation for contract analysis illustrates the power of cross-functional collaboration. Rather than having technologists build an AI system and impose it on lawyers, the bank created integrated teams that included software engineers, legal experts, compliance officers, and business analysts. The lawyers helped identify which types of contract clauses were most important to analyze, compliance officers ensured the AI system met regulatory requirements, and business analysts helped quantify the value of automated contract review. The result was an AI system that saved the bank thousands of hours of legal work while actually improving the quality and consistency of contract analysis.

Breaking down departmental silos allows organizations to maximize the potential of digital tools. When departments work in isolation, digital initiatives become disconnected from broader business objectives. Leaders must encourage knowledge-sharing, ensuring that every function understands how digital transformation aligns with the company's overall vision and goals.

AI implementations are particularly vulnerable to silo problems because the technology often requires data and insights from multiple business functions to work effectively. A retail company's attempt to implement AI-powered demand forecasting failed spectacularly when the algorithm was trained only on historical sales data provided by the IT department. The system couldn't account for marketing campaigns, seasonal promotions, supplier delays, or competitive actions because marketing, procurement, and business intelligence teams weren't involved in the development process. When the AI system predicted demand that bore no resemblance to actual market conditions, the company was left with massive inventory imbalances and significant financial losses.

Empowering employees is another key driver of digital success. Instead of dictating every aspect of transformation from the top, leaders should involve employees in decision-making, giving them ownership over specific digital initiatives. Employees who feel included in shaping digital strategies are more engaged, innovative, and proactive in ensuring their success.

The approach taken by ING Bank during their digital transformation demonstrates the power of employee empowerment. Rather than implementing a top-down digital strategy, ING created cross-functional "squads" of employees who were given autonomy to identify opportunities for digital improvement in their areas of expertise. These squads were empowered to experiment with new technologies, including AI tools, and implement solutions that improved their daily work. One squad of mortgage specialists identified how machine learning could streamline loan approval processes, while another squad of customer service representatives developed AI-powered tools to better handle customer inquiries. Because employees had ownership over these initiatives, adoption rates were extremely high and the solutions actually addressed real business problems rather than theoretical improvements.

Recognizing and rewarding employee contributions further strengthens engagement and motivation. Digital transformation is a collective effort, and leaders who acknowledge employees' ideas, experiments, and successes encourage a culture of continuous improvement.

However, recognition and rewards in AI-driven transformation require new approaches because traditional performance metrics may not capture the value of human-AI collaboration. Progressive organizations are developing new recognition systems that reward employees for effectively collaborating with AI systems, identifying AI opportunities, and maintaining human judgment in AI-augmented processes.

Collaboration should extend beyond internal teams to include external partners, vendors, and customers. The digital ecosystem is interconnected, and organizations that leverage strategic partnerships and external expertise can accelerate their digital initiatives. Whether working with technology providers, consultants, or industry peers, successful leaders create alliances that strengthen their organization's digital capabilities.

The partnership between Walmart and Microsoft for AI-powered supply chain optimization exemplifies how external collaboration can accelerate digital transformation. Rather than attempting to develop AI capabilities internally, Walmart leveraged Microsoft's Azure AI services while contributing their deep supply chain expertise. This collaboration produced AI systems that could predict demand fluctuations, optimize inventory placement, and reduce waste across Walmart's massive retail network. The partnership succeeded because both organizations contributed their core strengths—Walmart's operational knowledge and Microsoft's AI technology—rather than trying to replicate each other's capabilities.

Ultimately, collaboration and empowerment are the building blocks of sustainable digital transformation. Leaders who foster teamwork, inclusivity, and shared responsibility ensure that employees are actively engaged in transformation efforts rather than passive recipients of change. A collaborative approach leads to greater efficiency, creativity, and long-term success in the digital era.

The failure of many AI implementations can be traced to leaders who treated digital transformation as a technology deployment rather than a collaborative change management process. When employees are excluded from AI development and implementation decisions, they often find creative ways to work around systems they don't understand or trust, ultimately undermining the entire initiative.

A Real-World Example: How Leadership Drives Digital Success

One of the most compelling examples of leadership-driven digital transformation is Microsoft's remarkable turnaround under Satya Nadella's leadership. When Nadella took over as CEO in 2014, Microsoft was facing stagnation. Once the dominant force in computing, the company was struggling to keep up with the rise of cloud computing, mobile technology, and new digital business models. Competitors like Amazon Web Services (AWS) and Google were gaining ground, and Microsoft's focus on legacy software products was becoming a liability in an increasingly cloud-driven market.

Recognizing the urgency for change, Nadella redefined Microsoft's vision, shifting it from a product-centric company to a cloud-first, customer-centric enterprise. This strategic transformation was not just about technology upgrades—it required a fundamental shift in company culture, leadership mindset, and business strategy. Under Nadella's leadership, Microsoft embraced digital transformation at its core, ensuring that technology served not just as an enabler of efficiency but as a driver of innovation and long-term growth.

Shifting from a Product-Centric to a Cloud-First Strategy

One of Nadella's most significant contributions was pivoting Microsoft's business model toward cloud computing. At the time, Microsoft's traditional Windows and Office software licensing model was profitable but outdated, limiting the company's ability to compete in a rapidly changing digital world. Nadella introduced a cloud-first strategy, focusing on subscription-based services such as Microsoft Azure and Office 365, which enabled businesses to access computing power, storage, and productivity tools on demand.

This transformation positioned Microsoft as a leading cloud provider, competing directly with AWS and Google Cloud. Under Nadella's leadership, Microsoft Azure became one of the fastest-growing cloud platforms, powering thousands of businesses, governments, and startups worldwide. The shift to software-as-a-service (SaaS) offerings also ensured that Microsoft's products remained flexible, scalable, and relevant in an increasingly mobile and connected world.

However, Nadella understood that digital transformation was not just about deploying cloud services—it was about ensuring that technology was used to create real value for customers. This led Microsoft to integrate AI, automation, and machine learning into its services, enabling businesses to leverage data analytics, enhance collaboration, and improve security.

The integration of AI across Microsoft's product portfolio demonstrates how strategic leadership can accelerate technology adoption. Under Nadella's direction, Microsoft didn't just add AI features to existing products—they reimagined how AI could enhance human productivity. Copilot, Microsoft's AI assistant integrated across Office applications, exemplifies this approach. Rather than replacing human workers, Copilot augments human capabilities by handling routine tasks like formatting documents, generating meeting summaries, and analyzing data patterns, freeing employees to focus on creative and strategic work.

Driving a Cultural Shift: The Growth Mindset

Beyond technological changes, Nadella recognized that a successful digital transformation required a cultural shift. Under his leadership, Microsoft moved away from a rigid, internally competitive corporate culture toward a more collaborative, growth-oriented environment. He encouraged employees to adopt a "growth mindset," a concept developed by psychologist Carol Dweck, which emphasizes continuous learning, adaptability, and the ability to learn from failure.

This shift was crucial in breaking down silos between departments, fostering cross-functional collaboration, and accelerating innovation. Employees were encouraged to experiment, share ideas, and collaborate across teams, ensuring that new digital initiatives were not just confined to isolated business units but were implemented holistically across the organization.

The cultural transformation at Microsoft provides important lessons for AI implementation. Nadella recognized that employees needed to feel safe experimenting with AI tools and potentially failing as they learned. The company created "AI innovation challenges" where employees could propose and test AI applications in their work areas without fear of negative consequences if the experiments didn't succeed. This approach led to breakthrough innovations like AI-powered code completion in Visual Studio and intelligent scheduling in Outlook.

Nadella also introduced more inclusive leadership practices, emphasizing diversity, transparency, and empathy. He championed the idea that technology should empower people, both within Microsoft and in its customer base. This people-first approach ensured that Microsoft's digital transformation was not just about financial performance but about creating a meaningful impact on businesses, developers, and consumers worldwide.

Customer-Centric Digital Transformation

Rather than simply implementing new technologies for the sake of innovation, Nadella prioritized customer-centricity, ensuring that digital initiatives enhanced user experience and met real-world business needs. He led Microsoft to shift its focus from short-term sales goals to long-term customer relationships, recognizing that the true value of technology lies in its ability to solve customer challenges.

This customer-first approach led to major improvements in Microsoft's product offerings. Instead of launching isolated software updates, the company began developing integrated, cloud-based solutions that enabled customers to be more productive, collaborative, and secure. For example, Microsoft Teams, a collaboration and communication platform, became a game-changer in the digital workplace, especially during the COVID-19 pandemic, when businesses required remote work solutions.

The development of Microsoft Teams illustrates how customer-centric AI development can drive adoption. Rather than building AI features that showcased technical capabilities, Microsoft focused on AI applications that solved real problems for remote and hybrid workers. AI-powered features like real-time transcription, meeting summaries, and intelligent scheduling addressed the actual pain points that customers experienced in virtual collaboration, leading to rapid adoption and high satisfaction rates.

Additionally, Microsoft expanded its AI-driven capabilities across products like Cortana, Dynamics 365, and Power BI, enabling businesses to harness data for better decision-making, automation, and predictive analytics. These innovations reflected Microsoft's commitment to digital transformation as a continuous journey, not just a one-time shift.

Learning from Failure: The Cortana Case Study

Not all of Microsoft's AI initiatives succeeded, and Nadella's leadership approach to failure provides valuable lessons for digital transformation. Cortana, Microsoft's consumer AI assistant, failed to gain significant market share against Amazon's Alexa and Google Assistant. Rather than continuing to invest in a losing consumer strategy, Nadella pivoted Cortana toward enterprise applications where Microsoft had stronger competitive advantages.

This strategic flexibility—the ability to acknowledge failure quickly and redirect resources toward more promising opportunities—exemplifies the agile leadership mindset necessary for successful digital transformation. Many organizations become trapped by sunk costs and continue investing in failing AI initiatives rather than learning from setbacks and adapting their approach.

The Results: A Transformed Microsoft

Nadella's leadership and strategic vision revitalized Microsoft, turning it into one of the most valuable companies in the world. The company's market capitalization grew from around $300 billion in 2014 to over $2 trillion by 2022, making it one of the most financially successful digital transformations in modern business history.

By embracing a cloud-first strategy, prioritizing cultural transformation, and fostering a customer-centric mindset, Microsoft successfully repositioned itself as a leader in enterprise cloud services, AI, and digital workplace solutions. Under Nadella's guidance, the company reinvented itself, demonstrating how leadership, adaptability, and a commitment to continuous learning can drive successful digital transformation.

Key Lessons from Microsoft's Digital Transformation

Microsoft's evolution under Nadella provides several critical lessons for businesses undergoing digital transformation:

Visionary leadership is essential — Digital transformation must start with a clear, long-term vision that aligns with business goals and market demands. Nadella's ability to redefine Microsoft's purpose and direction was a key factor in its success.

Cultural transformation is just as important as technology — A growth mindset, collaboration, and inclusivity drive innovation and digital adoption. Breaking down silos and fostering a culture of continuous learning and adaptability enables businesses to thrive in the digital age.

Customer-centricity must be the priority — Digital transformation should enhance user experience, improve business outcomes, and solve customer pain points, rather than simply implementing technology for its own sake.

Agility and adaptability ensure long-term success — Technology, markets, and customer needs are constantly evolving. Organizations that embrace change, iterate quickly, and remain flexible will stay ahead of disruption.

Digital transformation is a journey, not a destination — Businesses must commit to continuous innovation, real-time data-driven decision-making, and iterative improvements to sustain success.

Lessons from AI Implementation Failures

While Microsoft's success story provides inspiration, examining AI implementation failures offers equally valuable insights for leaders navigating digital transformation. The pattern of AI failures often reveals fundamental misunderstandings about the human elements required for successful technology adoption.

IBM Watson's highly publicized struggles in healthcare provide a sobering case study. Despite billions in investment and tremendous technical capability, Watson for Oncology failed to achieve widespread adoption because IBM's leadership underestimated the complexity of medical decision-making and the importance of physician trust in AI recommendations. The system was trained primarily on data from Memorial Sloan Kettering Cancer Center, but medical practices vary significantly across institutions and patient populations. When Watson's recommendations conflicted with local medical expertise, physicians lost confidence in the system.

More critically, IBM's approach treated AI implementation as primarily a technical challenge rather than a change management process. They focused on algorithmic accuracy while neglecting the cultural and workflow changes necessary for physicians to effectively collaborate with AI systems. Doctors weren't adequately trained on how to interpret Watson's recommendations within the context of individual patient circumstances, leading to frustration and resistance rather than adoption.

The failure of Zillow's AI-powered home buying program, Zillow Offers, demonstrates how even sophisticated AI can fail when human factors are ignored. Zillow's algorithms were trained on vast amounts of housing data and could predict home values with impressive accuracy under normal market conditions. However, the AI system couldn't account for the complex human factors that influence real estate markets during periods of volatility.

When the COVID-19 pandemic disrupted housing markets, Zillow's AI continued making purchase decisions based on historical patterns that no longer applied. The algorithms couldn't adapt to rapidly changing buyer preferences, supply chain disruptions affecting home renovations, or the psychological factors driving pandemic-era housing decisions. Zillow's leadership had become overly confident in their AI capabilities and failed to maintain adequate human oversight for unusual market conditions. The result was billions in losses and the complete shutdown of the Zillow Offers program.

These failures highlight a critical pattern: AI implementations succeed when they enhance human decision-making and fail when they attempt to replace human judgment entirely. The most successful AI applications are those that create effective human-machine collaboration rather than human-machine competition.

The Future of Human-AI Collaboration

As AI capabilities continue to advance, the challenge for leaders shifts from whether to implement AI to how to create effective human-AI partnerships. The organizations that will thrive in the AI era are those that develop superior capabilities for human-machine collaboration rather than those with the most sophisticated algorithms.

This evolution requires leaders to think differently about both technology and human development. Traditional approaches to digital transformation focused on training employees to use new tools. AI transformation requires developing employees' abilities to work with intelligent systems that can learn, adapt, and sometimes produce unexpected results.

Progressive organizations are beginning to develop "AI collaboration skills" as a core competency. These include the ability to effectively prompt AI systems, critically evaluate AI recommendations, identify when human judgment should override algorithmic suggestions, and seamlessly hand off tasks between human and artificial intelligence.

The accounting firm EY's approach to AI implementation illustrates this collaborative model in action. Rather than using AI to replace auditors, EY developed AI systems that enhance auditor capabilities by automatically identifying anomalies in financial data, flagging potential risk areas, and analyzing complex transactions across multiple systems. Auditors remain responsible for professional judgment about the significance of AI findings and making final determinations about audit conclusions.

This human-AI partnership approach has proven more successful than implementations that attempted to automate auditing decisions entirely. Auditors trust the AI recommendations because they understand how the systems work and maintain control over final decisions. The AI systems improve over time because they receive feedback from experienced auditors about which findings are most significant. Both human and artificial intelligence capabilities are enhanced through collaboration.

Microsoft's transformation under Satya Nadella is a powerful example of how strong leadership, strategic vision, and a commitment to cultural change can drive digital success. By embracing a cloud-first strategy, prioritizing customer needs, and fostering innovation, Nadella not only revitalized Microsoft but also set a new standard for digital leadership.

This case study demonstrates that technology alone does not drive transformation—it is how organizations integrate, adapt, and leverage technology to create real value that defines long-term success. Leaders who prioritize vision, collaboration, and continuous learning will be best positioned to navigate digital disruption and create resilient, future-ready organizations.

The integration of AI into business processes adds new dimensions to these leadership challenges, but the fundamental principles remain constant: successful digital transformation requires leaders who understand that technology serves people, not the reverse. The organizations that will thrive in the AI era are those whose leaders create cultures where human and artificial intelligence enhance each other's capabilities rather than compete for relevance.

The Human Side of Digital Transformation

At its core, digital transformation is about people. While technology provides the tools to innovate, it is leadership that determines whether those tools are used effectively. Strong leaders guide organizations through the uncertainties of transformation, ensuring that technology serves a greater purpose rather than becoming an end in itself.

Leaders who prioritize vision, agility, communication, and collaboration create an environment where employees feel engaged and empowered rather than overwhelmed. By fostering a culture of adaptability and learning, organizations can not only implement new technologies but also ensure that these tools drive long-term business success.

The emergence of AI has intensified both the opportunities and challenges of digital transformation. AI can automate routine tasks, provide unprecedented insights from data, and enable new forms of customer engagement. However, AI implementation failures demonstrate that sophisticated technology cannot compensate for poor change management, inadequate training, or cultures that resist collaboration between human and artificial intelligence.

As businesses continue to navigate the complexities of the digital era, those with strong, people-centered leadership will be best positioned to thrive. In an ever-changing digital landscape, technology alone is not enough—the human element remains the most powerful catalyst for transformation.

The most successful digital transformations are those that enhance human potential rather than replace it. Leaders who understand this principle and create organizations where people and technology work together synergistically will drive innovation, inspire their teams, and build sustainable competitive advantages in the digital economy.

The Leadership Mindset for the Digital Age

Leadership in the digital age is no longer about maintaining strict control over processes and outcomes; it is about empowerment, collaboration, and adaptability. The traditional command-and-control leadership model has become obsolete in a world where digital transformation is constant and unpredictable. Instead, leaders must embrace a mindset that encourages agility, innovation, and shared ownership of change.

To successfully lead digital transformation, leaders must first establish a clear and strategic vision that aligns digital initiatives with broader business objectives. Without a well-defined purpose, digital efforts can become fragmented, leading to wasted resources and disengaged employees. A strong leader ensures that every technological advancement contributes to the company's long-term goals, enhancing operations, customer experience, and overall competitiveness.

In a rapidly evolving landscape, agility and adaptability are essential qualities for modern leaders.

The digital economy moves quickly, and strategies that work today may become irrelevant tomorrow. Leaders must remain flexible, willing to pivot their approach when necessary, and open to new opportunities that arise from emerging technologies and shifting market conditions. Rather than rigid long-term planning, they must embrace continuous learning and iteration, adjusting their strategies based on data, feedback, and real-world performance.

The rise of AI has made this adaptability even more critical. AI technologies evolve rapidly, with new capabilities emerging monthly rather than yearly. Leaders must develop the ability to quickly evaluate new AI tools and applications while maintaining focus on fundamental business objectives. This requires a delicate balance between embracing innovation and avoiding the trap of implementing technology for its own sake.

Communication plays a crucial role in successful digital leadership. Transformation often introduces uncertainty, making employees feel uneasy about the future of their roles. Effective leaders communicate with empathy and transparency, addressing concerns openly and fostering trust among their teams. When employees understand the purpose behind digital initiatives and feel included in the process, they are far more likely to embrace change rather than resist it.

AI implementations require particularly sophisticated communication approaches because the technology can seem mysterious or threatening to employees who don't understand how machine learning systems work. Leaders must be able to demystify AI capabilities while addressing both rational concerns about job displacement and emotional concerns about human relevance in an increasingly automated workplace.

Beyond communication, collaboration is a cornerstone of effective digital leadership. Transformation is not the responsibility of a single department or executive—it requires buy-in and participation across the entire organization. Leaders must encourage cross-functional teamwork, ensuring that employees at all levels feel empowered to contribute. When digital transformation becomes a shared effort, it is more likely to succeed because those implementing the changes feel personally invested in the outcome.

The most successful AI implementations demonstrate this collaborative principle clearly. Rather than having technical teams develop AI systems in isolation, successful organizations create integrated teams that include domain experts, end users, and business stakeholders alongside data scientists and engineers. This collaborative approach ensures that AI applications actually solve real business problems rather than showcasing technical capabilities that don't translate to business value.

Even the most advanced technology will fail to deliver meaningful change without strong leadership to guide its implementation. The organizations that thrive in the digital age will be those whose leaders recognize that transformation is not just about adopting new tools—it is a fundamental shift in how people work, collaborate, and create value. Leaders who embrace this cultural and strategic evolution will be the ones who drive innovation, inspire their teams, and position their organizations for long-term success.

The integration of AI into business processes represents both the greatest opportunity and the greatest challenge for digital leaders. AI has the potential to augment human capabilities in unprecedented ways, but only when implemented by leaders who understand that successful transformation requires both technological sophistication and deep human insight. The future belongs to leaders who can create organizations where human creativity, judgment, and empathy work seamlessly with artificial intelligence to achieve outcomes that neither could accomplish alone.

Part II: PLANNING AND PREPARATION

Digital transformation is not just about implementing new technologies—it requires careful planning, strategic foresight, and organizational readiness. Too often, businesses rush into digital initiatives without fully understanding their goals, the risks involved, or the resources needed for success. Without a well-defined roadmap, even the most promising innovations can lead to disruptions, inefficiencies, and employee resistance.

The statistics surrounding digital transformation failures are sobering. Recent industry research reveals that between 55% and 75% of ERP projects either fail outright or fail to meet their intended objectives. The average cost overrun for ERP implementations reaches a staggering 189%, while only 23% of all ERP implementations are considered successful. Perhaps most telling, 54% of companies experience operational disruption when their new systems go live. These numbers represent more than statistical anomalies—they reflect fundamental breakdowns in planning, preparation, and execution.

Consider the cautionary tale of SPAR Group's SAP S/4HANA implementation, where over $100 million was invested in a system that ultimately failed to deliver its intended benefits. Or examine Lidl's even more dramatic failure, where the German retailer spent seven years and approximately €500 million on an SAP implementation before abandoning the project entirely and reverting to their legacy systems. These failures weren't caused by faulty technology—both SAP and S/4HANA are proven platforms used successfully by thousands of organizations worldwide. Instead, they stemmed from inadequate planning, insufficient stakeholder engagement, resistance to change, and poor governance structures.

The emergence of artificial intelligence adds another layer of complexity to modern digital transformations. While AI promises to revolutionize enterprise systems through predictive analytics, intelligent automation, and personalized user experiences, it also introduces new challenges around data quality, integration complexity, and organizational readiness. Companies are grappling with questions about whether AI in ERP is truly materializing beyond the marketing hype, how to prepare their organizations for AI-driven workflows, and what the real implications are for their workforce and business processes.

This section serves as the foundation for a successful digital transformation journey. Before moving into execution, organizations must take the time to align strategies, assess current capabilities, and ensure that leadership and employees are prepared for change. Digital transformation is a multi-layered process, and skipping the critical planning phase can result in failed implementations and wasted resources.

Why Planning Matters

Digital transformation is much like constructing a skyscraper. Without a solid blueprint, clear objectives, and the right materials, the structure may collapse under its own weight. Similarly, digital initiatives require a well-defined vision, a strategic approach to technology selection, and a culture that is ready to embrace change. Businesses must clearly define their objectives, ensuring that digital efforts align with their overall mission and provide measurable impact. Choosing the right digital tools is equally important, as they must integrate with existing systems and support long-term growth rather than simply adding complexity.

The failure patterns we observe across industries are remarkably consistent. Organizations that struggle with digital transformation typically exhibit common characteristics: unclear business objectives from the outset, inadequate stakeholder engagement, insufficient change management, over-reliance on external consultants without building internal capabilities, and resistance to adapting business processes to align with new systems. These patterns emerge whether we're examining massive retailers like Lidl, industrial conglomerates, or mid-market manufacturers.

Organizational readiness plays a key role in determining the success of transformation efforts. Leaders must ensure that teams are aligned with transformation goals, that company culture supports innovation, and that employees are equipped with the necessary skills to adapt. This becomes even more critical as artificial intelligence capabilities are integrated into enterprise systems. AI-driven transformations require not only technical readiness but also a workforce prepared to collaborate with intelligent systems, interpret AI-generated insights, and adapt to workflows that increasingly blend human expertise with machine intelligence.

Alongside these factors, risk management is essential, as every transformation comes with potential challenges. The rise of AI introduces additional risk dimensions, including data privacy concerns, algorithmic bias, cybersecurity vulnerabilities, and the need for continuous monitoring of AI model performance. Identifying these risks in advance and creating contingency plans can prevent costly setbacks and ensure a smoother transition into digital workflows. By investing in thorough preparation, organizations minimize risks, maximize return on investment, and create a stronger foundation for digital transformation.

Chapter 5

Strategic Alignment

In the current business environment, digital transformation is no longer optional—it is a necessity. Companies that embrace digital initiatives gain efficiencies, improve customer experiences, and drive innovation. However, the success of transformation depends on more than just implementing new technologies; it hinges on ensuring that digital initiatives align with overarching business objectives.

Strategic alignment ensures that digital strategies serve a greater purpose within the organization rather than existing as isolated IT projects. When digital initiatives are integrated with business priorities, companies can streamline operations, increase agility, and gain a competitive advantage. Without alignment, digital investments can result in wasted resources, costly failures, and operational disruptions. The challenge for many organizations is bridging the gap between technological advancements and business goals. Understanding how to align digital strategies with business objectives is critical for long-term success.

The consequences of misalignment extend far beyond financial losses. When digital initiatives lack strategic coherence, they create organizational confusion, employee frustration, and fragmented systems that often work against each other rather than supporting unified business goals. This fragmentation becomes even more problematic as organizations attempt to integrate artificial intelligence capabilities across their enterprise systems, where misaligned

AI implementations can perpetuate and amplify existing inefficiencies.

Aligning Digital Strategies with Business Objectives

Successful digital transformation requires more than just the adoption of technology—it demands intentional planning, collaboration across teams, and governance structures that ensure digital initiatives truly support the organization's goals. Without a structured approach, businesses risk investing in technology without realizing its full potential, leading to inefficiencies, wasted resources, and missed opportunities.

Defining Clear Business Objectives

One of the first and most critical steps in aligning digital strategies with business objectives is defining clear and measurable goals. Before launching any digital initiative, organizations must have a strong understanding of their priorities and strategic direction. Business leaders need to identify what they want to achieve through digital transformation, whether it is cost reduction, revenue growth, improved customer satisfaction, operational efficiency, market expansion, or a combination of these objectives.

When digital initiatives are launched without a clear purpose, they often become fragmented, failing to deliver meaningful value. The Lidl case provides a perfect illustration of this problem. Despite investing €500 million over seven years, the company failed to establish a clear vision for how the new SAP system would fundamentally improve their business operations. Instead of defining specific, measurable outcomes, the project became focused on technical implementation without adequate consideration of business impact.

To avoid this pitfall, organizations must ensure that each digital investment is purpose-driven and directly tied to strategic business outcomes. A well-articulated vision enables teams to prioritize projects effectively and allocate resources where they will have the greatest impact. This becomes particularly important when considering AI integration, where the temptation to adopt "AI for AI's sake" must be balanced against clear business value propositions.

Establishing key performance indicators (KPIs) is equally important in ensuring alignment. These measurable metrics allow businesses to track progress and evaluate the effectiveness of digital efforts. For example, if the primary goal is customer satisfaction, relevant KPIs might include Net Promoter Score (NPS), customer retention rates, and response times for customer support. If revenue growth is a key focus, then sales conversion rates, average order value, and customer acquisition costs could serve as indicators of success. By setting clear benchmarks, organizations can continuously assess the impact of digital transformation initiatives and make necessary adjustments along the way.

The integration of artificial intelligence into these measurement frameworks requires additional consideration. AI-driven KPIs might include model accuracy rates, prediction confidence levels, automation efficiency gains, and user adoption of AI-powered features. Organizations must establish baselines for these new metrics while ensuring they remain connected to overarching business objectives rather than becoming purely technical measures.

Developing a Comprehensive Digital Strategy

A comprehensive digital strategy serves as a blueprint for transformation efforts. A well-defined strategy ensures that digital transformation is not viewed as an isolated IT initiative but rather as an organization-wide effort that touches every department and function. This approach fosters collaboration among teams, breaks down silos, and ensures that digital investments are seamlessly integrated into business operations.

Selecting the right technologies is a key component of an effective digital strategy. Rather than adopting the latest trends simply for the sake of innovation, organizations should carefully evaluate which technologies align with their business needs and long-term vision. Cloud computing, artificial intelligence, data analytics, and automation tools are among the many digital solutions that can drive transformation, but their implementation must be thoughtfully planned to ensure they enhance business performance.

The current AI landscape presents both unprecedented opportunities and significant challenges for strategic technology selection. While vendors promote embedded AI, generative insights, and predictive automation capabilities, organizations must look beyond the marketing hype to evaluate whether these AI features solve real business problems. Many companies are discovering that their data infrastructure and organizational processes are not yet ready to fully leverage AI capabilities, requiring foundational improvements before advanced AI features can deliver meaningful value.

Beyond technology, optimizing processes is essential for improving efficiency and creating a more agile organization. Digital transformation often involves reengineering existing workflows to eliminate bottlenecks, streamline operations, and improve overall productivity. For example, automating repetitive tasks can free up employees to focus on higher-value work, while digital collaboration tools can enhance communication across teams. However, process optimization becomes more complex when AI is involved, as it requires rethinking how humans and machines will collaborate within new workflows.

Company culture also plays a critical role in digital transformation success. Change management strategies should be incorporated into the digital roadmap to ensure employees are engaged and equipped to embrace new technologies and ways of working. This cultural dimension becomes even more significant with AI integration, where employees may harbor concerns about job displacement, algorithmic decision-making, or the reliability of AI-generated insights. Resistance to change is a common challenge, so organizations should invest in training, provide clear communication, and create an environment where innovation is encouraged. Leadership must set the tone by championing digital initiatives and demonstrating a commitment to transformation.

Ensuring Long-Term Alignment

Aligning digital strategies with business objectives is not a one-time effort—it requires continuous evaluation and adaptation. The business landscape is constantly evolving, and digital strategies must remain flexible to accommodate new market trends, customer expectations, and technological advancements. The rapid pace of AI development exemplifies this challenge, as capabilities that seemed futuristic just months ago are now becoming standard features in enterprise software platforms.

Organizations should establish governance structures to oversee digital initiatives, ensuring that all projects remain aligned with corporate goals. Regular performance reviews, feedback loops, and strategic assessments can help identify areas for improvement and keep transformation efforts on track. Additionally, fostering a culture of innovation enables businesses to stay ahead of the competition by continuously exploring new opportunities for digital advancement.

The governance of AI-powered initiatives requires particular attention to ethical considerations, data privacy, model performance monitoring, and compliance with evolving regulations. As AI becomes more prevalent in business operations, organizations must develop frameworks for responsible AI deployment that balance innovation with risk management.

A successful digital transformation is not just about implementing technology but about strategically integrating digital initiatives into the core business strategy. By clearly defining objectives, developing a comprehensive roadmap, selecting the right technologies, optimizing processes, and fostering a digital-first culture, organizations can ensure that their digital investments drive meaningful business outcomes. When executed effectively, digital transformation has the power to enhance efficiency, improve customer experiences, and create sustainable competitive advantages in an increasingly digital world.

Engaging Stakeholders Across the Organization

One of the most common reasons for digital transformation failures is the lack of stakeholder involvement. Digital initiatives impact every department, from finance and HR to marketing and operations. When leaders fail to engage key stakeholders early in the process, transformation efforts can face resistance, inefficiencies, and siloed decision-making. Ensuring that leaders and employees across the organization are involved in the planning process creates a unified approach that prevents misalignment and increases adoption.

The Lidl failure provides a stark example of what happens when stakeholder engagement breaks down. Throughout the seven-year project, the company experienced significant executive turnover, including changes in CEO and Head of IT positions. This leadership instability created confusion about project priorities and strategic direction. Without consistent stakeholder commitment at the highest levels, the project lost momentum and coherence, ultimately contributing to its abandonment.

Stakeholder engagement begins with leadership buy-in, as executives must support digital transformation efforts to ensure successful implementation. A strong commitment from leadership sets the tone for the entire organization, demonstrating that digital transformation is a priority. Without this commitment, employees and department heads may not see the value of new initiatives or may even resist change due to uncertainty or skepticism.

The challenge becomes more complex when AI capabilities are introduced into digital transformation initiatives. Stakeholders across the organization need to understand not just what AI can do, but how it will change their daily work, decision-making processes, and collaboration patterns. This requires more sophisticated communication and training programs that help stakeholders envision their roles in an AI-augmented workplace.

Involving department heads and employees in early planning discussions provides valuable insights, allowing companies to refine their strategies based on real-world needs. Each department has unique challenges and processes, and involving representatives from all functions ensures that digital initiatives address those specific needs. For example, HR might require streamlined employee onboarding systems, while finance might need automated reporting tools that can integrate AI-powered analytics for better forecasting and decision support. Without stakeholder input, digital transformation efforts might lead to solutions that are impractical or inefficient for end users, ultimately resulting in poor adoption rates.

To foster stakeholder engagement, organizations should implement structured feedback mechanisms. Gathering feedback through workshops, surveys, and pilot programs helps employees feel involved and invested in the transformation process. Workshops provide a platform for employees to voice their concerns and ideas, allowing organizations to tailor solutions that truly enhance workflows. Surveys can capture broader sentiment across the organization, highlighting potential areas of resistance or enthusiasm. Pilot programs enable a phased approach to implementation, allowing teams to test digital solutions on a smaller scale before full deployment. This iterative process helps organizations make necessary refinements while also giving employees confidence in the effectiveness of the changes.

When AI components are part of the digital transformation, pilot programs become even more critical. They allow organizations to test AI model performance in real-world conditions, gather feedback on user interfaces, and identify potential biases or errors before full-scale deployment. These pilots also help build organizational confidence in AI capabilities while providing valuable data for refining implementation approaches.

Another key component of stakeholder engagement is transparency. Organizations should communicate the purpose, benefits, and expected outcomes of digital transformation initiatives clearly and consistently. Employees who understand why changes are being made and how they will benefit from them are more likely to embrace new technologies and workflows. This transparency becomes crucial when discussing AI integration, where employees may have concerns about job security, decision-making autonomy, or the reliability of AI-generated insights. Change management strategies, including training programs and ongoing support, further enhance adoption by ensuring employees feel equipped to navigate digital tools effectively.

Digital tools should be practical, user-friendly, and aligned with the daily workflows of employees. When digital initiatives are implemented with input from those who will be using them, they are far more likely to succeed. A user-centric approach prioritizes functionality and ease of use, ensuring that technology serves as an enabler rather than a burden. This principle extends to AI-powered features, which must be designed with intuitive interfaces and clear explanations of how AI-generated insights support human decision-making. Additionally, organizations should foster a culture of continuous learning, where employees feel encouraged to experiment with and adapt to new technologies.

Cross-functional collaboration is another critical aspect of stakeholder engagement. Digital transformation should not be confined to IT departments or senior leadership; it must involve employees at all levels. Cross-departmental teams should be formed to oversee and champion digital initiatives, ensuring that knowledge and insights are shared across the organization. These teams can identify common challenges, align on best practices, and collectively drive innovation. Encouraging a culture of collaboration breaks down silos and fosters a shared sense of ownership over digital transformation efforts.

Moreover, organizations must recognize that digital transformation is an ongoing journey rather than a one-time project. Stakeholder engagement should be sustained beyond the initial implementation phase to ensure long-term success. Regular check-ins, open forums, and continuous feedback loops enable organizations to address evolving challenges and capitalize on emerging opportunities. Leaders should also celebrate successes and milestones, reinforcing the value of digital transformation efforts and keeping employees motivated.

Ultimately, engaging stakeholders across the organization is essential for the success of digital transformation initiatives. By securing leadership buy-in, involving employees in decision-making, implementing effective feedback mechanisms, ensuring transparency, fostering collaboration, and maintaining ongoing engagement, organizations can drive meaningful and sustainable digital change.

Implementing Effective Governance Structures

Digital transformation is not a one-time event—it is an ongoing process that requires continuous oversight and refinement. To maintain alignment between digital initiatives and business objectives, organizations must establish governance structures that provide strategic direction and accountability.

A strong governance framework includes the establishment of a digital transformation steering committee responsible for overseeing major initiatives. This committee should consist of key stakeholders from various departments, including IT, finance, operations, HR, and marketing. By involving a diverse group of decision-makers, organizations can ensure that digital transformation efforts align with overall business goals and address the needs of different functional areas.

The steering committee plays a crucial role in setting the vision for digital transformation, defining priorities, and ensuring that projects remain on track. It is responsible for establishing clear objectives, setting key performance indicators (KPIs), and monitoring progress against predefined milestones. Regular meetings and status updates help maintain momentum and allow for course corrections when necessary.

When AI capabilities are integrated into digital transformation initiatives, governance structures must evolve to address unique challenges such as algorithm transparency, data ethics, model performance monitoring, and regulatory compliance. Organizations need specialized AI governance committees or subcommittees that can oversee the responsible development and deployment of AI systems while ensuring they remain aligned with business objectives and ethical standards.

One of the most important aspects of governance is accountability. Clearly defining roles and responsibilities within the organization prevents digital initiatives from stalling due to miscommunication or lack of ownership. Each digital initiative should have designated project leads who are responsible for execution, monitoring progress, and reporting outcomes. Establishing a hierarchy of accountability ensures that digital transformation efforts are actively managed and not deprioritized amidst competing business demands.

The SPAR Group case Illustrates the dangers of weak governance structures. The company's SAP S/4HANA implementation suffered from poor project oversight, which resulted in scope creep, budget overruns, and technical challenges that were not adequately addressed. Without strong governance frameworks and clear accountability mechanisms, critical issues such as data migration errors and system compatibility problems went unresolved, ultimately contributing to the project's failure.

Resource allocation is another critical function of governance structures. Digital transformation requires investment in technology, personnel, and training. Governance committees must ensure that resources are allocated efficiently, balancing short-term needs with long-term strategic objectives. Budget considerations, technology procurement, and workforce planning should all be addressed within the governance framework to avoid overspending or underutilization of digital tools.

Regular performance reviews should be conducted to assess the success of digital initiatives, allowing organizations to make adjustments based on data and feedback. Key metrics such as user adoption rates, efficiency gains, customer satisfaction, and financial impact should be tracked to measure the effectiveness of digital transformation efforts. Data-driven decision-making enables organizations to refine strategies, optimize digital solutions, and maximize return on investment.

Governance structures provide the necessary oversight to ensure that digital transformation efforts remain relevant, scalable, and aligned with the organization's evolving needs. Without proper governance, digital initiatives can become inconsistent, lack direction, and fail to deliver on their intended goals. A lack of governance can also lead to fragmented technology adoption, where different departments implement separate solutions that do not integrate effectively, resulting in inefficiencies and data silos.

Additionally, risk management is a key component of digital governance. Digital transformation introduces potential risks, including cybersecurity threats, data privacy concerns, and operational disruptions. These risks become more complex with AI integration, where additional considerations include algorithmic bias, model drift, explainability requirements, and regulatory compliance. Governance committees should proactively identify and mitigate these risks by implementing robust security measures, ensuring compliance with regulatory requirements, and developing contingency plans for potential disruptions.

Change management strategies should also be embedded within governance structures. Digital transformation often involves significant shifts in workflows, business processes, and employee roles. Governance committees should oversee change management efforts, ensuring that employees receive adequate training, support, and communication throughout the transition. Effective change management reduces resistance and enhances overall adoption rates.

Finally, organizations should recognize that governance is not a static framework; it should evolve in response to changing business environments, technological advancements, and organizational needs. Governance structures should be periodically reviewed and refined to ensure continued effectiveness. By remaining agile and adaptable, organizations can sustain digital transformation efforts and drive long-term success.

Implementing effective governance structures is essential for maintaining alignment, accountability, and scalability in digital transformation initiatives. A well-defined governance framework, supported by a steering committee, clear accountability, resource allocation, performance monitoring, risk management, and change management strategies, ensures that digital transformation efforts deliver tangible business value. By prioritizing governance, organizations can navigate the complexities of digital change and achieve sustainable growth in an increasingly digital world.

Maintaining Flexibility and Adaptability

The digital landscape is constantly evolving, and businesses must be prepared to adjust their strategies as new technologies and market conditions emerge. The rapid pace of digital transformation means that organizations cannot afford to remain static in their approach. Companies that fail to embrace change risk falling behind their competitors, losing market share, and struggling to meet the expectations of an increasingly tech-savvy customer base. Organizations that remain rigid in their digital plans may struggle to compete with more adaptable competitors who are quicker to innovate and respond to shifts in consumer behavior, industry trends, and technological advancements.

The emergence of artificial intelligence as a mainstream business capability exemplifies the need for strategic flexibility. Organizations that planned their digital transformations just two years ago could not have fully anticipated the rapid advancement and democratization of generative AI technologies. Companies that maintained flexible architectures and adaptive governance structures have been better positioned to integrate AI capabilities as they became available, while those with rigid systems and processes have struggled to adapt.

To maintain flexibility, businesses must continuously evaluate emerging technologies and assess their potential impact on operations. This process requires ongoing research, investment in learning and development, and a willingness to experiment with new digital solutions. By actively monitoring industry trends and advancements, organizations can make informed decisions about when and how to integrate new technologies into their operations. The AI landscape, in particular, requires careful monitoring as capabilities evolve rapidly and new use cases emerge regularly.

Additionally, fostering a proactive mindset across teams helps businesses anticipate potential disruptions and respond effectively to changes in the market. This becomes particularly important as AI technologies mature and create new possibilities for automation, decision support, and customer engagement that may not have existed when initial digital strategies were developed.

Encouraging a culture of experimentation is crucial for businesses aiming to stay ahead in the digital space. Employees should be empowered to test and refine digital tools without fear of failure. When failure is seen as a learning opportunity rather than a setback, innovation thrives, and organizations become more resilient in the face of change. This experimental mindset is essential for AI adoption, where organizations need to test different AI models, approaches, and use cases to determine what works best for their specific context.

Providing employees with the resources and autonomy to explore new ideas fosters creativity and drives continuous improvement. Companies that embrace a test-and-learn approach can identify the most effective digital strategies, optimize existing processes, and remain competitive in a dynamic environment. This approach becomes even more valuable when experimenting with AI capabilities, where pilot programs and controlled testing can reveal unexpected insights and applications.

Another essential aspect of maintaining flexibility is regularly reviewing digital investments to ensure they continue to align with business objectives. Technology that was effective a few years ago may no longer meet the organization's needs, and failing to update systems can lead to inefficiencies and missed opportunities. This challenge is particularly acute with AI technologies, where models can become outdated quickly, new capabilities emerge regularly, and integration patterns evolve rapidly.

Businesses should implement structured evaluation processes to assess the performance of their digital tools and determine whether adjustments are necessary. Regularly auditing digital investments helps organizations avoid obsolescence and ensures that resources are allocated effectively. This includes evaluating whether existing systems can accommodate AI enhancements or whether more fundamental architectural changes are needed.

Adaptability is key to sustaining long-term digital success, allowing organizations to pivot when necessary and seize new opportunities as they arise. Companies that are willing to reassess their strategies, restructure operations, or reallocate resources in response to industry shifts will be better equipped to thrive in a rapidly changing environment. The organizations that successfully integrate AI capabilities into their operations are often those that maintained flexible digital architectures and governance structures that could accommodate new technologies as they matured.

Flexibility in decision-making and operational processes enables businesses to respond to challenges with agility, making them more resilient to disruptions such as economic downturns, technological advancements, or changes in consumer expectations. This agility becomes particularly valuable as AI technologies continue to evolve and create new opportunities for competitive advantage.

The success of digital transformation is not determined by technology alone but by the careful planning and preparation that precedes it. Implementing new digital tools without a clear strategy or alignment with business goals can lead to wasted resources and suboptimal results. Organizations that take the time to define clear objectives, align digital strategies with business goals, engage stakeholders, establish governance structures, and maintain flexibility will be far better positioned for success. Digital transformation requires a holistic approach that involves leadership, employees, and external partners working together to create a unified vision and execute it effectively.

Digital transformation is a continuous journey that requires strategic foresight, collaboration, and the ability to evolve with the changing digital landscape. It is not a one-time initiative but an ongoing process that must be embedded in the organization's culture. Companies that view digital transformation as an iterative process rather than a destination will be more successful in adapting to future changes, including the ongoing evolution of AI capabilities. By investing in the planning phase, businesses can minimize risks, optimize resources, and create a strong foundation for sustainable digital growth.

Ultimately, organizations that embrace flexibility and adaptability will be well-positioned to navigate the complexities of the digital age. By fostering a culture of innovation, continuously evaluating digital strategies, and maintaining a proactive approach to change, businesses can enhance their competitiveness and drive long-term success in an ever-evolving digital landscape.

Case Studies: Lessons in Strategic Alignment

Successful Alignment: Procter & Gamble's OGSM Framework

Procter & Gamble (P&G) is a global consumer goods giant known for its ability to innovate and remain competitive in an increasingly digital business environment. With a vast portfolio of brands, P&G continuously adapts to changing market dynamics, consumer behaviors, and technological advancements. The company's success in digital transformation can be attributed to its disciplined use of the

Objectives, Goals, Strategies, and Measures (OGSM) framework. This structured approach ensures that every digital initiative is directly tied to the company's overarching business objectives, preventing wasted investments and misaligned efforts.

Understanding the OGSM Framework

The OGSM framework is a strategic planning tool that helps organizations define their key priorities and execute them efficiently. It consists of four key elements:

- Objectives: The broad vision or mission the company aims to achieve.
- Goals: Measurable targets that define what success looks like.
- Strategies: The specific actions and initiatives undertaken to meet the goals.
- Measures: The key performance indicators (KPIs) used to track progress and ensure accountability.

P&G has embraced this framework to align its digital initiatives with long-term business strategy, ensuring that innovation translates into tangible business results. By breaking down broad objectives into actionable goals and strategies, the company has been able to maintain its competitive edge while driving efficiency and profitability.

Digital Transformation at P&G: A Structured Approach

AI-Driven Analytics for Supply Chain Optimization

One of the most significant areas where strategic alignment has paid off for P&G is supply chain optimization. With a vast and complex supply chain spanning multiple continents, ensuring efficiency in production, inventory management, and logistics is critical.

To enhance operational efficiency, P&G has implemented sophisticated data analytics tools powered by artificial intelligence (AI). These tools predict demand patterns, optimize inventory levels, and improve logistics, ensuring products reach the right markets at the right time. By leveraging real-time data and machine learning algorithms, P&G can anticipate market fluctuations and adjust production schedules accordingly.

This data-driven approach has led to several benefits:

- Reduced Costs: AI-driven insights allow P&G to minimize excess inventory and reduce warehousing expenses.

- Minimized Waste: By optimizing supply chain processes, the company significantly decreases product obsolescence and resource wastage.

- Improved Product Availability: Better demand forecasting ensures that products are readily available to consumers, enhancing customer satisfaction.

Through the OGSM framework, P&G ensures that its AI-driven supply chain initiatives align with its broader objective of operational excellence. Every technological investment is assessed based on its contribution to efficiency, sustainability, and cost reduction.

Digital Marketing and Personalized Customer Engagement

Another key area where strategic alignment has played a crucial role is digital marketing and personalized customer engagement. Consumer expectations have shifted dramatically with the rise of digital platforms, requiring companies to adopt more targeted and data-driven marketing strategies.

P&G has leveraged AI-powered insights to refine its marketing approach. By analyzing consumer data and purchasing behaviors, the company tailors advertising campaigns to deliver relevant content to the right audience at the right time. This personalized approach is implemented across multiple digital channels, including social media, e-commerce platforms, and programmatic advertising.

Key benefits of P&G's data-driven marketing strategy include:

- Increased Customer Engagement: Targeted marketing ensures that customers receive content that resonates with their preferences, leading to higher engagement rates.
- Enhanced Brand Loyalty: Personalization fosters a stronger emotional connection between consumers and brands, increasing customer retention.
- Optimized Marketing Spend: AI-driven analytics allow P&G to allocate marketing budgets more effectively, reducing unnecessary expenses and improving return on investment (ROI).

The OGSM framework ensures that these marketing efforts align with broader business objectives, such as market expansion, brand differentiation, and revenue growth. Every marketing initiative is evaluated based on its contribution to customer experience and business performance.

Cloud-Based Collaboration for Enhanced Efficiency

In addition to optimizing supply chains and marketing strategies, P&G has embraced cloud-based collaboration tools to improve internal efficiency. With a workforce spread across multiple regions, seamless communication and collaboration are essential for driving innovation and operational success.

By moving key operations and communication platforms to the cloud, P&G enables employees to collaborate in real time, share insights, and work more effectively. Cloud-based solutions facilitate:

- Faster Decision-Making: Teams have instant access to critical data, allowing for quicker responses to market changes.
- Reduced Operational Bottlenecks: Eliminating silos and streamlining workflows enhance overall productivity.
- Increased Agility and Innovation: Employees can work flexibly, fostering a culture of continuous improvement and innovation.

By integrating cloud solutions within the OGSM framework, P&G ensures that its digital collaboration initiatives support its overarching goals of operational efficiency, employee empowerment, and agile decision-making.

Key Takeaways from P&G's Strategic Alignment

P&G's success in digital transformation offers valuable lessons for other organizations seeking to align technology with business objectives. The key takeaways from P&G's strategic approach include:

- Intentional Digital Transformation: Digital initiatives should be purpose-driven and directly linked to business goals.

Implementing technology for the sake of innovation alone can lead to misalignment and wasted resources.

- Structured Planning with OGSM: Using a structured framework like OGSM ensures that objectives, goals, strategies, and measures are clearly defined. This approach prevents fragmented efforts and fosters cross-functional collaboration.

- Data-Driven Decision-Making: Leveraging AI and analytics enables organizations to make informed decisions, optimize operations, and enhance customer engagement. Data should be at the core of digital strategies to drive meaningful business outcomes.

- Agility and Adaptability: In a rapidly changing business landscape, companies must remain agile and adaptable. P&G's ability to pivot and integrate new technologies while staying aligned with its long-term strategy has been a key driver of success.

- Customer-Centric Approach: Personalized marketing and customer engagement strategies enhance brand loyalty and market competitiveness. Understanding consumer behavior through data analytics ensures that digital efforts deliver maximum impact.

Procter & Gamble's strategic alignment through the OGSM framework has been instrumental in driving its digital transformation success. By ensuring that digital initiatives are aligned with overarching business objectives, P&G has optimized its supply chain, enhanced customer engagement, and improved internal efficiency.

The company's approach demonstrates that successful digital transformation is not just about adopting the latest technology but about integrating digital strategies into the core business framework. As industries continue to evolve, organizations that prioritize strategic alignment—ensuring that every technological investment serves a clear business purpose—will be best positioned for long-term success.

By following P&G's example, companies can develop a roadmap for digital transformation that is both structured and adaptable, ultimately achieving sustainable growth and competitive advantage in an increasingly digital world.

Unsuccessful Alignment: Lidl's €500 Million SAP Disaster

While Procter & Gamble's success demonstrates the power of strategic alignment in digital transformation, the failure of Lidl's SAP implementation serves as one of the most cautionary tales in modern enterprise software history. The German discount retailer spent seven years and approximately €500 million on a SAP for Retail implementation before ultimately abandoning the project and reverting to their legacy systems. This massive failure provides critical insights into what happens when strategic alignment breaks down and organizational readiness is insufficient.

The Ambitious Vision That Went Wrong

In 2011, Lidl made the decision to replace its homegrown legacy system "Wawi" with a new solution based on SAP for Retail, powered by HANA. The project, code-named "eLWIS" (electronic Lidl merchandise management and information system), was intended to be transformative for the company. With close to €100 billion in annual revenue and operations spanning thousands of stores across multiple countries, Lidl needed a modern, scalable system to support its rapid growth and complex inventory management requirements.

The project assembled approximately 1,000 internal staff members and hundreds of external consultants, making it one of the largest retail system implementations ever attempted. SAP, recognizing the significance of the engagement, even awarded Lidl a prize in April 2017 for being one of their best customers. The system was designed to centralize and simplify worldwide inventory management across Lidl's network of over 10,000 stores and more than 140 logistics centers.

Fundamental Misalignment from the Start

The first critical failure in Lidl's implementation was the lack of clear strategic objectives and alignment between the technology solution and the company's business processes. Unlike P&G's disciplined OGSM approach, Lidl never established a clear framework for how the new system would fundamentally improve their business operations beyond technical modernization.

The most glaring example of this misalignment emerged around inventory valuation methods. Lidl had built its business model around purchase price-based inventory valuation, which allowed them to maintain their low-cost structure and rapid decision-making processes. However, SAP for Retail used a retail price-based valuation model as its standard approach. This seemingly technical difference represented a fundamental clash between Lidl's core business operations and the software's built-in assumptions.

Rather than adapting their business processes to align with SAP's proven methodology—used successfully by numerous other retailers worldwide—Lidl insisted on customizing the system to mirror their legacy approach. This decision revealed a critical failure in strategic thinking: the company was not willing to change their processes to leverage the benefits of a modern, standardized system. Instead, they tried to recreate their old system using expensive new technology.

Organizational Chaos and Leadership Instability

Throughout the seven-year implementation, Lidl experienced significant executive turnover that further undermined strategic alignment. The company appointed a new CEO in 2014 who subsequently stepped down in 2017, during the most critical phases of the project. The Head of IT also departed during this period, creating a leadership vacuum at precisely when strong, consistent direction was most needed.

This executive instability meant that key strategic decisions—such as whether all stores should operate under the same process model or whether certain geographies should maintain autonomous operations—were left unresolved. Without consistent leadership championing the transformation and making difficult decisions about process changes, the project lost momentum and coherence.

The contrast with successful implementations is stark. Companies that achieve digital transformation success typically maintain stable leadership throughout the process, with executives who are willing to make tough decisions about changing business processes to align with new systems. Lidl's leadership instability created a vacuum where no one had the authority or commitment to drive necessary organizational changes.

Over-Customization and Technical Complexity

When organizations resist changing their business processes to align with standard software functionality, they inevitably face the costly path of over-customization. Lidl fell into this trap, creating a heavily modified version of SAP that was described by industry experts as "not suitable for high-turnover countries" after all the adaptations and amendments required.

This over-customization created a cascade of problems. The heavily modified system became more complex to implement, test, and maintain. Integration with other systems became more difficult. Upgrades to newer versions of SAP became nearly impossible. Most critically, the customized system failed to deliver the efficiency gains and best practices that come with standard implementations.

Industry research shows that companies achieving the greatest success with ERP implementations are those that minimize customization and adapt their processes to leverage software best practices. Lidl's approach violated this fundamental principle, creating a solution that combined the worst aspects of both worlds: the complexity and cost of modern enterprise software without the benefits of proven business processes.

The Role of Change Management Failure

Perhaps the most critical factor in Lidl's failure was inadequate change management and organizational resistance to adopting new ways of working. The company's employees and management teams were simply not prepared to embrace the fundamental changes required for successful ERP implementation.

Research from industry experts reveals that change management failures are present in virtually every major ERP disaster. Organizations that fail to invest in proper change management strategies inevitably struggle with user adoption, process compliance, and system utilization. Lidl's case exemplifies this pattern, where the technology worked as designed, but the organization was not ready to change how it operated.

The company's decision to ultimately abandon the project and revert to developing their old "Wawi" system further illustrates this resistance to change. Rather than adapting to modern business practices embedded in SAP, Lidl chose to continue with outdated approaches that may have worked in the past but created strategic vulnerabilities for the future.

Financial and Strategic Consequences

The €500 million write-off represents more than just a financial loss—it reflects seven years without meaningful system modernization during a period of intense retail industry transformation. While Lidl's competitors were implementing modern systems that enabled better analytics, improved customer insights, and more efficient operations, Lidl remained stuck with outdated technology.

This strategic setback occurred during a critical period when artificial intelligence and advanced analytics were becoming important competitive differentiators in retail. Companies with modern, integrated systems were better positioned to leverage these emerging technologies, while Lidl's legacy infrastructure limited their ability to compete on data-driven insights and automated processes.

The reputational damage extended beyond financial losses. The high-profile failure sent signals to investors, partners, and competitors about Lidl's ability to execute complex strategic initiatives. In an industry where operational excellence and technological capability are increasingly important competitive factors, such failures can have lasting strategic implications.

Lessons from the Disaster

Lidl's SAP failure provides several critical lessons for organizations embarking on digital transformation initiatives:

Strategic Alignment is Non-Negotiable: Organizations must be willing to adapt their business processes to align with proven software methodologies.

When companies insist on replicating legacy processes in new systems, they forfeit the benefits of modernization while incurring all the costs and complexity.

Leadership Stability and Commitment: Successful digital transformations require consistent, committed leadership throughout the entire process. Executive turnover during critical phases can derail even well-planned initiatives. Leaders must be prepared to make difficult decisions about process changes and organizational adaptation.

Change Management is Critical: Technical implementation is only half the battle. Organizations must invest heavily in change management, training, and organizational development to ensure employees are prepared to embrace new ways of working. Without this investment, even perfectly functional systems will fail.

Avoid the Customization Trap: While some level of configuration is necessary, extensive customization undermines the value proposition of enterprise software. Organizations should prioritize process adaptation over system modification.

Governance and Accountability: Clear project governance, defined roles, and accountability mechanisms are essential for maintaining focus and momentum throughout lengthy implementations. Without strong governance, projects can lose direction and fall victim to scope creep and shifting priorities.

Consider Organizational Readiness: Before embarking on major digital transformations, organizations must honestly assess their readiness for change. This includes cultural factors, leadership commitment, and the organization's track record of successfully implementing major changes.

The Broader Implications

Lidl's failure illustrates that successful digital transformation is fundamentally about organizational change, not just technology implementation. The most sophisticated software in the world cannot succeed in an organization that is not prepared to embrace new ways of working.

This lesson becomes even more critical as organizations consider integrating artificial intelligence capabilities into their operations. AI implementation requires even more fundamental changes to business processes, decision-making approaches, and organizational roles than traditional ERP systems. Organizations that cannot successfully adapt to standard ERP functionality will likely struggle even more with AI integration.

The Lidl case also demonstrates the importance of strategic patience and commitment. Digital transformation is a long-term process that requires sustained effort and consistent leadership. Organizations that approach these initiatives with short-term thinking or without full commitment to change are setting themselves up for expensive failures.

Comparing Success and Failure Patterns

The contrast between P&G's success and Lidl's failure reveals fundamental patterns that determine digital transformation outcomes. These patterns transcend specific technologies or industries, applying equally to traditional ERP implementations and modern AI-enhanced systems.

Strategic Clarity: P&G's OGSM framework provided clear linkage between technology investments and business objectives. Every digital initiative had defined purposes and measurable outcomes. Lidl, by contrast, lacked clear strategic objectives for their transformation beyond technical modernization, leading to confusion about success criteria and project priorities.

Organizational Readiness: P&G demonstrated willingness to adapt business processes to leverage technology capabilities effectively. The company embraced change as a necessary component of transformation. Lidl resisted changing their business processes, instead attempting to customize technology to replicate legacy approaches.

Leadership Commitment: P&G maintained consistent leadership commitment throughout their transformation initiatives, with executives championing change and making necessary decisions. Lidl experienced significant leadership turnover during critical phases, creating instability and loss of momentum.

Change Management Investment: P&G invested in comprehensive change management, ensuring employees were prepared for new ways of working. Lidl underestimated the importance of change management, leading to organizational resistance and poor adoption.

Governance and Execution: P&G employed structured governance frameworks that maintained alignment and accountability. Lidl lacked effective governance structures, leading to scope creep, budget overruns, and loss of strategic focus.

These patterns provide a roadmap for organizations embarking on digital transformation initiatives. Success requires more than selecting the right technology—it demands strategic clarity, organizational readiness, committed leadership, effective change management, and strong governance throughout the process.

As organizations increasingly consider artificial intelligence integration, these foundational principles become even more critical. AI implementations require greater organizational adaptation, more sophisticated change management, and stronger governance than traditional system implementations. Organizations that master these fundamentals will be better positioned to succeed with AI-enhanced digital transformations, while those that ignore these lessons may face even more costly failures than traditional ERP disasters.

Frameworks for Achieving Strategic Alignment

To ensure that digital transformation efforts are not just technology-driven but strategically sound, organizations can turn to proven frameworks that align digital strategies with overarching business objectives. These frameworks provide structured methodologies that help businesses integrate technology investments into their long-term vision, ensuring that every digital initiative contributes to measurable success.

One widely used approach is the GQM+Strategies framework, which connects organizational goals with specific, measurable strategies. This method ensures that every digital transformation effort is directly linked to key business objectives, preventing misalignment and wasted investments. By establishing clear goals, defining targeted strategies, and measuring outcomes, organizations can create a structured path to digital success. GQM+Strategies provides a way to systematically evaluate whether digital initiatives are truly driving value and contributing to the company's broader mission.

Another critical framework is Business-IT Alignment, which integrates information technology into business strategy rather than treating IT as a separate function. This approach recognizes that digital transformation is not just about upgrading technology but about embedding IT into the core of business operations. Organizations that successfully align IT with their business strategy ensure that technology initiatives enhance efficiency, drive innovation, and deliver tangible business value rather than becoming isolated technical projects with no direct impact on growth or profitability.

A well-defined Technology Strategy is also essential for businesses looking to structure their digital transformation efforts. This framework involves developing a comprehensive roadmap for technology adoption, clearly defining objectives, principles, and tactics for implementation. By taking a strategic approach to technology planning, organizations can make informed decisions about which digital tools to invest in, how to integrate them with existing systems, and how to scale their digital capabilities over time. A strong technology strategy ensures that digital transformation efforts are sustainable, adaptable, and capable of evolving alongside industry trends and business needs.

The integration of artificial intelligence capabilities requires additional framework considerations. AI Governance Frameworks help organizations establish policies and procedures for responsible AI development, deployment, and monitoring. These frameworks address critical concerns such as algorithmic transparency, bias detection and mitigation, data privacy, regulatory compliance, and performance monitoring. As AI becomes more prevalent in business operations, having structured governance frameworks becomes essential for managing risks while maximizing benefits.

Digital Maturity Models provide another valuable framework for organizations seeking to understand their current capabilities and plan their transformation journey. These models help companies assess their digital readiness across multiple dimensions—technology infrastructure, data capabilities, organizational culture, skills and talent, and governance structures. By understanding their current maturity level, organizations can develop realistic roadmaps for advancement and identify areas requiring focused investment.

These frameworks play a crucial role in helping organizations maintain strategic coherence throughout their digital transformation journey. Rather than investing in technology for the sake of modernization, businesses that apply structured methodologies ensure that their digital initiatives drive long-term business success. By using these frameworks, companies can remain focused on their strategic goals, measure the impact of digital investments, and continuously refine their approach to ensure ongoing alignment with evolving market conditions.

The importance of these frameworks becomes even more pronounced as artificial intelligence capabilities mature and become more accessible to organizations of all sizes. Without structured approaches to AI integration, companies risk implementing powerful technologies without clear business purposes, leading to wasted resources and missed opportunities. Organizations that establish strong governance frameworks early in their AI journey will be better positioned to scale these capabilities effectively while managing associated risks.

The Importance of Strategic Alignment in Digital Transformation

Strategic alignment is the foundation of successful digital transformation. When digital initiatives are closely tied to business objectives, organizations can enhance efficiency, improve customer experiences, and maximize the return on investment in digital tools and technologies. Without this alignment, businesses risk launching disconnected IT projects that fail to deliver measurable results, leading to wasted resources and operational disruptions.

The evidence from industry research and case studies consistently demonstrates that strategic alignment is the primary differentiator between successful and failed digital transformations. Organizations that prioritize alignment between digital strategy and business goals are better equipped to drive innovation, remain competitive, and adapt to changing market demands. They can streamline operations, reduce inefficiencies, and use technology as a true enabler of business growth.

This alignment becomes even more critical as artificial intelligence capabilities become standard features in enterprise software platforms. AI-driven transformations require not only technical readiness but also clear understanding of how intelligent systems will support business objectives. Organizations must define specific use cases where AI can drive measurable business value, establish metrics for evaluating AI performance, and ensure that AI implementations support rather than complicate existing business processes.

By ensuring that every digital investment supports a clear and measurable business purpose, companies can avoid the common pitfalls of misalignment and create a sustainable roadmap for digital success. This requires ongoing attention to changing business priorities, evolving market conditions, and emerging technological capabilities. Organizations that maintain strong alignment between their digital strategies and business objectives will be better positioned to leverage new technologies, including AI, as they become available.

Amid today's realities, businesses that take a strategic approach to transformation will not only survive but thrive. By leveraging proven frameworks, fostering collaboration between IT and business teams, and continuously refining digital strategies, organizations can turn technology into a powerful catalyst for long-term growth and competitive advantage. The companies that master strategic alignment in their digital transformation efforts will be best positioned to capitalize on emerging opportunities, including the transformative potential of artificial intelligence, while avoiding the costly failures that plague organizations lacking strategic focus.

Chapter 6

Selecting the Right Tools

Choosing the right technologies is critical for ensuring operational efficiency and maintaining a competitive edge. Enterprise Resource Planning (ERP) systems, for example, serve as a centralized platform for managing various functions, from finance and supply chain to human resources and customer relationships. However, traditional monolithic ERP systems may not always align with the specific needs of every organization.

The statistics paint a sobering picture of technology selection challenges. McKinsey research indicates that digital transformations fail to meet expectations 70 percent of the time, with success rates in traditional industries like oil and gas, automotive, and pharmaceuticals falling between 4 and 11 percent. These failures often stem not from technological inadequacies but from poor selection processes that fail to align technology capabilities with business objectives.

As businesses increasingly demand agility, flexibility, and scalability, the process of selecting the right tools has become more complex. Companies must carefully evaluate technologies based on how well they align with their long-term goals and operational needs. Making the wrong choice—no matter how advanced the solution—can result in inefficiencies, employee frustration, and significant financial loss. This section outlines key strategies for selecting the most suitable tools and explores alternatives to conventional ERP solutions, offering a more adaptable approach to digital transformation.

Defining Business Objectives and Requirements

The foundation of any successful technology selection process begins with a clear understanding of business objectives. Before committing to a new system, organizations must conduct a thorough analysis of their current workflows to identify inefficiencies, bottlenecks, and processes that could benefit from automation. By assessing these pain points, businesses can pinpoint the features they need in a new system, ensuring it addresses existing challenges rather than adding unnecessary complexity.

The case of Haribo, the German confectionery manufacturer, illustrates the critical importance of thorough business requirements analysis. In 2018, Haribo began implementing SAP S/4HANA across 16 candy factories in 10 countries, intending to replace decades-old standalone ERP systems. However, the implementation initially failed to map old business processes and workflows to the new ERP system. Shortly after going live, Haribo was unable to track raw materials and inventory, leading to product shortages at grocery stores and a 25 percent decline in sales of its signature Gold Bear gummy candy. The failure stemmed from inadequate upfront analysis of how the company's unique manufacturing processes would translate to the new system.

Clearly defined business goals play a crucial role in guiding technology decisions. Whether the objective is to enhance customer satisfaction, reduce operational costs, improve decision-making through data analytics, or enable expansion into new markets, every technology investment should directly contribute to a strategic priority. Without alignment between business goals and technology capabilities, organizations risk implementing systems that fail to deliver meaningful improvements.

Once objectives are established, companies must determine the specific functional requirements their new technology must support. Integration with existing systems, cloud-based versus on-premise deployment, scalability for future growth, and user-friendliness all factor into this decision. Choosing the right technology means selecting a solution that fits seamlessly into existing operations while providing room for future advancements.

The integration of artificial Intelligence Into this requirements analysis process is becoming increasingly valuable. AI-powered analytics can assess historical business data to predict future needs, ensuring that businesses select scalable solutions that align with growth trajectories. Machine learning algorithms can analyze patterns in current system usage, identify bottlenecks, and recommend features that would provide the greatest operational impact. This data-driven approach to requirements gathering helps organizations move beyond subjective preferences to make objective, evidence-based technology decisions.

Exploring Alternatives to Traditional ERP Systems

Enterprise Resource Planning (ERP) systems have long been the backbone of business operations, offering integrated solutions for managing various processes such as finance, human resources, supply chain, and customer relationship management. These systems promise to streamline workflows, enhance efficiency, and provide real-time data access for informed decision-making. However, despite their extensive capabilities, traditional ERP systems are not always the best fit for every organization. Many businesses, especially small to mid-sized enterprises (SMEs) and niche industries, struggle with the high cost, complexity, and rigidity of traditional ERP solutions. Consequently, organizations are increasingly exploring alternative solutions that provide greater flexibility, customization, and cost efficiency.

The spectacular failure of Lidl's SAP implementation serves as a cautionary tale about the risks of traditional ERP systems. After seven years and an investment of over €500 million, the German discount supermarket chain abandoned its SAP project entirely and reverted to its original in-house inventory management system. The primary issue was the system's inability to handle Lidl's unique discount pricing structures and operational processes. For instance, Lidl's existing inventory management system used purchase prices, whereas the standard retail ERP used retail prices. Rather than adapting their processes to fit the system's best practices, Lidl attempted to customize the software extensively to match their existing workflows. This approach led to complex customizations, extended timelines, and ultimately project failure.

The Challenges of Traditional ERP Systems

Traditional ERP systems are often large-scale software solutions that require significant investment in licensing, implementation, and ongoing maintenance. Many organizations face challenges such as:

High Initial Costs: Traditional ERP solutions demand substantial upfront investment in software licenses, infrastructure, and implementation. This can be prohibitive for small businesses or startups that operate on limited budgets, making it difficult to allocate funds to other critical business functions such as marketing, product development, or hiring. The case of Travis Perkins, a UK construction supplier, demonstrates this challenge. The company faced significant difficulties with an Infor ERP implementation that was initially announced with high expectations but encountered numerous issues due to inadequate planning and insufficient IT department involvement.

Long Deployment Timelines: Implementing a comprehensive ERP system can take months or even years, causing disruptions to business operations. This prolonged implementation period can lead to lost productivity, increased costs, and employee frustration as they wait for the new system to become fully operational. The U.S. Navy's ERP project, which began in 1998 and consumed over a billion dollars across four iterations, exemplifies this challenge. Despite massive investment and multiple attempts, the organization has yet to see material improvements, with project scope continuously changing and shortening over the years.

Limited Flexibility: These systems are typically designed with a one-size-fits-all approach, making customization difficult and costly. Many businesses find themselves forced to adapt their processes to fit the system rather than the system adapting to their unique workflows, which can lead to inefficiencies and reduced competitiveness. The National Grid case illustrates this problem perfectly. The power distribution company serving customers in New York, Rhode Island, and Massachusetts pushed forward with an SAP ERP project despite clear signs that the system wasn't ready, citing that further delays would be too costly. This decision to prioritize timeline over proper customization resulted in system instabilities and operational disruptions.

Complex Maintenance and Upgrades: Businesses must continuously invest in updates, patches, and training to ensure the system remains functional and up-to-date. This ongoing maintenance can require dedicated IT staff or external consultants, adding to the total cost of ownership and creating dependencies on software vendors.

Due to these challenges, businesses are looking for more agile and cost-effective alternatives. Below are some of the most promising alternatives to traditional ERP systems that companies are increasingly adopting.

Best-of-Breed Solutions

One of the most popular alternatives is the best-of-breed approach, which involves selecting specialized software applications for different business functions rather than relying on a single, all-encompassing ERP suite. This method allows companies to adopt the best software for each department, ensuring higher functionality and efficiency in specific business areas.

For example, a manufacturing company might use Salesforce for customer relationship management, QuickBooks for accounting, BambooHR for human resources, and TradeGecko for inventory management. Each of these solutions excels in its specific domain, often providing more sophisticated features and better user experiences than what would be available in a monolithic ERP system.

Benefits of Best-of-Breed Solutions include greater flexibility, as businesses can mix and match software applications to meet their unique needs. Unlike monolithic ERP systems, this approach allows companies to scale and add functionalities as needed without committing to an all-in-one system. Lower upfront costs make these solutions more accessible to small and medium-sized businesses, while faster deployment enables quicker results and adaptation to market changes. Specialized applications often offer better user interfaces, more focused functionalities, and intuitive workflows that improve employee adoption and productivity.

Workflow and Interoperability Tools

Another alternative to traditional ERP systems is the use of workflow and interoperability tools, which enable businesses to integrate multiple software applications without undergoing a complete system overhaul. These tools help connect disparate systems, facilitating seamless data flow and process automation.

Modern integration platforms like MuleSoft, Zapier, Microsoft Power Automate, and Boomi allow organizations to create sophisticated automation workflows that connect multiple applications. These tools can synchronize data between systems, trigger actions based on specific events, and provide unified dashboards that give users a comprehensive view of their operations across multiple platforms.

Benefits of Workflow and Integration Tools include cost efficiency, as businesses can extend and enhance existing software rather than replacing entire systems. Minimal disruption allows companies to integrate new tools without major operational interruptions, while scalability ensures organizations can easily add or remove applications as their business evolves. Better data flow between applications reduces silos, improves efficiency, and enhances collaboration across departments.

Custom Software Platforms and AI-Enhanced Solutions

For businesses seeking fully customized solutions, custom software platforms provide an attractive option. These platforms allow companies to develop tailored applications that meet their specific operational needs. The rise of low-code and no-code development platforms has made custom software development more accessible and cost-effective than ever before.

Modern custom platforms often incorporate artificial intelligence capabilities from the ground up. AI can be embedded into custom solutions to provide predictive analytics, automated decision-making, and intelligent process optimization. For instance, a custom inventory management system might use machine learning algorithms to predict demand patterns, optimize stock levels, and automatically trigger reorder points based on seasonal trends and market conditions.

Benefits of Custom Software Platforms include full control over features and functionality, scalability that grows with the business, competitive advantage through unique capabilities, and seamless integration with existing systems. When enhanced with AI capabilities, these custom solutions can provide intelligent automation, predictive insights, and adaptive learning that improves performance over time.

Cloud-Based ERP Alternatives

In response to the challenges of traditional ERP systems, many businesses are also opting for cloud-based ERP solutions, which offer greater flexibility and lower costs compared to on-premise systems. Cloud-based ERP platforms provide the benefits of traditional ERP systems while addressing key concerns such as deployment time, scalability, and maintenance.

Benefits of Cloud-Based ERP Solutions include lower infrastructure costs, faster implementation, automatic updates, and remote accessibility. Cloud solutions eliminate the need for expensive on-premise servers and reduce overall IT expenses. Deployment is significantly quicker than traditional ERP systems, automatic updates reduce IT maintenance efforts, and users can access the system from anywhere, enabling better collaboration and productivity.

While traditional ERP systems have been the standard for enterprise management, they are not always the most practical or cost-effective solution for every business. By considering alternative solutions such as best-of-breed applications, workflow integration tools, custom-built platforms, and cloud-based ERP systems, businesses can create a flexible, scalable, and cost-effective technology stack tailored to their unique operational needs.

Engaging Neutral Industry Experts

Selecting an Enterprise Resource Planning (ERP) system or other digital tools can be a complex and daunting process. The market is saturated with vendors eager to showcase their solutions, each presenting polished sales pitches that highlight benefits while minimizing or completely omitting potential challenges. These sales-driven presentations can make it difficult for organizations to discern which solution truly aligns with their operational and strategic needs. In such an environment, engaging neutral industry experts can provide a level of objectivity that ensures technology decisions are based on business fit rather than marketing claims.

The importance of independent guidance becomes clear when examining high-profile failures like Revlon's SAP S/4HANA implementation. In 2018, following its acquisition of Elizabeth Arden, Revlon decided to implement SAP S/4HANA to integrate processes across both companies. Instead of building on one of the two ERP systems that had previously worked well for each company (Elizabeth Arden's Oracle Fusion and Revlon's Microsoft Dynamics AX), they chose an entirely new system. The implementation was so disruptive that it shut down a core manufacturing facility in North Carolina, resulting in millions of dollars in lost sales and ultimately triggering multiple shareholder lawsuits when the company's stock fell nearly 7 percent within 24 hours of announcing the failure.

The Importance of Objectivity In Technology Selection

When organizations embark on the journey of selecting an ERP system or other digital tools, they are often confronted with a barrage of vendor claims. Each vendor naturally positions their product as the best solution, emphasizing strengths while downplaying weaknesses. Without independent guidance, companies may make choices based on persuasive marketing rather than a thorough and objective assessment of their actual needs.

Industry experts, particularly those without vendor affiliations, offer an impartial perspective that is invaluable in navigating this complex landscape. Their primary objective is to help businesses make well-informed decisions based on thorough analysis rather than promotional rhetoric. By leveraging their deep understanding of the industry, technology landscape, and vendor ecosystem, these experts ensure that businesses focus on practical considerations such as functionality, scalability, integration capabilities, and long-term sustainability.

The Role of Independent Consultants

Neutral industry consultants play a crucial role in the ERP and digital tool selection process by providing unbiased market insights and strategic guidance. Unlike vendors who have a vested interest in selling their products, independent consultants work solely in the interest of the organization, offering an objective evaluation of available options.

Assessing Business Needs and Gathering Requirements: Before evaluating ERP solutions or other digital tools, organizations must clearly define their business requirements. Consultants help in this process by working closely with key stakeholders across departments to understand current workflows, pain points, and future growth objectives. This ensures that the selection process is driven by organizational needs rather than vendor-driven narratives.

A well-documented list of requirements helps businesses filter out solutions that may lack critical functionalities. Without this initial assessment, companies risk investing in a system that requires extensive customization, leading to increased costs, extended implementation timelines, and potential operational disruptions.

Evaluating Vendors and Technologies: Once business requirements are established, neutral consultants bring extensive market knowledge and industry experience, allowing them to assess ERP systems and digital tools without bias. They help organizations compare various solutions based on factors such as functionality and features, scalability, integration capabilities, user experience and training requirements, long-term viability, and total cost of ownership.

By systematically analyzing these factors, consultants help organizations avoid costly missteps and ensure they invest in a solution that aligns with their long-term objectives.

Facilitating Vendor Demonstrations and Proof of Concept: Vendor demonstrations and proof-of-concept (PoC) implementations are critical components of the selection process. However, without expert oversight, these presentations can become sales-driven showcases rather than practical evaluations of system capabilities.

Neutral experts structure these sessions to focus on real-world use cases specific to the organization's needs. They ensure that demonstrations are not just high-level overviews but include in-depth scenarios that test system functionality in practical applications. By facilitating structured assessments, consultants help organizations distinguish between surface-level promises and genuine operational fit.

Negotiating Contracts and Ensuring Favorable Terms: Selecting an ERP system or digital tool is a significant investment, often involving complex contracts with licensing terms, service-level agreements, and long-term commitments. Industry experts assist in contract negotiations, ensuring that businesses secure favorable terms, avoid hidden fees, and establish clear service expectations. Their experience in dealing with vendors enables them to identify potential risks and negotiate terms that safeguard the organization's interests.

Avoiding Common Pitfalls in ERP Selection

ERP implementations can be costly and time-consuming, with potential risks that can disrupt business operations if not managed properly. Some common pitfalls include choosing a system based on brand recognition rather than suitability, underestimating implementation complexity, over-customization leading to long-term maintenance issues, failure to involve key stakeholders, and ignoring long-term scalability.

The case of Nike's demand planning software failure in 2000 illustrates several of these pitfalls. The company spent $400 million to overhaul its supply chain and ERP software, but rushed implementation led to improper handling of the system. The new demand planning software disastrously misforecasted market demand, leading to excessive inventory for some products while others faced shortages. Nike reported $100 million in lost sales, coupled with a 20 percent stock price dip. The company had to invest another five years and hundreds of millions of dollars to overcome the problems.

By working with neutral consultants, businesses can proactively identify and mitigate these risks, ensuring a smoother and more successful ERP implementation.

Engaging neutral industry experts in ERP and digital tool selection is a strategic move that can save organizations time, money, and operational disruptions. By offering unbiased insights, facilitating structured evaluations, and assisting with vendor negotiations, these experts help businesses make informed technology decisions that align with their long-term goals.

As technology continues to evolve, the role of independent consultants becomes even more critical in ensuring that organizations select solutions that are not only suitable for their current needs but also adaptable to future challenges. In an environment where vendor-driven sales pitches can be misleading, leveraging expert guidance provides the clarity and confidence needed to choose the right technology investments.

Leveraging Artificial Intelligence in the Selection Process

Artificial intelligence is transforming the ERP selection and implementation process by offering data-driven insights that enable smarter decision-making. AI-powered analytics can assess historical business data to predict future needs, ensuring that businesses select scalable solutions that align with growth trajectories.

Modern AI systems can analyze vast amounts of organizational data to identify patterns, bottlenecks, and opportunities that human analysts might miss. Machine learning algorithms can evaluate how different software solutions might perform within a specific organizational context by analyzing similar implementations across industries. This capability allows businesses to move beyond generic vendor promises to understand how a particular solution is likely to perform in their unique environment.

AI also streamlines the selection process by automating routine tasks such as data entry, evaluation, and reporting. Natural language processing can analyze vendor documentation, extracting key features and capabilities for easier comparison. Automated scoring systems can evaluate vendors against weighted criteria, providing objective rankings based on organizational priorities rather than subjective impressions.

Furthermore, AI-driven insights allow businesses to compare ERP solutions based on real-world performance metrics rather than relying solely on vendor promises. Predictive analytics can forecast implementation timelines, costs, and potential risks based on historical data from similar projects. This level of analysis helps organizations set realistic expectations and prepare for challenges before they arise.

Integrating AI into technology selection ensures a more informed, objective approach to choosing digital tools. As AI capabilities continue to advance, organizations that leverage these technologies in their selection processes will be better positioned to make decisions that drive long-term value and competitive advantage.

Adopting a Phased Implementation Approach

Rolling out a new ERP system or digital tool in one large-scale deployment can create operational disruptions and resistance to change. To mitigate these risks, businesses should adopt a phased implementation approach that allows for gradual transition and continuous assessment.

The failure of Hershey's ERP implementation in 1999 demonstrates the dangers of rushed, monolithic deployments. The chocolate manufacturer aimed to revamp its IT systems by integrating ERP, supply chain management, and customer relationship management systems all at once. The company set an unrealistic timeline and chose to go live during Halloween—their peak sales season. The result was catastrophic: Hershey's was unable to fulfill $100 million worth of orders for its iconic Kisses and Jolly Ranchers, leading to an 8 percent drop in stock price and significant lost market share during their most critical selling period.

A pilot program can serve as a preliminary test, enabling businesses to evaluate system functionalities and identify potential issues before a full-scale rollout. An incremental implementation strategy extends the system gradually across different departments, giving employees time to adjust and adopt new processes without feeling overwhelmed. Regular performance assessments throughout the implementation ensure that adjustments can be made as needed, optimizing system effectiveness.

A phased approach reduces disruptions, improves user adoption, and increases the likelihood of a successful transition. Organizations that implement systems incrementally can learn from early phases, refine their processes, and avoid the catastrophic failures that often result from big-bang implementations.

Focusing on Data Governance and Integration

One of the biggest challenges in ERP implementation is maintaining data consistency across multiple systems. Poor data governance can lead to duplicated records, security vulnerabilities, and inaccurate reporting. To prevent these issues, organizations must develop a strong data governance framework that ensures data integrity, security, and seamless integration between systems.

Standardizing data formats and definitions across all platforms improves accuracy and ensures consistency in reporting. Establishing a clear integration plan allows new software to interact efficiently with existing applications, preventing data silos and process inefficiencies. Additionally, robust security measures such as encryption and access controls protect sensitive business information, ensuring compliance with regulatory standards.

Effective data governance ensures that ERP implementation enhances efficiency without disrupting existing workflows. Organizations must treat data as a strategic asset, establishing clear ownership, quality standards, and access protocols that support both operational efficiency and regulatory compliance.

Considering Timing and Organizational Readiness

The success of a new technology implementation depends largely on organizational readiness. Before selecting and deploying an ERP system, businesses must assess whether their teams, processes, and infrastructure are prepared for change.

Employee training plays a critical role in determining adoption rates. Organizations must provide comprehensive training programs that equip employees with the skills needed to transition smoothly into new systems. The IT infrastructure must also be capable of supporting the new technology, ensuring compatibility and scalability.

Timing is another crucial factor—implementing a new system during peak operational periods can cause unnecessary disruptions, so businesses should strategically schedule transitions to minimize impact. By carefully evaluating readiness factors, organizations can ensure a smoother and more effective adoption process.

Ensuring Long-Term Success

Selecting the right tools is a critical step in digital transformation. Businesses that approach technology selection with strategic intent and careful planning set themselves up for long-term success. A well-defined selection process begins with clear business objectives and extends to exploring flexible alternatives, engaging industry experts, leveraging AI-driven insights, and implementing systems in manageable phases. Strong data governance and an assessment of organizational readiness further ensure that new technologies integrate seamlessly and enhance operational efficiency.

By adopting a structured approach to selecting digital tools, businesses can optimize processes, drive growth, and position themselves for sustained success in an increasingly digital world. Those that take the time to make informed decisions will not only maximize their return on investment but also build a foundation for continued innovation and competitiveness.

Chapter 7

Project Governance and Leadership

In the era of digital transformation, establishing robust project governance and leadership structures is essential for ensuring that initiatives align with organizational objectives and deliver measurable benefits. Governance provides a structured framework for accountability, decision-making, and oversight, while effective leadership ensures that digital projects stay on track, manage risks, and drive meaningful outcomes. Without well-defined governance structures, digital projects often suffer from ambiguity, inefficiencies, and misalignment with business goals. Similarly, a lack of strong leadership can result in poor stakeholder engagement, resource mismanagement, and resistance to change.

The statistics underscore the critical Importance of strong governance and leadership in digital transformation success. McKinsey research reveals that fewer than one-third of organizational transformations succeed at improving a company's performance and sustaining those gains, with digital transformations showing even lower success rates. Only 16 percent of organizations report that their digital transformations successfully improved performance while equipping them to sustain changes long-term. This sobering reality highlights the need for exceptional governance and leadership to beat the odds.

Ensuring digital transformation success requires more than just implementing new technology. It demands clear governance frameworks that maintain control over project execution, define accountability, and provide a roadmap for achieving strategic business objectives. Leadership must inspire teams, facilitate cross-functional collaboration, and ensure that digital initiatives are embraced across the organization. Strong governance and leadership together create the foundation for a seamless and sustainable digital transformation journey.

Establishing Governance Structures for Digital Projects

Project governance refers to a structured set of policies, functions, processes, and procedures that define how digital projects are established, managed, and controlled. Effective governance ensures that projects are executed in a structured manner, that there is clear accountability at every level, and that risks are identified and proactively mitigated. It also ensures that stakeholders remain engaged throughout the project lifecycle, allowing for better collaboration, informed decision-making, and alignment with business goals. Without strong governance, projects risk inefficiencies, scope creep, delays, and failure to meet business expectations.

The case of MillerCoors illustrates the critical importance of strong governance structures. The Chicago-based brewery aimed to streamline its operations by unifying its SAP environment, consolidating seven different instances of SAP ECC into a more cohesive system. MillerCoors hired HCL Technologies to create the unified platform, but quickly expressed concerns about implementation quality. In response, HCL issued a new work order that extended the timeline and added $9 million to implementation costs. Unfortunately, these changes did little to resolve the underlying issues, which stemmed from inadequate governance structures that failed to provide clear oversight and quality controls from the project's inception.

A key principle of project governance is ensuring that each digital initiative has a single point of accountability. Every project must have a designated project owner or executive sponsor who is responsible for strategic oversight, ensuring that project objectives align with business goals, facilitating collaboration across departments, and securing the necessary resources for execution. The project owner must also serve as the champion of the initiative at the executive level, reinforcing its importance and keeping momentum going.

To maintain neutrality and objectivity in decision-making, project ownership should remain independent from asset or service ownership. This separation ensures unbiased governance, minimizes conflicts of interest, and allows the focus to remain on the long-term success of the transformation rather than short-term operational concerns.

A common pitfall in digital transformation is inefficient decision-making due to excessive involvement of large committees, leading to delays and confusion. To mitigate this, organizations must clearly separate stakeholder management from project decision-making. While stakeholders should be actively engaged in providing input and feedback, the actual decision-making authority should reside within a defined governance body that can swiftly resolve issues and make critical calls when necessary. A well-defined escalation path ensures that problems are addressed promptly without causing bottlenecks.

Another essential aspect of governance is maintaining distinct structures for project governance and broader organizational governance. Digital projects often require a more agile and flexible decision-making process than traditional corporate governance allows. By establishing a dedicated governance model for digital transformation, organizations can avoid bureaucratic slowdowns and maintain the adaptability needed for evolving technological environments.

Implementing Governance Frameworks

A structured governance framework enhances project transparency, accountability, and efficiency. One of the most widely used frameworks in digital transformation is PRINCE2 (Projects IN Controlled Environments). This methodology ensures that projects maintain business justification throughout their lifecycle, that roles and responsibilities are clearly defined, and that progress is assessed at structured checkpoints to enable timely interventions. Organizations that implement PRINCE2 or similar governance frameworks create an environment where digital transformation projects are structured, transparent, and results-driven.

Modern governance frameworks are increasingly incorporating artificial intelligence to enhance decision-making and oversight capabilities. AI-powered project management tools can analyze project performance data in real-time, identify potential risks before they materialize, and recommend corrective actions based on patterns from successful implementations. These tools can track key performance indicators across multiple projects simultaneously, providing governance bodies with comprehensive dashboards that enable data-driven oversight.

Machine learning algorithms can also analyze historical project data to predict implementation timelines, resource requirements, and potential bottlenecks more accurately than traditional estimation methods. This predictive capability allows governance bodies to make more informed decisions about resource allocation, timeline adjustments, and risk mitigation strategies.

Roles and Responsibilities of Project Leaders

Leadership plays a crucial role in guiding digital transformation efforts. Successful digital initiatives require leaders who possess both technical and strategic expertise, ensuring that technology adoption aligns with broader business goals while also fostering innovation and collaboration across teams.

The Chief Digital Officer (CDO) is responsible for overseeing the organization's digital strategy, ensuring that digital initiatives align with business objectives, and identifying emerging technologies that provide a competitive advantage. A CDO plays a key role in cultivating a digital-first culture across teams and departments, bridging the gap between technology and business strategy. Modern CDOs increasingly leverage artificial intelligence to inform strategic decisions, using AI-powered analytics to identify market trends, predict customer behavior, and optimize digital initiatives for maximum business impact.

A Digital Strategy Manager Is task”d wi’h Integrating digital initiatives across multiple business units. This role involves developing digital transformation roadmaps, coordinating cross-functional teams to ensure smooth adoption, and prioritizing technology investments based on their potential to drive business impact. Digital Strategy Managers increasingly rely on AI-driven insights to evaluate the potential return on investment of various digital initiatives and to optimize resource allocation across competing priorities.

An Executive Sponsor acts as the project's champion at the executive level. Their role is essential in providing strategic direction, securing senior leadership support, and ensuring that the project receives the necessary budget, technology, and personnel resources. The executive sponsor also plays a vital role in addressing resistance to change, ensuring that transformation initiatives are met with organizational buy-in rather than skepticism.

Responsibilities of Project Leaders

One of the most important responsibilities of project leaders is defining and communicating a clear vision for the digital initiative. Leaders must ensure that digital transformation efforts align with long-term business strategy, creating a scalable roadmap that allows for phased implementation and continuous improvement. This vision must be compelling enough to motivate employees through the inevitable challenges of transformation while remaining flexible enough to adapt to changing circumstances.

The case of Avon's failed SAP ERP project in 2013 demonstrates the consequences of unclear vision and poor leadership communication. Instead of making processes easier for the organization, the SAP ERP implementation made operations too intricate for users to handle. The system's complexity had a snowball effect—when high-level sales representatives couldn't operate the system, other workers gave up on the ERP entirely. Part of the failure stemmed from employees showing no patience for the system's complexity and beginning to leave the company. This failure could have been prevented with clearer communication about the system's benefits and more comprehensive change management.

Stakeholder engagement is another crucial responsibility. Leaders must identify key internal and external stakeholders early in the project, proactively address concerns, and foster collaboration across different business units. By maintaining open communication and ensuring that all voices are heard, they can build strong support for digital initiatives and minimize resistance to change.

Effective resource allocation is critical to the success of any digital transformation effort. Leaders must secure adequate funding, technology, and human resources while optimizing budget allocations to avoid overspending. Ensuring that the right talent is assigned to key project roles is essential, as digital transformation requires expertise in technology, data analytics, business operations, and change management.

Risk management must also be a priority. Identifying potential risks early in the project allows for proactive mitigation strategies. Leaders must establish contingency plans to address disruptions and leverage data analytics and AI-driven insights to assess risk impact and make informed decisions. Modern risk management increasingly relies on artificial intelligence to predict potential issues and recommend preventive measures based on analysis of similar projects and market conditions.

Performance monitoring is essential to ensuring that digital initiatives remain on track. Leaders must define Key Performance Indicators (KPIs) to measure success, use real-time dashboards for data-driven decision-making, and conduct regular performance evaluations to adjust strategies as needed. Monitoring progress enables organizations to identify areas for improvement, address challenges before they escalate, and continuously refine their approach.

AI-powered performance monitoring tools can provide real-time insights into project health, automatically flagging deviations from planned timelines or budgets and recommending corrective actions. These tools can analyze vast amounts of project data to identify patterns that predict success or failure, enabling leaders to make proactive adjustments rather than reactive corrections.

Adaptability and agility are critical traits for digital project leaders. Given the rapid pace of technological change, strategies must remain flexible, allowing for adjustments as market conditions evolve. Leaders must encourage continuous innovation and process improvement, ensuring that digital initiatives remain relevant and effective. Implementing agile methodologies accelerates decision-making, fosters cross-functional collaboration, and enables teams to pivot quickly when necessary.

Learning from Leadership Failures

The importance of strong leadership becomes particularly evident when examining high-profile failures. The case of Waste Management's lawsuit against SAP provides valuable insights into leadership challenges. In 2005, Waste Management initiated an enterprise-wide ERP project intended to go live in 2007. The goal was to automate and simplify the company's order-to-cash processes, which were largely handled by legacy systems and outdated workflows.

The contract was awarded to SAP based on claims that the solution was out-of-the-box, adapted to U.S. standards, and could fulfill the company's goals with minimal customization. However, Waste Management found these claims to be false. The company was unable to glean any benefit from the software and filed a $100 million lawsuit against SAP in 2008, later raising that amount to $500 million before settling out of court in 2010.

This failure highlights several leadership shortcomings: inadequate due diligence in vendor evaluation, insufficient technical oversight during implementation, and poor risk management that failed to identify fundamental misalignments between vendor promises and organizational reality. Strong leadership would have demanded proof-of-concept demonstrations, insisted on detailed technical evaluations, and maintained independent oversight throughout the implementation process.

The Role of AI in Modern Leadership

Artificial intelligence is increasingly becoming a critical tool for digital transformation leaders. AI can analyze vast amounts of organizational data to provide insights into employee sentiment, project performance, and market trends that inform strategic decisions. Machine learning algorithms can identify patterns in successful transformations, helping leaders understand what strategies are most likely to succeed in their specific context.

AI-powered predictive analytics can help leaders anticipate challenges before they become critical issues. For example, AI can analyze employee engagement data to predict resistance to change, evaluate system performance metrics to identify potential integration problems, and assess market conditions to recommend timing adjustments for implementation phases.

Natural language processing capabilities enable leaders to analyze vast amounts of unstructured feedback from employees, customers, and stakeholders, providing insights into sentiment and concerns that might not be captured through traditional surveys or meetings. This real-time feedback analysis allows leaders to address issues proactively and adjust communication strategies to maintain stakeholder support.

AI also enhances decision-making speed and accuracy. Machine learning algorithms can process complex scenarios with multiple variables, evaluating thousands of potential outcomes to recommend optimal strategies. This capability is particularly valuable in fast-moving digital transformation projects where delays in decision-making can compound into significant problems.

Building AI-Ready Leadership Capabilities

As artificial intelligence becomes increasingly integrated into business operations, digital transformation leaders must develop new competencies to effectively leverage these technologies. Leaders must understand not only how AI can support their decision-making but also how to manage AI-driven initiatives and communicate their value to stakeholders.

Modern leaders need to develop data literacy skills that enable them to interpret AI-generated insights and make informed decisions based on algorithmic recommendations. This doesn't require deep technical knowledge of machine learning algorithms, but rather an understanding of how AI systems work, their limitations, and how to validate their outputs.

Leaders must also become comfortable with AI-augmented decision-making processes. Rather than replacing human judgment, AI should enhance leadership capabilities by providing data-driven insights that inform strategic choices. The most effective leaders learn to combine their experience and intuition with AI-generated analysis to make more informed decisions than either could achieve alone.

Change management in AI-driven transformations requires special attention. Employees may feel threatened by AI implementation, fearing job displacement or skill obsolescence. Leaders must communicate clearly about AI's role in augmenting rather than replacing human capabilities, provide training opportunities for employees to develop AI-related skills, and demonstrate how AI can make their work more interesting and valuable.

Ensuring Long-Term Digital Transformation Success

The success of digital projects is deeply dependent on well-structured governance frameworks and strong leadership. Effective governance ensures clear accountability, structured decision-making, and proactive risk management, preventing inefficiencies and costly missteps. At the same time, strong leadership fosters strategic execution, stakeholder collaboration, and a culture of innovation that allows digital initiatives to thrive.

The integration of artificial intelligence into governance and leadership practices represents a significant evolution in how organizations manage digital transformation. AI-powered tools provide leaders with unprecedented visibility into project performance, risk factors, and stakeholder sentiment, enabling more informed and timely decision-making. However, the human element remains crucial—AI enhances but does not replace the need for visionary leadership, emotional intelligence, and strategic thinking.

For organizations to achieve successful digital transformation, they must establish comprehensive governance structures such as PRINCE2, appoint competent digital leaders like CDOs, strategy managers, and executive sponsors, and implement structured decision-making processes that enable agility and responsiveness. Continuous monitoring of performance, risk factors, and stakeholder engagement ensures that digital initiatives remain aligned with business objectives and deliver sustainable value.

The organizations that will thrive in the digital age are those that combine the rigor of structured governance with the vision of transformational leadership and the power of artificial intelligence. By integrating these elements, companies can navigate the complexities of digital transformation, drive sustainable innovation, and secure long-term business success.

By combining structured governance with visionary leadership and AI-enhanced decision-making capabilities, organizations can navigate the complexities of digital transformation, drive sustainable innovation, and secure long-term business success. Those that establish strong governance frameworks and cultivate effective leadership will not only execute digital initiatives successfully but will also position themselves for ongoing adaptability and growth in an increasingly digital world.

Chapter 8

Risk Management and Contingency Planning in Digital Transformation

Digital transformation presents businesses with an opportunity to enhance efficiency, improve customer experiences, and drive innovation. However, along with these benefits comes an array of risks that can derail even the most well-planned initiatives. Without a comprehensive risk management and contingency planning strategy, organizations may find themselves struggling with integration challenges, resistance to change, scope creep, cybersecurity threats, and vendor-related issues. Identifying potential risks early and developing proactive contingency plans are essential for mitigating disruptions and ensuring the long-term success of digital initiatives.

The magnitude of transformation failures underscores the critical importance of robust risk management. Research consistently shows that 70 percent of business transformations fail to meet their objectives, with digital transformations facing even greater challenges. Gartner estimates that 80 percent of organizations seeking to scale digital business will fail through 2025, often due to inadequate risk management and poor governance. These sobering statistics highlight that risk management is not merely a best practice but a fundamental requirement for transformation success.

Modern risk management in digital transformation must account for both traditional project risks and emerging challenges posed by artificial intelligence, cybersecurity threats, and rapidly evolving technology landscapes. Organizations that fail to adapt their risk management approaches to address these contemporary challenges find themselves vulnerable to failures that could have been prevented through proactive planning and comprehensive contingency strategies.

Identifying Potential Risks in Digital Transformation Projects

The introduction of new technologies into an organization's ecosystem is often accompanied by technological integration challenges. Many businesses rely on legacy systems that were not designed to seamlessly connect with modern digital tools. Compatibility issues, data inconsistencies, and operational disruptions can arise when attempting to merge old and new technologies without a well-structured plan. If integration is not managed properly, digital transformation efforts may lead to inefficiencies rather than improved workflows.

The spectacular failure at Revlon provides a stark example of integration challenges gone wrong. When the cosmetics company implemented SAP S/4HANA in 2018 to integrate operations following its acquisition of Elizabeth Arden, the new system caused major problems in the supply chain. The company was unable to successfully manufacture enough goods to meet customer demand, resulting in approximately $64 million in unfulfilled orders. The integration failure was so severe that it shut down a core manufacturing facility in North Carolina, leading to expedited shipping costs, customer service disruptions, and ultimately a $70.3 million net loss in the fourth quarter of 2018.

Another significant risk factor is employee resistance to change. Digital transformation is not just about upgrading technology—it is also about shifting organizational culture. Employees accustomed to traditional workflows may feel threatened by automation, artificial intelligence, or entirely new systems that require them to relearn processes. If they perceive the transformation as a disruption rather than an improvement, they may resist adoption, leading to productivity declines and a lack of enthusiasm for digital initiatives.

The case of Avon's SAP ERP failure in 2013 illustrates how employee resistance can doom even well-intentioned projects. The system was so complex that sales representatives couldn't log into the website, and when high-level sales staff couldn't operate the system, other workers simply gave up on the ERP entirely. Employee frustration reached such levels that many began leaving the company rather than adapting to the new system. This cascade of resistance ultimately forced Avon to abandon the project entirely.

Inadequate planning and scope creep can severely impact the success of a digital transformation project. Without a clear roadmap and defined objectives, organizations risk expanding the scope of their digital initiatives beyond what was originally intended. As new features and capabilities are added, costs can spiral out of control, timelines may extend indefinitely, and the project can lose sight of its original purpose. Poorly managed scope expansion often leads to implementation delays and budget overruns, making it crucial for businesses to establish a structured planning framework that sets boundaries while allowing for necessary adaptations.

The increasing reliance on digital platforms also exposes businesses to cybersecurity threats. As more data is stored and processed online, organizations become more vulnerable to data breaches, ransomware attacks, and hacking attempts. Failing to implement adequate cybersecurity measures can lead to financial losses, reputational damage, and regulatory penalties. In the digital age, cybersecurity must be a top priority, integrated into every phase of transformation planning.

Organizations that depend on external vendors for critical aspects of their digital transformation also face third-party risks. ERP providers, cloud service providers, and software vendors may experience their own security breaches, service outages, or financial difficulties that impact the organizations they serve. Businesses must carefully vet their technology partners and develop contingency plans in case a vendor fails to meet expectations or becomes unreliable.

The emergence of artificial intelligence introduces new categories of risk that organizations must address. AI-related risks include algorithmic bias that could lead to discriminatory outcomes, data privacy concerns as AI systems process vast amounts of personal information, and over-reliance on AI decision-making without adequate human oversight. Organizations implementing AI must consider these risks carefully and develop specific mitigation strategies.

Model degradation represents another AI-specific risk where machine learning models become less accurate over time as underlying data patterns change. Without proper monitoring and retraining protocols, AI systems may provide increasingly unreliable outputs, potentially leading to poor business decisions based on faulty algorithmic recommendations.

To systematically identify these and other potential risks, organizations can utilize a Risk Breakdown Structure (RBS). This structured framework categorizes risks into distinct areas such as technological, organizational, external, project management, and AI-specific risks. By breaking down risks in this manner, organizations can perform a more comprehensive assessment and ensure that no critical threats are overlooked. An RBS provides clarity on where vulnerabilities lie and allows teams to develop targeted mitigation strategies to address specific risk factors before they escalate into larger problems.

Developing Effective Contingency Plans

Once potential risks have been identified, the next crucial step is developing contingency plans that allow businesses to respond effectively if those risks materialize. A contingency plan provides predefined strategies to mitigate disruptions and ensure business continuity, reducing the negative impact of unforeseen events.

The first step in contingency planning is conducting a risk assessment and prioritization process. Not all risks carry the same level of severity, so organizations must evaluate each risk based on its likelihood and potential impact. A minor integration delay may not require an extensive contingency plan, while a major cybersecurity breach would demand immediate and well-coordinated action. Businesses should focus their resources on mitigating high-priority risks that pose the greatest threat to project success.

Modern risk assessment increasingly leverages artificial intelligence to improve accuracy and speed. Machine learning algorithms can analyze historical data from similar projects to predict risk likelihood more accurately than traditional estimation methods. AI can process vast amounts of market data, regulatory information, and organizational metrics to identify emerging risks that human analysts might miss. Predictive analytics can model various scenarios to determine which risks are most likely to materialize and what their potential impact would be.

Once risks have been prioritized, organizations must define contingency strategies tailored to each risk. If technological integration challenges arise, for example, a contingency strategy might involve hiring specialized IT consultants or implementing phased deployment to gradually test system compatibility. For employee resistance, the strategy may involve developing a comprehensive change management program that includes training sessions, feedback loops, and clear messaging about the benefits of digital transformation.

The failure of Nike's supply chain transformation in 2000 demonstrates the importance of having robust contingency plans for technology integration issues. Nike spent $400 million to implement new demand planning software, but the system disastrously misforecasted market demand, leading to excessive inventory for some products while others faced shortages. The company lost $100 million in sales and saw its stock price drop 20 percent. Had Nike developed contingency plans for system integration problems—such as parallel running of old and new systems or phased rollouts—they could have identified and corrected these issues before they caused such massive disruption.

A key aspect of effective contingency planning is establishing clear roles and responsibilities. When an unexpected issue arises, employees must know exactly who is responsible for executing contingency measures. Assigning clear ownership of each contingency plan to designated team members or departments ensures accountability and prevents confusion. Without clearly defined roles, businesses may struggle to respond effectively in the face of a crisis, wasting valuable time and resources.

Communication is another critical element of contingency planning. Organizations must develop communication protocols to ensure that all stakeholders are informed promptly when a risk event occurs. In the case of a cybersecurity breach, for instance, IT teams, executives, and legal departments must be notified immediately to take coordinated action. Transparent communication helps maintain trust within the organization and allows teams to respond swiftly to mitigate potential damage.

A contingency plan is only as effective as its testing and updating process. Businesses should regularly conduct simulations, drills, or scenario-based testing to evaluate how well contingency plans work in practice. By running mock exercises, organizations can identify weaknesses in their plans and make necessary improvements. Additionally, as the digital landscape evolves, new risks may emerge, requiring contingency plans to be periodically reviewed and updated.

The case of National Grid's SAP implementation provides an example of inadequate contingency planning. The utility company serving customers in New York, Rhode Island,

and Massachusetts faced a difficult situation when their three-year SAP implementation was overdue. Missing their go-live date would have resulted in cost overruns of tens of millions of dollars, so they pushed forward with the implementation despite clear signs that the system wasn't ready. The lack of proper contingency plans for dealing with an unready system led to significant operational disruptions and customer service issues that could have been avoided with better preparation.

Integrating contingency planning into overall project management helps maintain alignment between risk mitigation efforts and broader business goals. Contingency measures should not be isolated from the main transformation strategy but rather incorporated into project timelines, budgets, and resource allocations. A well-integrated approach ensures that contingency plans support, rather than disrupt, the organization's long-term objectives.

Leveraging AI for Enhanced Risk Management

Artificial intelligence is revolutionizing risk management in digital transformation by providing capabilities that far exceed traditional risk assessment methods. AI-powered risk management systems can continuously monitor multiple risk factors simultaneously, analyzing patterns and trends that would be impossible for human analysts to track manually.

Machine learning algorithms can analyze historical project data to identify leading indicators of potential problems. By examining thousands of previous implementations, AI can recognize patterns that typically precede specific types of failures, enabling organizations to take preventive action before problems fully materialize. This predictive capability transforms risk management from a reactive discipline to a proactive one.

Natural language processing enables AI systems to monitor news, social media, regulatory announcements, and internal communications for early warning signs of emerging risks. For example, AI can track mentions of supply chain disruptions, regulatory changes, or competitive threats that might impact digital transformation initiatives. This real-time monitoring provides organizations with early warning systems that enable faster response times.

AI can also optimize resource allocation for risk mitigation by analyzing the cost-effectiveness of different mitigation strategies. Machine learning models can evaluate multiple scenarios to determine which combination of preventive measures provides the best protection for the available budget. This optimization ensures that organizations invest their risk management resources where they will have the greatest impact.

Automated risk reporting powered by AI provides executives with real-time dashboards that track risk levels across all transformation initiatives. These systems can automatically escalate critical risks to appropriate decision-makers and recommend specific actions based on successful mitigation strategies from similar situations. This automation ensures that risk management remains consistent and thorough even as organizations manage multiple complex projects simultaneously.

Learning from Comprehensive Failure Analysis

Case Study: City of Oakland's Oracle Fusion ERP Implementation

In an effort to modernize its financial and administrative systems, the City of Oakland embarked on implementing Oracle Fusion ERP. This initiative aimed to enhance operational efficiency, streamline workflows, and provide better services to residents. The project was expected to replace aging legacy systems, improve data accuracy, and support better decision-making. However, despite the project's ambitious goals, it encountered numerous setbacks, ultimately leading to its failure.

Challenges and Failures

Inadequate Planning and Risk Assessment: The project suffered from insufficient upfront planning and a lack of comprehensive risk assessment. Without a detailed roadmap, project managers failed to anticipate potential risks such as integration complexities, cost overruns, and workforce disruptions. The absence of a robust risk management framework resulted in a reactive rather than proactive approach to problem-solving, further compounding implementation challenges.

The lack of AI-enhanced planning tools meant that the city couldn't leverage predictive analytics to identify potential bottlenecks or resource constraints. Modern AI systems could have analyzed similar municipal implementations to predict timeline risks, budget overruns, and integration challenges specific to Oakland's unique environment.

Scope Creep: One of the most significant issues was scope creep. As the project progressed, additional requirements and new functionalities were introduced without proper evaluation of their impact on budget, timeline, and resources. This unplanned expansion stretched resources thin and led to increased costs, extended deadlines, and an overcomplicated system that ultimately failed to meet the city's needs effectively.

AI-powered project management tools could have helped prevent scope creep by continuously analyzing the impact of proposed changes on project timelines and budgets. Machine learning algorithms could have evaluated whether additional requirements aligned with original objectives and recommended alternative approaches that would achieve desired outcomes without compromising project success.

Insufficient Stakeholder Engagement: A lack of effective communication and collaboration among key stakeholders, including city departments, IT personnel, and end-users, resulted in misaligned expectations. The lack of stakeholder involvement during critical decision-making phases meant that the system did not adequately address the specific needs of its intended users. This disconnect led to frustration, low adoption rates, and resistance to change.

Technical Challenges: Integrating Oracle Fusion ERP with the city's existing legacy systems proved to be a major technical hurdle. Many of the older systems were incompatible with the new platform, leading to data inconsistencies, frequent system outages, and operational disruptions. Additionally, inadequate testing before deployment resulted in unresolved software bugs that affected functionality and user experience.

Modern AI-powered testing tools could have identified integration issues earlier in the development process. Automated testing systems can simulate thousands of scenarios to identify potential compatibility problems, while machine learning algorithms can predict which system components are most likely to cause integration difficulties.

Inadequate Change Management: Change management was another weak link in the project's execution. Employees were not adequately trained or prepared for the transition, leading to confusion and inefficiencies in daily operations. Without a structured approach to change management—including proper training, support mechanisms, and phased implementation—the workforce struggled to adapt to the new system, further hindering its success.

Lessons Learned

The City of Oakland's experience offers valuable lessons for risk management and contingency planning in digital transformation projects:

Comprehensive Planning: Thorough planning, including detailed risk assessments and clearly defined project scopes, is essential. Organizations should conduct feasibility studies, anticipate potential roadblocks, and establish clear project goals to ensure smoother execution. AI-enhanced planning tools can provide predictive insights that help organizations anticipate challenges and develop more realistic project timelines.

Stakeholder Engagement: Active involvement of all stakeholders from the project's inception is crucial. Engaging department heads, end-users, and IT teams throughout the implementation process ensures alignment, minimizes resistance, and facilitates a user-friendly system design.

Technical Preparedness: Assessing the compatibility of new systems with existing infrastructure is a key factor in avoiding technical failures. Conducting rigorous system testing, pilot runs, and phased rollouts can help identify and address integration challenges before full-scale deployment. AI-powered testing tools can accelerate this process and improve testing coverage.

Effective Change Management: A robust change management strategy, including employee training, ongoing support, and clear communication, is necessary to facilitate adoption. Change champions should be identified within departments to guide and support their peers through the transition.

Contingency Planning: Developing contingency plans for potential setbacks ensures that the project can adapt to challenges without significant delays or failures. Organizations should have backup plans, alternative workflows, and crisis management protocols in place to mitigate risks and maintain operational stability.

The City of Oakland's failed Oracle Fusion ERP implementation underscores the complexities inherent in digital transformation projects. By emphasizing comprehensive planning, stakeholder engagement, technical readiness, change management, and contingency planning, organizations can navigate these challenges more effectively. The integration of AI-powered tools into these processes can significantly improve the likelihood of success by providing predictive insights, automated testing capabilities, and real-time risk monitoring.

Case Study: Haribo's SAP S/4HANA Implementation Challenges

Haribo, the German company famous for creating gummy bears a century ago, provides another instructive example of risk management challenges in digital transformation. In October 2018, Haribo began implementing SAP S/4HANA across 16 candy factories in 10 countries, planning to convert from standalone ERP systems, some of which were decades old.

The implementation initially failed to properly map existing business processes and workflows to the new ERP system. Shortly after going live, Haribo was unable to track raw materials and inventory, leading to product shortages at grocery stores. The company saw a 25 percent decline in sales of its signature Gold Bear gummy candy in 2018, representing millions of dollars in lost revenue.

The failure stemmed from inadequate business process analysis during the planning phase. Haribo's manufacturing processes had evolved over decades to optimize candy production, but these specialized workflows weren't properly documented or translated into the new system. The company lacked comprehensive contingency plans for handling process mapping failures, leaving them unable to quickly resolve the issues once they emerged.

Had Haribo employed AI-powered process mining tools, they could have automatically analyzed their existing workflows to create detailed process maps that would have facilitated more accurate system configuration. Machine learning algorithms could have identified critical process dependencies that human analysts might have missed, preventing the inventory tracking failures that plagued the implementation.

Ensuring a Resilient Approach to Digital Transformation

Organizations that approach digital transformation with a proactive risk management mindset are far better positioned to handle challenges and setbacks. Instead of viewing risks as roadblocks, businesses can treat them as opportunities to build resilience and adaptability. By identifying potential risks early, implementing targeted mitigation strategies, and developing well-structured contingency plans, companies can minimize disruptions and maintain momentum in their digital initiatives.

The integration of artificial intelligence into risk management processes represents a significant advancement in organizational capability. AI enables continuous risk monitoring, predictive risk assessment, and automated response protocols that far exceed the capabilities of traditional risk management approaches. Organizations that leverage these AI-enhanced capabilities gain significant advantages in identifying, assessing, and mitigating risks before they can impact project success.

Strong risk management practices not only protect organizations from financial and operational losses but also enhance stakeholder confidence. Investors, employees, and customers all benefit from a business that is well-prepared to navigate uncertainty. Digital transformation is a journey filled with complexities, but with the right safeguards in place, businesses can turn risks into manageable obstacles rather than insurmountable barriers.

Modern risk management must also account for the interconnected nature of digital systems and the cascading effects that failures can have across organizations. A failure in one system can quickly propagate to connected systems, potentially causing organization-wide disruptions. Understanding these interdependencies and developing contingency plans that account for systemic risks is crucial for maintaining operational resilience.

The most successful organizations develop risk management cultures where every employee understands their role in identifying and mitigating risks. This cultural approach to risk management, combined with AI-powered tools and comprehensive contingency planning, creates multiple layers of protection that significantly improve the likelihood of transformation success.

A successful digital transformation strategy is not one that avoids risks altogether, but one that acknowledges risks, prepares for them, and responds with agility when challenges arise. Organizations that integrate comprehensive risk management and contingency planning into their transformation efforts will be able to drive sustainable innovation while maintaining stability and operational excellence. Through foresight, preparation, continuous monitoring, and the strategic application of artificial intelligence, businesses can ensure that digital transformation becomes a catalyst for long-term success rather than a source of disruption and uncertainty.

The organizations that will thrive in the digital age are those that view risk management not as a constraint but as a competitive advantage. By developing superior risk identification, assessment, and mitigation capabilities—enhanced by artificial intelligence and supported by comprehensive contingency planning—these organizations can pursue more ambitious transformation initiatives with greater confidence and higher success rates. In an environment where digital transformation is essential for competitive survival, superior risk management capabilities become a key differentiator that enables organizations to innovate boldly while maintaining operational stability.

Chapter 9

Building a Competent Team for Digital Transformation

Digital transformation is not simply about implementing new technologies—it is about having the right people in place to drive innovation, adapt to change, and fully leverage digital tools. The success of any digital initiative hinges on the skills, knowledge, and adaptability of the workforce leading the transformation. However, as organizations worldwide have discovered, building and maintaining the right team for digital transformation remains one of the most challenging aspects of the entire endeavor.

Recent research reveals that 83% of organizations lack the necessary employees with change management skills to succeed in digital transformation initiatives. This startling statistic underscores a fundamental truth: technology alone does not drive transformation—people do. Organizations that invest in building a strong digital team will be far better positioned to achieve seamless transitions, increase efficiency, and maintain a competitive edge. Conversely, those that underestimate the human element face an alarming failure rate, with studies showing that 70% of digital transformation projects fail, often due to inadequate talent management and poor organizational change capabilities.

Recruiting Talent for Digital Transformation

As businesses embrace digital transformation, they often encounter a widening skills gap that threatens the very foundation of their initiatives. Traditional roles are evolving at an unprecedented pace, requiring employees to develop new digital competencies that didn't exist just a few years ago. The challenge is particularly acute when considering that only 26% of digital transformations in tech-savvy industries succeed, while traditional industries see success rates as low as 4-11%.

To ensure that digital initiatives succeed, companies must strategically recruit professionals with expertise in emerging technologies such as artificial intelligence, cloud computing, cybersecurity, data analytics, and automation. However, the recruitment challenge extends far beyond simply finding candidates with the right technical skills. Organizations must also navigate the complex landscape of AI implementation, where research indicates that more than 80% of AI projects fail—twice the rate of traditional IT projects.

The high failure rate of AI initiatives provides critical insights for digital transformation recruitment strategies. Many organizations rush to hire AI specialists without understanding the full scope of what makes these projects successful. A comprehensive study by RAND Corporation, which interviewed 65 data scientists and engineers with extensive AI experience, identified five root causes of AI project failure: unclear business objectives, poor data quality, inadequate collaboration between technical and business teams, insufficient organizational support, and unrealistic expectations about AI capabilities.

Recruiting for digital transformation goes beyond hiring IT specialists. Organizations must seek professionals with both technical and strategic capabilities. This includes data analysts who understand business context, UX designers who can bridge the gap between technology and user experience, cybersecurity experts who think holistically about risk, digital marketing strategists who understand customer journeys, cloud engineers who can architect scalable solutions, and AI specialists who can translate business problems into technical solutions.

However, technical proficiency alone is not enough. The most successful digital transformation teams combine technical expertise with critical soft skills. Candidates should possess problem-solving abilities that go beyond code debugging to include strategic thinking, adaptability that allows them to pivot when technologies or business requirements change, and a collaborative mindset that enables them to work across functions effectively. Digital transformation affects multiple departments, and employees must be able to communicate complex technical concepts to non-technical stakeholders while driving technological adoption throughout the organization.

Companies must also refine their recruitment strategies to attract top digital talent in an increasingly competitive market. One of the most effective approaches is positioning themselves as digital leaders rather than followers. Modern professionals, especially those in the technology sector, are drawn to organizations that prioritize innovation, offer meaningful career development opportunities, and provide flexibility in work arrangements. This is particularly important when recruiting AI and emerging technology specialists, who often have multiple options and are selective about the organizations they join.

Businesses should emphasize their commitment to digital transformation through their employer branding, job descriptions, and workplace culture. This means showcasing real projects, highlighting the impact of digital initiatives on business outcomes, and demonstrating a commitment to continuous learning and innovation. Offering remote work options, competitive compensation packages, and opportunities to work on cutting-edge projects can help attract skilled professionals in high-demand fields.

The challenge becomes more complex when organizations realize that many digital transformation failures stem from a fundamental misunderstanding of what these roles actually entail. For instance, hiring an AI specialist without ensuring they have experience in change management, data governance, and cross-functional collaboration often leads to technically sound solutions that fail to gain organizational adoption.

While external hiring is crucial for acquiring specialized skills, organizations should not overlook the potential of their existing workforce. Internal recruitment can be an effective way to fill critical digital roles by upskilling and reskilling employees who already have institutional knowledge and understand the organization's culture, processes, and challenges. Developing internal talent fosters loyalty, reduces hiring costs, and helps companies create a workforce that is adaptable to technological changes.

However, internal development programs must be carefully structured to avoid the common pitfall of assuming that traditional IT skills automatically translate to digital transformation capabilities. The skills required for modern digital initiatives—particularly those involving AI, automation, and data analytics—require specialized training and hands-on experience that goes far beyond traditional technical training programs.

Developing and Retaining Digital Talent

Recruiting the right talent is only the first step. Organizations must also focus on retaining and developing their workforce to ensure long-term success in digital transformation. Without clear career growth paths and continuous development opportunities, employees may become disengaged or seek opportunities elsewhere, leading to high turnover and disruptions in digital initiatives. This challenge is particularly acute in digital transformation projects, where the loss of key team members can derail entire initiatives.

The retention challenge is compounded by the reality that 68% of companies encounter difficulties in aligning ERP implementations with industry best practices, often because they lose critical team members mid-project. When experienced team members leave during implementation, organizations frequently discover that knowledge transfer was inadequate, documentation was incomplete, and the remaining team lacks the institutional knowledge necessary to complete the project successfully.

One of the most effective ways to retain digital talent is by fostering a culture of continuous learning and development.

This is not merely about offering training programs—it requires creating an environment where employees are encouraged to stay ahead of technological trends, explore new tools, and enhance their digital skill sets through meaningful, challenging work. Providing access to professional development opportunities such as online courses, industry certifications, mentorship programs, and participation in digital innovation projects empowers employees to expand their expertise and take on leadership roles in digital initiatives.

The importance of continuous learning becomes even more critical when considering the rapid evolution of digital technologies. AI capabilities that were cutting-edge just two years ago are now considered basic requirements, and new platforms, tools, and methodologies emerge constantly. Organizations that fail to invest in ongoing education quickly find that their teams' skills become obsolete, leading to project failures and competitive disadvantage.

In addition to technical training, employees should also be equipped with soft skills that support digital transformation. Critical thinking, problem-solving, adaptability, and collaboration are just as important as technical knowledge. As technology continues to evolve, employees must be able to adjust to new workflows, communicate complex concepts effectively, and collaborate across teams to implement digital solutions. The most successful digital transformation teams combine deep technical expertise with strong business acumen and change management capabilities.

Organizations should also invest in mentorship and leadership development programs that go beyond traditional management training. These programs should pair employees with experienced digital leaders who have successfully navigated complex transformations, understand the challenges of implementing emerging technologies, and can provide guidance on both technical and organizational aspects of digital change. By pairing employees with experienced digital leaders, businesses can accelerate learning, encourage knowledge-sharing, and create a pipeline of future digital transformation champions.

Effective mentorship programs in digital transformation contexts focus on real-world problem-solving rather than theoretical knowledge transfer. Experienced mentors help junior team members understand not just how to implement specific technologies, but how to navigate organizational resistance, communicate value propositions to stakeholders, manage project risks, and adapt when initial plans don't work as expected. Employees who feel supported and have access to career advancement opportunities are more likely to remain engaged and committed to their roles.

However, development programs must also address the unique challenges of digital transformation projects. Unlike traditional IT projects, digital transformation initiatives often require teams to work with experimental technologies, manage ambiguous requirements, and adapt to rapidly changing business conditions. Development programs should prepare employees for this uncertainty while building their confidence in making decisions with incomplete information.

The Importance of Training and Development

No digital transformation initiative can succeed without a workforce that is properly trained to use new technologies. Simply implementing new systems without providing adequate training will result in resistance, inefficiencies, and failed adoption. Yet research consistently shows that 95% of failed companies dedicate less than 10% of their total budget to education, training, and change management—a critical oversight that contributes to the 60-70% failure rate of change initiatives.

The training challenge becomes more complex when organizations implement AI and automation technologies that fundamentally change how work gets done. Unlike traditional software implementations where users learn new interfaces and workflows, AI implementations often require employees to rethink their entire approach to problem-solving and decision-making. This cognitive shift requires more sophisticated training approaches that go beyond traditional user manuals and video tutorials.

One of the most effective ways to train employees is through structured learning programs tailored to their specific roles and responsibilities. These programs can take various formats, including online courses, instructor-led workshops, hands-on training sessions, and self-paced learning modules. However, the most successful programs combine multiple formats and are designed around real-world use cases that employees will actually encounter in their daily work.

Many organizations partner with educational institutions, technical training providers, and online learning platforms to provide employees with access to up-to-date, industry-relevant content. However, partnership selection is critical—training providers must understand not just the technical aspects of new technologies, but also the organizational context in which they will be implemented. The most effective training programs combine technical instruction with change management principles, helping employees understand not just how to use new tools, but why the changes are necessary and how they fit into the broader organizational strategy.

Beyond structured training, organizations should create an environment that encourages on-the-job learning and experimentation. Employees often learn best by applying their skills in real-world scenarios, experimenting with new tools, and collaborating with colleagues who have different perspectives and expertise. By fostering a learning-by-doing approach, businesses can help employees integrate digital skills into their daily workflows more naturally while building confidence and competence simultaneously.

This experiential learning approach is particularly important for AI and automation implementations, where the technology's behavior can be unpredictable and context-dependent. Employees need opportunities to experiment with these tools in safe environments, understand their limitations, and develop judgment about when and how to apply them effectively. Traditional training approaches that focus on specific procedures and expected outcomes are inadequate for technologies that learn and adapt over time.

Change management is another crucial aspect of digital training that is often overlooked or underestimated. Employees may feel overwhelmed or resistant when faced with new technologies, especially if they perceive automation or AI as a threat to job security. Research shows that 39% of employee resistance stems from fear of job displacement, while another significant portion comes from concerns about their ability to master new skills.

To address these concerns, organizations should communicate the benefits of digital transformation clearly and transparently. Employees need to understand how digital tools will improve their efficiency, enhance job satisfaction, and create new career opportunities rather than replace their roles. This communication must be ongoing and supported by concrete examples of how the transformation will benefit both the organization and individual employees.

Training should not be a one-time event. As digital technologies continue to evolve, organizations must implement ongoing learning initiatives to keep employees up to date with the latest advancements. This is particularly challenging with AI technologies, where capabilities expand rapidly and new applications emerge constantly. Regular training refreshers, access to learning resources, and participation in industry conferences or webinars can help employees stay ahead of the curve and maintain their expertise over time.

The most successful organizations also establish internal communities of practice where employees can share experiences, troubleshoot challenges, and learn from each other's successes and failures. These communities become particularly valuable during digital transformation implementations, where formal training may not cover every scenario that employees encounter in their daily work.

Building a Collaborative and Agile Digital Workforce

Digital transformation is not a task for the IT department alone—it is an organization-wide effort that requires cross-functional collaboration at every level. Traditional silos must be dismantled, and employees from different departments must work together to integrate digital strategies effectively. However, achieving this level of collaboration is more challenging than many organizations anticipate, particularly when dealing with the cultural changes required for successful digital transformation.

Research indicates that 48% of companies face significant challenges in managing organizational change associated with digital implementations. This challenge stems partly from the fact that digital transformation affects different departments in different ways, creating winners and losers within the organization. Some roles may be enhanced by new technologies, while others may be eliminated or fundamentally changed. Managing these disparities requires sophisticated change management approaches that address both the technical and human aspects of transformation.

Encouraging a culture of collaboration ensures that digital initiatives align with business objectives and that technology is leveraged in a way that benefits the entire organization. However, collaboration cannot be mandated—it must be cultivated through structural changes, incentive alignment, and consistent leadership modeling. Organizations that successfully build collaborative digital workforces typically restructure reporting relationships, create cross-functional project teams, and establish shared metrics that encourage departments to work together toward common goals.

Organizations should also adopt agile work methodologies, where teams operate in iterative cycles, continuously testing and refining digital solutions. Agile frameworks such as Scrum and Kanban help teams respond quickly to technological changes, customer feedback, and market demands. However, implementing agile methodologies in digital transformation contexts requires more than adopting new meeting structures and project management tools—it requires a fundamental shift in how the organization thinks about planning, risk management, and decision-making.

The most successful digital transformation teams embrace uncertainty and view failures as learning opportunities rather than setbacks. This mindset is particularly important when implementing emerging technologies like AI, where the path to success is often unclear and requires significant experimentation. Encouraging an agile mindset among employees fosters adaptability, innovation, and a willingness to embrace change rather than resist it.

Creating digital centers of excellence can further support collaboration and knowledge-sharing across the organization. These dedicated teams serve as innovation hubs where employees can experiment with new technologies, share insights, and develop best practices for digital implementation. By providing a space for innovation and experimentation, businesses can empower employees to take ownership of digital transformation and drive meaningful change.

However, centers of excellence must be carefully designed to avoid becoming isolated from the broader organization. The most effective centers of excellence maintain strong connections with business units, regularly share their learnings, and actively work to scale successful innovations across the organization. They serve as bridges between cutting-edge technology and practical business applications, helping to translate innovative ideas into scalable solutions.

Digital centers of excellence also play a crucial role in managing the risks associated with emerging technologies. As organizations experiment with AI, automation, and other advanced technologies, they need safe spaces to test these tools, understand their limitations, and develop governance frameworks for broader implementation. Centers of excellence provide this testing ground while ensuring that lessons learned are captured and shared across the organization.

Learning from Digital Transformation Failures

While success stories often dominate discussions about digital transformation, learning from failures provides equally valuable insights for building competent teams. The high failure rates of digital transformation projects—with only 30% achieving their intended outcomes—offer important lessons about the critical role that talent plays in determining project success or failure.

One of the most instructive examples comes from the retail industry, where several major companies have struggled with digital transformation implementations despite having substantial resources and technical expertise. These failures often trace back to talent-related issues: insufficient change management capabilities, lack of cross-functional collaboration skills, and inadequate understanding of customer experience principles among technical teams.

Amazon's scrapped AI recruiting system provides another compelling case study about the importance of having the right team composition and skills. In 2014, Amazon began developing AI-powered recruiting software to help screen job candidates more efficiently. However, the system developed a bias against female candidates because it was trained on historical data that predominantly reflected male hires. The project was abandoned in 2018 after Amazon couldn't guarantee that the system wouldn't learn other discriminatory patterns.

This failure illustrates several critical points about building digital transformation teams. First, technical expertise alone is insufficient—teams need members who understand bias, ethics, and the broader implications of AI implementations. Second, diverse perspectives are essential when developing AI systems, as homogeneous teams may not recognize their own blind spots. Third, ongoing monitoring and evaluation capabilities are crucial, as AI systems can develop unexpected behaviors over time.

The IBM Watson for Oncology project offers another significant lesson about talent requirements for AI implementations. Despite substantial investment and technical capabilities, Watson for Oncology failed to deliver on its promises to revolutionize cancer treatment. The project was discontinued in 2023 after years of disappointing results and criticism from the medical community.

The Watson failure stemmed from several talent-related issues. The team lacked sufficient domain expertise in oncology, leading to recommendations that didn't align with real-world clinical practices. There was inadequate collaboration between AI developers and medical practitioners, resulting in a system that was technically sophisticated but clinically impractical. The marketing team overstated the system's capabilities, creating unrealistic expectations that the technical team couldn't meet.

These failures highlight the importance of building truly interdisciplinary teams for digital transformation projects. Technical expertise must be combined with domain knowledge, change management skills, and realistic understanding of organizational constraints. Teams need members who can bridge the gap between technical possibilities and business realities, ensuring that digital solutions address real problems rather than creating impressive demonstrations.

The utility sector provides additional insights into talent-related failures. Pacific Gas & Electric faced a significant security breach in 2016 when a third-party vendor hired to create a new asset management platform copied live customer data to its own network without implementing necessary security measures. This breach, which exposed over 30,000 data items for nearly 70 days, resulted in substantial costs and a nearly $3 million fine.

The PG&E incident illustrates the importance of having team members with both technical expertise and security awareness. It also demonstrates the risks of relying on external partners without ensuring they have appropriate skills and governance procedures. Organizations must ensure that all team members, including external consultants and vendors, understand security requirements and have the skills necessary to implement them effectively.

Ensuring Long-Term Success Through Talent Investment

Organizations that prioritize talent development in their digital transformation strategies will have a significant competitive advantage. Investing in recruitment, training, and professional growth ensures that employees are equipped with the skills and mindset needed to navigate the digital landscape effectively. However, this investment must be strategic and sustained rather than episodic and reactive.

Research consistently shows that organizations with strong change management practices are six times more likely to meet or exceed their performance expectations during digital transformation initiatives. This success stems from their investment in developing employees who can manage both the technical and human aspects of change, communicate effectively with diverse stakeholders, and adapt to evolving requirements throughout the transformation process.

By aligning talent development with business objectives, companies can build a workforce that is not only digitally competent but also capable of driving strategic innovation. This alignment requires ongoing dialogue between HR, IT, and business leaders to ensure that skill development priorities match both current needs and future strategic directions. Organizations must anticipate the skills they will need in three to five years and begin developing those capabilities today.

Leadership also plays a critical role in sustaining digital transformation success. Executives and managers must model the behaviors they want to see throughout the organization, champion digital initiatives even when facing short-term challenges, and create an environment that fosters continuous learning and adaptation. Research shows that 40% of organizations report lack of executive buy-in as a significant factor in digital transformation failures.

Effective leaders in digital transformation contexts demonstrate several key characteristics: they maintain realistic expectations about timelines and outcomes, they invest in building organizational capabilities rather than just implementing technologies, they communicate consistently about the vision and progress, and they adapt their strategies based on feedback and changing conditions. Employees are more likely to embrace digital transformation when they see leadership demonstrating genuine commitment to technological advancement and organizational change.

The most successful digital transformation leaders also understand that building a competent team is an ongoing process rather than a one-time effort. They establish systems for continuous skill assessment, create career paths that reward digital competency development, and foster cultures where learning from failure is valued as much as celebrating success. These leaders recognize that digital transformation is ultimately about enabling people to do their jobs more effectively, not about replacing people with technology.

Looking ahead, organizations must also prepare for the continued evolution of digital technologies and the changing skill requirements they bring. AI capabilities continue to advance rapidly, new platforms and tools emerge regularly, and customer expectations evolve constantly. Building a competent team for digital transformation means creating an organization that can adapt to these changes rather than simply implementing current technologies effectively.

Ultimately, digital transformation is about people, processes, and technology working in harmony. Companies that invest in their workforce—through strategic recruitment, comprehensive development programs, ongoing training, and supportive leadership—will not only enhance their digital capabilities but also create a culture of adaptability and innovation that ensures long-term success in an ever-evolving digital world. The organizations that recognize talent as the foundation of digital transformation success will be the ones that thrive in the decades to come.

Part III: IMPLEMENTATION AND EXECUTION

Chapter 10

The Implementation Process: A Step-by-Step Guide to Digital Transformation

Implementing digital technologies is a complex process that requires meticulous planning, strategic execution, and ongoing evaluation. Digital transformation affects not only technology but also people, processes, and the overall culture of an organization. Without a structured approach, businesses risk costly delays, misalignment with strategic goals, and resistance from employees. The stakes are particularly high when considering that research shows only 23% of all ERP implementations are considered successful, while the average cost overrun for digital implementation projects reaches 189%.

A well-defined implementation strategy ensures that digital initiatives deliver the intended benefits while minimizing disruptions to day-to-day operations. However, developing and executing such a strategy requires understanding not just what makes implementations successful, but also what causes them to fail catastrophically. The lessons learned from high-profile failures provide crucial insights that can help organizations avoid similar pitfalls and achieve better outcomes.

Understanding the Implementation Landscape

Before diving into the step-by-step implementation process, it's important to understand the current landscape of digital transformation success and failure. Recent studies indicate that 68% of businesses encounter issues with dependency on third-party vendors during implementations, while 52% struggle with maintaining system performance after go-live. These statistics reveal that implementation challenges extend far beyond the initial deployment phase and require sustained attention throughout the entire transformation journey.

The complexity of modern digital implementations has increased significantly with the integration of artificial intelligence and automation technologies. Unlike traditional software implementations, AI-powered systems introduce additional variables that can affect project outcomes. Organizations must account for data quality requirements, model training timelines, integration complexities, and the need for specialized expertise that may not exist within their current teams.

Research conducted by RAND Corporation found that over 80% of AI projects fail, with five primary root causes: poorly defined business objectives, inadequate data quality, insufficient cross-functional collaboration, lack of organizational readiness, and unrealistic expectations about AI capabilities. These findings highlight the importance of approaching digital implementations with a comprehensive understanding of both technical and organizational requirements.

Step 1: Define Clear Objectives and Scope

Before embarking on a digital transformation journey, organizations must first define their goals and objectives with unprecedented precision. This step lays the foundation for the entire implementation process and ensures that technology investments align with business needs. The objectives should be specific, measurable, achievable, relevant, and time-bound (SMART), but they must also account for the unique challenges introduced by emerging technologies.

For example, an organization may seek to enhance customer experience by implementing an AI-powered chatbot, streamline operations with a cloud-based ERP system, or improve decision-making through advanced data analytics. However, defining these objectives requires understanding not just what the technology can do, but how it will integrate with existing processes, what data it will require, and how it will affect different user groups throughout the organization.

The complexity of objective-setting becomes apparent when examining real-world failures. Lidl, the German grocery chain, provides a compelling example of how poor objective definition can derail even well-funded initiatives. In 2011, Lidl partnered with SAP to develop a modernized inventory management system with an initial budget of €500 million. However, the project's scope expanded continuously as stakeholders added new requirements without properly evaluating their impact on the overall system design or timeline.

The Lidl project ultimately consumed over €500 million and seven years before being abandoned in favor of a completely different approach. The failure stemmed partly from the initial objectives being too ambitious and poorly defined. Rather than focusing on specific, measurable improvements to inventory management, the project attempted to create a comprehensive retail management system that would revolutionize every aspect of the company's operations.

One of the most common challenges at this stage is scope creep, where additional features and functionalities are continuously added without proper planning. This often results in increased costs, extended timelines, and reduced project focus. Scope creep is particularly dangerous in AI implementations, where stakeholders may be tempted to expand the system's capabilities based on promising early results or new technological developments.

To avoid scope creep, organizations should develop a detailed project plan that outlines deliverables, milestones, and timelines with clear boundaries around what is and isn't included in the current phase. Engaging key stakeholders early in the process ensures alignment and prevents unnecessary modifications down the line. However, this engagement must be structured to prevent the project from becoming a wish list of everyone's desired features.

Effective objective definition also requires honest assessment of organizational readiness and constraints. Many digital transformation failures occur because organizations set objectives that exceed their current capabilities or resources. For instance, implementing sophisticated AI systems requires not just technical infrastructure, but also data governance processes, skilled personnel, and cultural readiness for data-driven decision-making.

Step 2: Conduct a Comprehensive Needs Assessment

Before implementing digital solutions, businesses must conduct a thorough assessment of their current systems, processes, and capabilities. This step helps identify gaps, inefficiencies, and areas that require improvement, but it must go beyond traditional IT assessments to include organizational readiness, cultural factors, and change management requirements.

A comprehensive needs assessment should evaluate several critical areas:

Technology Infrastructure: Does the organization have the necessary IT infrastructure to support new digital tools? This evaluation must consider not just current capacity, but also scalability requirements, security capabilities, and integration possibilities. For AI implementations, infrastructure assessment must include data storage and processing capabilities, as well as the ability to handle real-time analytics and machine learning workloads.

Workforce Readiness: Are employees equipped with the skills needed to work with new technologies? This assessment should go beyond technical skills to include change management capabilities, digital literacy levels, and cultural readiness for new ways of working. Research shows that 83% of organizations lack employees with the change management skills necessary for successful digital transformation.

Business Processes: Which workflows can be optimized through digital transformation? This evaluation should identify not just inefficient processes, but also processes that could be fundamentally reimagined through digital technologies. However, organizations must be careful not to simply automate existing inefficiencies—digital transformation often requires process reengineering before technology implementation.

Data Quality and Governance: What is the current state of data quality, accessibility, and governance? This assessment is particularly critical for AI implementations, where poor data quality is a leading cause of project failure. Organizations must evaluate not just the quantity of available data, but its quality, consistency, accessibility, and relevance to the intended use cases.

Security and Compliance: Are there regulatory requirements or cybersecurity risks to consider? This evaluation must account for evolving regulatory landscapes, particularly around data privacy and AI governance. Organizations must also assess their current security postures and identify any vulnerabilities that could be exacerbated by new digital systems.

A common pitfall in this phase is failing to assess organizational readiness comprehensively. Without understanding how digital transformation will impact employees, customers, and business processes, companies risk encountering significant resistance and implementation roadblocks. The assessment must go beyond technical capabilities to include cultural readiness, change management capacity, and stakeholder alignment.

The US Air Force's failed Oracle ERP implementation provides a sobering example of inadequate needs assessment. The $5 billion digital transformation project, which began in 2017, encountered significant challenges that ultimately led to the engagement of Accenture to attempt project recovery. The Air Force's initial assessment failed to adequately account for the complexity of integrating multiple legacy systems, the unique requirements of military operations, and the change management challenges associated with transforming processes across multiple commands and organizations.

The Air Force case illustrates how organizations can underestimate the complexity of their current environment and overestimate their readiness for change. The assessment phase revealed that existing data was stored in incompatible formats across different systems, business processes varied significantly between different units, and personnel lacked the training necessary to use the new system effectively.

To mitigate these risks, organizations should engage cross-functional teams during the assessment process. Gathering insights from employees, IT teams, department heads, and external stakeholders helps create a more realistic and actionable implementation plan. However, this engagement must be structured to ensure that all perspectives are captured while maintaining focus on the project's core objectives.

The needs assessment should also include evaluation of external factors that could affect implementation success. These might include supplier relationships, customer expectations, competitive pressures, and regulatory changes. For AI implementations, organizations must also assess the availability of training data, the potential for bias in existing datasets, and the explainability requirements for different use cases.

Step 3: Develop a Detailed Implementation Plan

Once the needs assessment is complete, organizations must develop a structured implementation roadmap that accounts for the complexity and interdependencies of modern digital systems. This plan should outline project phases, timelines, resource allocation, and key performance indicators, but it must also include contingency planning for the unexpected challenges that inevitably arise during digital implementations.

A comprehensive implementation plan should include several key components:

Project Phases: Breaking the implementation into smaller, manageable phases rather than attempting to roll out everything at once. This phased approach is particularly important for AI implementations, where iterative development and testing are essential for success. Each phase should have clear deliverables, success criteria, and decision points for proceeding to the next phase.

Timelines and Milestones: Setting realistic deadlines for each stage of implementation while building in buffer time for unexpected challenges. Research shows that 80% of ERP implementations exceed their original timelines, often by significant margins. Organizations must balance the desire for quick results with the reality that complex digital systems require thorough testing and user adoption.

Resource Allocation: Defining budgets, workforce requirements, and technology needs for each phase of the project. This allocation must account for both direct implementation costs and indirect costs such as training, change management, and temporary productivity losses during transition periods.

Risk Management: Identifying potential risks and developing mitigation strategies for each major category of risk. For AI implementations, this must include technical risks (such as model performance degradation), data risks (such as bias or privacy violations), and organizational risks (such as user resistance or skill gaps).

Key Performance Indicators (KPIs): Establishing metrics to measure success and impact throughout the implementation process. These metrics should include both technical measures (such as system performance and uptime) and business measures (such as process efficiency improvements and user adoption rates).

A phased implementation approach is often recommended, as it allows organizations to test systems in smaller environments before scaling. For example, an ERP system can first be deployed in a single department or business unit before expanding company-wide. This approach enables organizations to identify and resolve issues early, gather user feedback, and refine processes before broader deployment.

However, phased implementations require careful coordination to ensure that different phases work together effectively. Organizations must design interfaces and integration points carefully to avoid creating data silos or process inefficiencies. The temptation to customize each phase for specific departments must be balanced against the need for system consistency and maintainability.

One of the biggest pitfalls in this phase is attempting to implement the system all at once without proper testing. This "big bang" approach can lead to operational disruptions, employee frustration, and even project failure. Mission Produce provides a cautionary example of this approach gone wrong.

In 2022, Mission Produce, a major avocado distributor, implemented a new ERP system across its entire operation simultaneously. Despite spending hundreds of hours in planning and preparation, the company experienced significant operational disruptions that forced them to revert to manual processes to maintain customer service. The implementation delays and cost overruns totaled nearly $4 million over nine months, while the company also experienced a $22.2 million year-over-year drop in gross profit during the quarter following the go-live.

Mission Produce's CEO later admitted that "the extent and magnitude was greater than we anticipated," highlighting the importance of realistic planning and phased implementation approaches. The company's failure stemmed from underestimating the complexity of their business processes and overestimating their organizational readiness for change.

To avoid these risks, organizations should adopt a pilot program approach before full-scale implementation. This allows teams to identify technical issues, gather user feedback, and make necessary adjustments before the system goes live across the organization. Pilot programs should be designed to test not just technical functionality, but also user adoption, process integration, and performance under realistic operational conditions.

The implementation plan must also account for the unique characteristics of AI and automation technologies. Unlike traditional software implementations, AI systems require ongoing training, monitoring, and adjustment. The implementation plan should include provisions for data collection, model training, performance monitoring, and continuous improvement processes that extend far beyond the initial go-live date.

Step 4: Secure Executive Sponsorship and Assemble a Competent Team

Digital transformation requires strong leadership and executive buy-in to be successful. Without commitment from top management, digital initiatives may lack the necessary resources, authority, and organizational support required for success. Research consistently shows that 40% of organizations report lack of executive buy-in as a significant factor in digital transformation failures.

Organizations should secure executive sponsorship from key decision-makers, such as the CEO, CIO, or Chief Digital Officer. These leaders play a crucial role in driving the project forward, allocating budgets, removing organizational obstacles, and ensuring alignment with business strategy. However, executive sponsorship must go beyond initial approval to include ongoing engagement and support throughout the implementation process.

Executive sponsors must understand that digital transformation is not just a technology project—it's a business transformation that affects every aspect of the organization. They must be prepared to make difficult decisions about resource allocation, process changes, and organizational restructuring. They must also communicate consistently about the importance of the transformation and model the behaviors they expect from employees.

In addition to leadership support, assembling a competent project team is essential. This team should include individuals with both technical expertise and business knowledge, as well as change management capabilities. The team composition should include:

Project Managers with experience in complex digital implementations who can navigate the unique challenges of AI and automation projects. These individuals must understand both traditional project management principles and the iterative, experimental nature of emerging technology implementations.

IT Specialists to handle system integration, security, and technical support. For AI implementations, this must include data scientists, machine learning engineers, and AI specialists who understand not just the technical aspects of these systems, but also their business applications and limitations.

Change Management Experts to facilitate employee adoption and training. These individuals must understand the psychological and organizational aspects of technology adoption, particularly for AI systems that may fundamentally change how people work and make decisions.

Department Representatives to provide insights into how the system will impact different business functions. These representatives must have sufficient authority to make decisions about process changes and sufficient credibility to influence their colleagues' adoption of new systems.

Data Governance Specialists to ensure data quality, privacy, and compliance requirements are met throughout the implementation. This role becomes particularly critical for AI implementations, where data quality directly impacts system performance and regulatory compliance requirements are evolving rapidly.

The Waste Management versus SAP lawsuit provides a powerful example of what happens when executive sponsorship is insufficient and team composition is inadequate. In 2005, Waste Management launched an enterprise-wide ERP project with SAP, scheduled to go live in 2007. The project aimed to simplify and automate order-to-cash processes and replace outdated legacy systems.

However, the project encountered significant challenges from the beginning. SAP had suggested that Waste Management could achieve $106 million to $220 million in annual benefits from the consolidated ERP system, but the company failed to verify these claims adequately before making executive decisions. The implementation team lacked sufficient business knowledge to identify gaps between SAP's promises and the reality of Waste Management's operations.

The project ultimately failed so dramatically that Waste Management sued SAP for $100 million, claiming that SAP had misrepresented its software's capabilities and failed to deliver a functional system. The lawsuit revealed that the project team lacked the expertise necessary to evaluate vendor claims, assess system fit, and manage the complex integration requirements of Waste Management's diverse operations.

A major risk at this stage is lack of sustained leadership involvement, which can lead to low project priority and insufficient resources. To ensure executive commitment, organizations should regularly communicate the strategic benefits of the project, such as increased efficiency, cost savings, and competitive advantage. However, this communication must be based on realistic assessments of what the technology can actually achieve rather than vendor marketing promises.

The team assembly process must also account for the long-term nature of digital transformation projects. Unlike traditional IT implementations that have clear end points, digital transformation is an ongoing process that requires sustained attention and continuous improvement. Team members must be prepared for a multi-year commitment and should have the authority to make decisions that affect their areas of responsibility.

Organizations should also consider external expertise when assembling implementation teams. While internal knowledge is valuable, external consultants and specialists can provide experience with similar implementations, knowledge of best practices, and objective perspectives on organizational challenges. However, external resources must be carefully selected and managed to ensure they transfer knowledge to internal teams rather than creating dependency relationships.

Step 5: Engage Stakeholders and Communicate Effectively

Successful digital transformation requires clear and continuous communication with all stakeholders, including employees, customers, suppliers, and external partners. However, communication in digital transformation contexts is more complex than traditional change communications because the technologies involved may be unfamiliar to many stakeholders, the benefits may not be immediately apparent, and the changes may affect different groups in different ways.

One of the most common reasons digital initiatives fail is poor communication, which leads to misunderstandings, lack of buy-in, and resistance from employees. Research shows that 29% of employees report that changes aren't communicated clearly, leading to confusion and decreased engagement. This communication challenge is particularly acute for AI implementations, where stakeholders may have misconceptions about the technology's capabilities and implications.

Organizations should implement a structured communication plan that addresses different stakeholder groups' specific needs and concerns. This plan should include:

Regular Project Updates that keep stakeholders informed about progress, challenges, and next steps. These updates must be tailored to different audiences—technical updates for IT teams, business impact updates for department heads, and strategic progress updates for executives.

Feedback Mechanisms that encourage stakeholders to provide input and raise concerns. This feedback must be actively solicited and genuinely considered, as stakeholders often identify issues that project teams miss. For AI implementations, feedback mechanisms should also include ways for users to report unexpected system behavior or concerning outcomes.

Transparency about potential disruptions, timeline changes, and resource requirements. Stakeholders need realistic expectations about what the transformation will involve and how it will affect their work. This transparency must extend to acknowledging uncertainties and risks, particularly for experimental technologies like AI.

Education and Training that helps stakeholders understand new technologies and their applications. This education must go beyond technical training to include strategic context, business benefits, and addressing concerns about job security and changing role requirements.

The communication strategy must also address the unique challenges of AI implementations. Many stakeholders have preconceived notions about AI based on popular media representations, which may range from unrealistic optimism to unfounded fears. Organizations must provide balanced, factual information about AI capabilities and limitations while addressing specific concerns about privacy, job displacement, and decision-making transparency.

Revlon's failed SAP implementation illustrates the consequences of inadequate stakeholder communication. In 2020, Revlon embarked on an ambitious ERP consolidation project intended to integrate systems from two separate business units into a single SAP S/4HANA platform. However, the project encountered significant challenges that ultimately contributed to the company's bankruptcy filing in 2022.

Early in the implementation, Revlon realized the ERP consolidation project was likely to fail. The company cited poor ERP design, inadequate process mapping, insufficient integration planning, and lack of effective change management as core reasons for the failure. However, investigation revealed that these technical issues were compounded by communication failures that left stakeholders unprepared for the complexity and impact of the transformation.

Revlon's communication strategy failed to adequately prepare stakeholders for the challenges of integrating two entirely separate business workflows into one centralized system. Employees were not properly informed about how their roles would change, customers were not prepared for potential service disruptions, and suppliers were not adequately briefed on new processes and systems. These communication failures amplified the technical challenges and made recovery much more difficult.

The Revlon case demonstrates that communication must begin early and continue throughout the implementation process. Stakeholders need time to understand, process, and prepare for changes. They also need opportunities to provide feedback and influence the implementation approach before critical decisions are made.

By fostering open communication, businesses can increase stakeholder engagement and improve the overall success rate of digital initiatives. However, this communication must be authentic and substantive rather than merely promotional. Stakeholders can quickly identify when communication is designed to sell them on predetermined decisions rather than genuinely engage them in the transformation process.

Step 6: Invest in Training and Change Management

Implementing digital technologies is not just a technical shift—it's a cultural change that requires employee buy-in and participation. Without proper training and change management, employees may feel overwhelmed, leading to low adoption rates and reduced productivity. Research consistently shows that change management is cited as the biggest challenge by CIOs and project teams, and inadequate change management is a primary factor in the 70% of digital transformation projects that fail.

A strong training and change management strategy ensures that employees feel confident in using new systems and understand how these systems benefit both their individual work and the organization's strategic objectives. However, training for digital transformation, particularly AI implementations, requires more sophisticated approaches than traditional software training.

Organizations should develop comprehensive training programs that include:

Hands-On Training Sessions that allow employees to practice with new systems in realistic scenarios. For AI implementations, this training must include understanding how to interpret AI outputs, when to trust AI recommendations, and how to escalate issues when AI systems behave unexpectedly.

Online Learning Modules for self-paced education that employees can access as needed. These modules should be regularly updated as systems evolve and new features are added. For AI systems that learn and adapt over time, training materials must also evolve to reflect changing system capabilities.

Digital Champions Programs where selected employees receive advanced training and serve as peer support resources. These champions can provide day-to-day assistance, answer questions, and help identify issues before they become major problems. Digital champions are particularly valuable for AI implementations, where users may encounter unexpected situations that aren't covered in formal training materials.

Continuous Learning Opportunities that keep employees updated on new features, best practices, and emerging capabilities. This is particularly important for AI systems, where capabilities can expand significantly through software updates and model improvements.

The training strategy must also address the emotional and psychological aspects of technological change. Many employees experience anxiety about learning new systems, particularly AI technologies that may seem complex or threatening to job security. Training programs must create safe environments where employees can ask questions, make mistakes, and build confidence gradually.

One common pitfall is underestimating employee resistance to change. Research shows that 39% of employee resistance stems from fear of job displacement, while additional resistance comes from concerns about ability to master new skills, changes to familiar routines, and uncertainty about future role requirements. To overcome this resistance, organizations should involve employees early in the process, seek their input on system design and implementation approaches, and clearly communicate how new technologies will benefit them personally.

HP's ERP implementation failure in the early 2000s provides a cautionary example of inadequate change management. The company attempted to implement a comprehensive ERP system across multiple business units but encountered significant resistance from employees who were not adequately prepared for the changes. HP's CIO later blamed the implementation team for not collaborating effectively across organizational silos and relying too heavily on manual processes during the transition.

The HP failure illustrates how technical competence alone is insufficient for digital transformation success. The implementation team had the technical skills necessary to configure and deploy the ERP system, but they lacked the change management expertise needed to help employees adapt to new processes and workflows. The failure to invest adequately in training and change management ultimately undermined the entire project.

Change management for AI implementations requires additional considerations beyond traditional software implementations. Employees must understand not just how to use AI tools, but also their limitations, potential biases, and appropriate applications. They need training on when to trust AI recommendations, how to identify potential problems, and how to maintain human oversight of AI-driven processes.

Organizations must also address concerns about transparency and explainability in AI systems. Employees need to understand how AI systems make decisions, what data they use, and how to interpret their outputs. This understanding is particularly important for regulated industries where employees may need to explain AI-driven decisions to auditors, customers, or regulatory authorities.

Step 7: Monitor Progress and Adapt

After implementation, businesses must continuously track performance and make necessary adjustments to ensure that digital systems deliver expected benefits and continue to meet evolving business needs. Establishing a monitoring system helps detect early warning signs and allows for timely interventions before small issues become major problems.

However, monitoring digital transformation initiatives requires more sophisticated approaches than traditional IT project monitoring. Organizations must track not just technical performance metrics, but also business impact measures, user adoption indicators, and longer-term strategic outcomes. For AI implementations, monitoring must also include model performance tracking, bias detection, and continuous validation of decision-making accuracy.

Organizations should implement comprehensive monitoring approaches that include:

Key Performance Indicator (KPI) Measurement to assess the impact of digital transformation on business outcomes.

These KPIs should include both leading indicators (such as user adoption rates and system utilization) and lagging indicators (such as productivity improvements and cost savings). For AI implementations, KPIs should also include model accuracy, prediction confidence levels, and decision-making transparency measures.

Regular Performance Reviews to evaluate system effectiveness and identify areas for improvement. These reviews should involve both technical assessments and business impact evaluations. They should also include user feedback sessions to understand how the systems are actually being used in practice versus how they were designed to be used.

User Feedback Collection to identify issues, improvement opportunities, and emerging requirements. This feedback should be actively solicited through surveys, focus groups, and usage analytics. For AI systems, user feedback is particularly important because these systems may behave in unexpected ways or identify patterns that users don't understand.

Continuous Adaptation based on real-world data and changing business conditions. Digital systems should be designed for continuous improvement rather than static operation. This is particularly important for AI systems, which can improve their performance through additional training data and algorithm refinements.

The monitoring approach must also account for the evolving nature of digital technologies. AI systems learn and adapt over time, which means their behavior may change in ways that weren't anticipated during initial implementation. Organizations need monitoring systems that can detect these changes and alert administrators when systems begin behaving differently than expected.

Hershey's ERP implementation disaster in 1999 provides a stark example of what happens when organizations fail to monitor progress adequately and adapt to emerging problems. The company attempted to implement a comprehensive ERP system, advanced planning system, and warehouse management system simultaneously during their peak shipping season leading up to Halloween.

The implementation encountered significant problems from the beginning, but the company failed to recognize the severity of these issues or take corrective action quickly enough. Orders were delayed, shipments were incorrect, and customer service deteriorated dramatically. The company lost approximately $100 million in sales during the critical Halloween season, and it took months to fully resolve the system issues.

Hershey's failure stemmed partly from inadequate monitoring and an unwillingness to adapt when early warning signs indicated serious problems. The company was so committed to meeting its go-live deadline that it ignored indicators that the system wasn't ready for full-scale deployment. Better monitoring systems and more willingness to delay the launch could have prevented much of the damage.

The Hershey case illustrates the importance of establishing clear go/no-go criteria before implementation and having the courage to delay launches when systems aren't ready. Organizations must balance the pressure to meet deadlines with the need to ensure system stability and user readiness.

For AI implementations, monitoring becomes even more critical because these systems can develop unexpected behaviors or biases over time. Organizations need automated monitoring systems that can detect when AI models are performing differently than expected, when they're making decisions based on inappropriate data, or when they're producing outcomes that violate business rules or ethical guidelines.

Ignoring early warning signs is a common mistake that can lead to project failure and significant business disruption. To prevent this, companies must adopt an agile approach—continuously refining processes based on real-world data and user experiences. This agility requires organizational cultures that value adaptation over adherence to original plans and that view course corrections as signs of responsiveness rather than failure.

Learning from Implementation Failures

While the steps outlined above provide a framework for successful digital transformation implementation, understanding why implementations fail provides equally valuable insights. Research shows that most ERP failures are self-inflicted, resulting from preventable mistakes rather than inherent technology limitations.

Common implementation failure patterns include:

Insufficient Planning and Assessment: Organizations that rush into implementation without thoroughly understanding their current state, requirements, and readiness for change consistently encounter problems. The complexity of modern digital systems requires comprehensive planning that accounts for technical, organizational, and strategic factors.

Unrealistic Expectations: Many failures stem from organizations expecting too much from digital technologies or underestimating the time and effort required for successful implementation. This is particularly common with AI implementations, where marketing hype often exceeds current technological capabilities.

Inadequate Resource Allocation: Organizations that underfund training, change management, or ongoing support consistently struggle with adoption and performance issues. Digital transformation requires sustained investment beyond initial technology costs.

Poor Vendor Management: Many implementations fail because organizations don't adequately evaluate vendor capabilities, verify marketing claims, or establish appropriate contractual protections. The relationship between organizations and technology vendors must be managed carefully to ensure successful outcomes.

Lack of Organizational Readiness: Organizations that attempt digital transformation without adequate change management capabilities, leadership commitment, or cultural preparation consistently encounter resistance and adoption problems.

Nike's supply chain software failure in the early 2000s illustrates how multiple implementation mistakes can compound to create disaster. The company implemented demand planning software from i2 Technologies that was supposed to optimize inventory management and reduce costs. However, the implementation encountered significant problems that led to a $100 million loss in sales and a 20% drop in stock value.

The Nike failure resulted from several implementation mistakes: inadequate testing of the software before go-live, insufficient training for users who would operate the system, poor integration with existing systems, and unrealistic expectations about the software's capabilities. The company also failed to have adequate backup plans when the system didn't perform as expected.

Nike's experience demonstrates how implementation failures can cascade—technical problems led to inventory shortages, which led to customer dissatisfaction, which led to financial losses and reputational damage. The company's recovery required not just fixing the technical issues, but also rebuilding customer relationships and restoring confidence in its supply chain capabilities.

The lessons from these failures emphasize the importance of following structured implementation processes, maintaining realistic expectations, and being prepared to adapt when things don't go according to plan. Organizations that learn from others' failures and implement comprehensive risk management strategies are much more likely to achieve successful digital transformation outcomes.

Driving Digital Transformation Success

Digital transformation is a journey, not a one-time project. Organizations that follow a structured implementation process—from defining objectives and assessing needs to training employees and monitoring progress—are more likely to achieve sustainable success. However, this success requires understanding that digital transformation affects every aspect of the organization and demands sustained attention and investment.

By avoiding common pitfalls such as scope creep, poor planning, lack of leadership support, inadequate training, and weak communication, businesses can seamlessly integrate digital technologies while maintaining operational efficiency. The organizations that succeed in digital transformation are those that approach it as a comprehensive business transformation rather than just a technology upgrade.

The integration of AI and other emerging technologies adds new dimensions to implementation complexity, but also creates new opportunities for innovation and competitive advantage. Organizations that develop capabilities for implementing and managing these advanced technologies will be better positioned to adapt to future technological developments and market changes.

Ultimately, successful digital transformation requires collaboration, adaptability, and a long-term vision. Companies that invest in strategic implementation capabilities, build comprehensive change management competencies, and maintain focus on business outcomes rather than just technology deployment will not only streamline processes but also position themselves for future growth, innovation, and competitive advantage in the digital age.

The organizations that master digital transformation implementation will be those that recognize it as an ongoing capability rather than a series of discrete projects. They will build internal expertise, establish robust governance processes, and create cultures that embrace continuous improvement and adaptation. These organizations will not just survive the digital transformation wave—they will ride it to new levels of success and market leadership.

Chapter 11

Change Management Strategies: Leading Successful Transformation

In any digital transformation initiative, technological upgrades and system implementations are only one part of the equation. The real challenge lies in managing the people side of change. Employees must adapt to new workflows, leadership must foster a culture of innovation, and the entire organization must navigate uncertainty while maintaining operational effectiveness. Without effective change management strategies, even the most well-planned transformation efforts can fail due to resistance, misalignment, and lack of engagement.

The statistics surrounding change management are sobering. Research consistently shows that 70% of change initiatives fail, with employee resistance and inadequate management support being primary factors. When examining digital transformation specifically, the failure rates are even more concerning—only 30% of digital transformation initiatives achieve their intended outcomes, and organizations with poor change management practices are six times less likely to meet their performance expectations.

Change management is the structured approach that helps organizations transition smoothly through transformation. It ensures that employees understand, accept, and adopt changes in a way that minimizes disruption while maximizing efficiency and long-term success. However, change management for digital transformation, particularly initiatives involving artificial intelligence and automation, requires more sophisticated approaches than traditional organizational change efforts.

The Complexity of Modern Change Management

The landscape of organizational change has evolved dramatically in recent years. Where traditional change management focused primarily on process improvements and organizational restructuring, modern digital transformation requires employees to adapt to technologies that may fundamentally alter how they work, make decisions, and interact with customers and colleagues.

Artificial intelligence implementations present particularly complex change management challenges. Unlike traditional software that automates existing processes, AI systems can make decisions, identify patterns, and recommend actions that humans might not understand or anticipate. This requires employees to develop new skills around interpreting AI outputs, maintaining appropriate oversight, and collaborating with intelligent systems.

Research conducted by RAND Corporation found that over 80% of AI projects fail, with organizational and change management issues being significant contributing factors alongside technical challenges. Many organizations focus heavily on the technical aspects of AI implementation while underestimating the human factors that determine whether these systems will be successfully adopted and effectively utilized.

The pace of technological change also complicates modern change management efforts. While traditional organizational changes might be implemented over months or years and then remain stable for extended periods, digital transformation requires ongoing adaptation as technologies evolve, new capabilities emerge, and market conditions change. Organizations must develop change management capabilities that support continuous transformation rather than discrete change events.

Furthermore, the scope of digital transformation affects multiple stakeholder groups simultaneously—employees, customers, suppliers, and partners—each with different needs, concerns, and levels of technological readiness. Change management strategies must account for these diverse perspectives while maintaining coherent organizational direction and messaging.

The Key to Effective Change Management

Successful change management begins with a clear vision and well-defined objectives that address both the technical and human aspects of transformation. Leaders must articulate not just what is changing and how it will work, but why the change is necessary, what benefits it will bring, and how it aligns with the organization's long-term strategy. This is particularly important for AI implementations, where employees may have misconceptions about the technology's capabilities and implications.

Employees need to see the bigger picture—how the changes will impact their roles, how the organization will support them through the transition, and what success will look like both for the organization and for them personally. When leadership provides a compelling case for change that addresses individual concerns and demonstrates clear benefits, it fosters greater buy-in and enthusiasm among employees.

However, creating a compelling vision requires more than inspirational messaging. Organizations must demonstrate that they understand the challenges employees face and have concrete plans for addressing them. This includes acknowledging that some jobs may change significantly or disappear entirely, while also showing how new opportunities will be created and how employees will be supported in developing new skills.

Engaging stakeholders early and often is critical to gaining support and reducing resistance. People are naturally resistant to change, especially when they feel excluded from decision-making or uncertain about how changes will affect them. Research shows that 39% of employee resistance stems from fear of job displacement, while additional resistance comes from concerns about ability to master new skills and uncertainty about future role requirements.

Organizations that involve employees from the outset create a sense of ownership, making it more likely that employees will embrace transformation rather than resist it. This involvement must go beyond token consultation to include meaningful opportunities to influence implementation approaches, system design decisions, and change timelines. By actively listening to concerns, answering questions, and incorporating employee feedback into the change process, leaders can ease fears and build trust.

For AI implementations, early engagement is particularly important because employees may have preconceived notions about artificial intelligence based on popular media representations or previous experiences. Organizations must provide balanced, factual information about AI capabilities and limitations while addressing specific concerns about privacy, job security, and decision-making transparency.

Clear and consistent communication is one of the most important aspects of change management, but it's also one of the most challenging to execute effectively. Employees need timely updates on what is changing, when it will happen, and how it will affect them. However, communication about complex digital transformations must balance providing sufficient detail with avoiding information overload.

Leaders must use multiple communication channels—including meetings, emails, training sessions, town halls, and digital platforms—to reinforce messages and accommodate different communication preferences. The communication strategy must also account for different stakeholder groups' varying levels of technical sophistication and different concerns about the transformation.

Misinformation and uncertainty breed anxiety and resistance, so organizations must ensure that messages remain transparent and accessible to all employees. This transparency must extend to acknowledging uncertainties and risks while maintaining confidence in the overall direction and approach. For AI implementations, transparency is particularly important because these systems may make decisions in ways that aren't immediately apparent to users.

Beyond communication, proper training and support are crucial to helping employees adjust to new technologies and processes. When employees lack the knowledge or confidence to use new systems effectively, productivity suffers, and frustration increases. This is particularly challenging for AI implementations, where employees must learn not just how to use new tools, but how to interpret their outputs and maintain appropriate human oversight.

Training programs should be tailored to different roles and skill levels, recognizing that employees in various departments have unique needs when adapting to digital transformation. Training must also be ongoing rather than a one-time event, as digital systems evolve and new capabilities are added over time.

A phased approach to adoption allows organizations to implement change gradually rather than all at once, giving employees time to adapt, provide feedback, and suggest improvements. This phased approach also helps organizations identify and resolve potential challenges before full-scale implementation. However, phased implementations require careful coordination to ensure that different phases work together effectively and that employees don't become confused by inconsistent processes or capabilities.

Monitoring progress and remaining adaptable are essential for ensuring that transformation stays on course and continues to meet employee and business needs. Organizations must track key performance indicators to assess whether changes are achieving their intended outcomes and whether employees are successfully adapting to new ways of working.

Leaders should remain flexible and be prepared to adjust strategies if initial plans do not yield expected results or if new challenges emerge during implementation. This adaptability is particularly important for AI implementations, where system behavior may change over time as models learn and adapt, requiring corresponding adjustments to processes and training.

Case Studies of Successful Change Initiatives

Learning from organizations that have successfully navigated complex change initiatives provides valuable insights for digital transformation efforts. These examples demonstrate how comprehensive change management strategies can overcome resistance, build employee engagement, and achieve sustainable transformation outcomes.

One compelling example of effective change management comes from the application of structured change theory at a Vietnamese university seeking to improve teaching effectiveness and student outcomes. The university's leadership team recognized that simply mandating new teaching methods would likely encounter resistance from faculty members who were comfortable with existing approaches.

Instead, the university conducted extensive research using observations, questionnaires, and interviews to assess current teaching methods and understand faculty perspectives on potential improvements. This research revealed specific challenges that faculty faced and identified opportunities where new approaches could address real problems rather than simply implementing change for its own sake.

Based on this feedback, university leadership introduced professional development seminars and alternative instructional approaches that directly addressed the issues faculty had identified. The change process included ongoing support, peer collaboration opportunities, and regular feedback sessions that allowed faculty to share experiences and refine approaches.

After implementing these changes, evaluations showed significant improvements in student satisfaction and learning outcomes. The university's success illustrates several important principles: the importance of involving affected individuals in identifying problems and solutions, the value of listening to concerns and addressing them directly, and the need for providing targeted training and ongoing support throughout the change process.

Another instructive case study comes from a federally qualified health center in Kentucky that worked with the Centers for Disease Control and Prevention to enhance preventive care services and reduce health disparities. This initiative faced significant challenges because it required changing established medical practices and convincing healthcare providers to adopt new approaches to patient care.

Leaders began the change process by conducting comprehensive assessments of current practices through employee interviews and observation. This assessment revealed specific barriers to preventive care delivery and identified opportunities where new approaches could improve patient outcomes while making healthcare providers' work more effective.

Based on these findings, leadership implemented higher quality standards and worked closely with healthcare providers to facilitate adoption of new practices. The change process included extensive training, peer support systems, and regular feedback mechanisms that allowed providers to share experiences and learn from each other.

By securing executive sponsorship and continuously gathering employee feedback, the organization was able to make lasting improvements in patient care quality and preventive service delivery. This case highlights the importance of securing leadership commitment, involving employees in problem identification and solution development, and fostering a culture of continuous improvement rather than one-time change events.

Harwood Manufacturing offers another compelling example of change management in action, demonstrating how employee involvement and leadership development can drive significant performance improvements. The company faced high employee turnover and declining productivity, prompting a series of change initiatives led by researchers including Kurt Lewin.

One of their key strategies was implementing group decision-making processes where workers participated in setting their own production goals rather than having targets imposed by management. This involvement led to increased job satisfaction and higher productivity levels because employees felt ownership of the goals they were working to achieve.

The company also experimented with self-management approaches, allowing workers to control their workflow and make decisions about how to organize their work. This resulted in improved efficiency compared to traditional management-led production lines, demonstrating that employees often have valuable insights about how to improve processes when given the opportunity to contribute.

Another critical intervention was leadership training, where supervisors were taught cooperative leadership styles that emphasized collaboration and support rather than command and control. This led to better communication between managers and employees, fewer disciplinary issues, and higher overall performance across the organization.

The success of Harwood Manufacturing's initiatives underscores the power of employee involvement and leadership development in driving organizational change. The company's approach demonstrated that treating employees as partners in change rather than subjects of change leads to better outcomes and more sustainable improvements.

In the healthcare sector, University Physicians Group in New York successfully implemented an Electronic Medical Records system through a carefully planned phased adoption approach. Recognizing the risks associated with implementing new systems across the entire organization simultaneously, UPG chose to introduce the new system gradually.

The transition began with small-scale testing and pilot programs that allowed staff to become familiar with the system and provide feedback before it was expanded to additional departments. This step-by-step strategy minimized disruption to patient care, ensured smooth adoption, and allowed the organization to refine processes and training based on real-world experience.

Each phase of implementation included comprehensive training, ongoing support, and opportunities for staff to share feedback and suggest improvements. The organization also established clear success criteria for each phase and required sign-off from users before proceeding to the next phase.

UPG's experience demonstrates the effectiveness of phased implementation in reducing risk and increasing employee confidence in new systems. The approach also allowed the organization to build internal expertise and change management capabilities that supported future technology implementations.

A different but equally instructive approach was taken by Daman Products, a manufacturing company that adopted lean manufacturing principles to enhance efficiency and reduce waste. The company's transformation required significant changes to production processes, quality control methods, and employee responsibilities.

Daman achieved remarkable improvements, including a 97% reduction in cycle times, a 50% decrease in setup times, and a 90% reduction in production flow distance. Their success was driven by comprehensive change management techniques that included focused workspace redesign, visual management systems, and extensive employee empowerment initiatives.

The transformation process emphasized collaboration and continuous learning, with employees at all levels involved in identifying improvement opportunities and implementing solutions. The company also invested heavily in training and development, ensuring that employees had the skills and knowledge necessary to succeed in the new operating environment.

Through sustained collaboration and continuous learning initiatives, Daman successfully transformed its operational model while maintaining high levels of employee engagement and satisfaction. The company's experience proves that structured change management can lead to significant business improvements when it addresses both technical and human factors comprehensively.

Some organizations choose a "big bang" approach where all changes are implemented simultaneously, which can be successful when properly managed. A large supermarket chain that upgraded its checkout system across all locations adopted this strategy, replacing its old point-of-sale system entirely in a single weekend.

While this method carries greater risks than phased implementation, the company mitigated potential issues through detailed planning, extensive employee training, and strong technical support. The preparation process included months of training for employees, comprehensive testing of the new system, and detailed contingency plans for addressing potential problems.

The transition was successful because the organization invested heavily in preparation and support, showing that even high-risk implementation approaches can work when organizations are committed to comprehensive change management. The key was ensuring that employees felt prepared and supported throughout the transition, with clear escalation procedures when problems arose.

Resistance to Change

Digital transformation is not just about upgrading technology; it requires a fundamental cultural shift that pushes organizations to rethink their processes, workflows, and overall mindset. However, implementing change is often met with resistance as employees and stakeholders struggle with uncertainty, fear, and skepticism. Without a well-structured change management strategy, even the most advanced digital initiatives risk failure. Research consistently shows that 70% of digital transformation projects fail, making effective change management not just important but critical for organizational survival.

Successfully managing change requires understanding where resistance comes from and implementing strategies that ensure smooth adoption and long-term success. The stakes have never been higher, particularly as organizations increasingly integrate artificial intelligence and advanced automation into their operations, fundamentally altering how work gets done and creating new anxieties among employees about their future roles.

Understanding Resistance to Change

One of the biggest obstacles to digital transformation is employee resistance. When change disrupts established routines, introduces new learning curves, and creates uncertainty about job security, employees may become hesitant to adopt new systems. Even when leadership recognizes the benefits of digital transformation, skepticism at various levels of the organization can slow down progress.

The failure of Target Canada's ambitious expansion serves as a stark reminder of what happens when change management is inadequate. Despite investing over $7 billion in their Canadian operations, Target failed to address the fundamental cultural and operational differences between their US and Canadian markets. The company's rushed timeline, coupled with inadequate change management processes, led to supply chain disasters, pricing errors, and ultimately the complete withdrawal from the Canadian market within two years. Employees were left feeling disconnected from the transformation, and customers never experienced the Target brand they expected.

Fear of the unknown is a significant factor in resistance. Employees who do not fully understand how a new technology, system, or process will impact their roles may feel anxious and hesitant to embrace change. This anxiety is particularly pronounced with AI implementations, where employees often worry about being replaced by machines. When uncertainty takes hold, it often leads to disengagement or outright pushback. The best way to address this concern is through clear and consistent communication. When employees see how transformation will improve efficiency, enhance workflow, and even provide job security through upskilling opportunities, they are more likely to approach it with an open mind.

A perceived loss of control can also contribute to resistance. Employees who feel that change is being imposed on them without their input may worry about their expertise being undervalued or their roles being diminished by automation and artificial intelligence. The introduction of AI-powered systems often amplifies these concerns, as employees fear their decision-making authority will be transferred to algorithms. To counter this, organizations must involve employees early in the decision-making process, seek their input, and make them feel like active participants in the transformation rather than passive recipients of change.

The pharmaceutical giant Johnson & Johnson learned this lesson during their global ERP implementation. Initial resistance was high because employees felt the new system would eliminate their ability to make nuanced decisions based on local market knowledge. However, by involving key users in the design process and demonstrating how AI-enhanced analytics would actually augment their decision-making capabilities, the company was able to transform skeptics into advocates.

Workload concerns further add to resistance. Many employees already feel stretched thin, and the idea of learning new tools or adapting to new processes while maintaining their existing responsibilities can feel overwhelming. This challenge becomes even more complex when introducing AI systems that require employees to learn new ways of working alongside intelligent automation. Organizations can ease this transition by providing comprehensive training, ongoing support, and phased implementation plans to prevent employees from feeling overloaded.

Past failures can also foster skepticism. If an organization has attempted digital transformation before and struggled due to poor implementation, lack of leadership support, or significant employee resistance, employees may be doubtful about new efforts. The healthcare sector provides numerous examples of failed ERP implementations that have created lasting skepticism. One major hospital system's $300 million ERP failure not only resulted in financial losses but also created a culture where employees actively resisted subsequent technology initiatives for years. Acknowledging previous mistakes, highlighting the changes in approach, and providing concrete examples of successful transformations within the industry can help rebuild confidence in the initiative.

Developing an Effective Change Management Strategy

Successfully navigating digital transformation requires a structured approach to change management that incorporates proactive planning, transparent communication, and continuous employee support. One of the most important aspects of this process is creating a clear vision for change and effectively communicating it throughout the organization. Employees need to understand not only what is changing but why it matters and how it benefits them. Without a well-defined vision, digital initiatives can feel directionless, leading to confusion and disengagement.

The contrast between successful and failed transformations often lies in vision clarity. Consider the difference between General Electric's failed digital transformation under former CEO Jeff Immelt and Microsoft's successful reinvention under Satya Nadella. GE's attempt to become a "digital industrial company" lacked clear messaging about what this meant for individual employees and departments. The vision was grand but abstract, leading to confusion and ultimately the abandonment of the strategy. Microsoft, conversely, articulated a clear vision of becoming a "productivity and platform company" with specific implications for how employees would work differently and the skills they would need to develop.

Effective communication goes beyond a single announcement. It requires a sustained effort through multiple channels, such as town halls, emails, internal platforms, and one-on-one meetings. Leaders should clearly define the goals, benefits, and expected outcomes of the transformation while using storytelling and real-world examples to illustrate how digital initiatives will lead to positive change. Transparency is essential, as employees are more likely to embrace transformation when they trust that leadership is being open and honest about the process.

This communication becomes even more critical when implementing AI technologies. Employees need to understand not just how AI will change their work, but how it will enhance their capabilities rather than replace them. Organizations that successfully implement AI often share specific examples of how the technology will eliminate mundane tasks while enabling employees to focus on higher-value, more strategic work.

Employee engagement is another critical element of successful change management. People are more willing to support change when they feel involved rather than dictated to. Organizations can encourage employee engagement by conducting surveys and focus groups to gather insights and concerns before rolling out new technology. Creating forums for discussion where employees can ask questions and offer feedback fosters a sense of ownership and inclusion. Additionally, pilot programs and test phases that allow employees to experiment with new technology and provide input on its implementation increase buy-in and enthusiasm.

The global consulting firm Accenture exemplifies this approach in their own digital transformation. Rather than imposing new AI tools company-wide, they created innovation labs where employees could experiment with emerging technologies. This hands-on approach allowed employees to discover the benefits of AI firsthand and become internal advocates for broader adoption.

Providing training and ongoing support is essential in reducing resistance. Many employees struggle with digital transformation simply because they lack confidence in using new technologies. This challenge is particularly acute with AI implementations, where employees may feel intimidated by sophisticated algorithms and machine learning capabilities. Hands-on training sessions, self-paced online courses, and mentorship programs help employees develop the skills they need to succeed in a digital environment. Digital coaches or internal knowledge-sharing platforms where employees can ask questions and exchange best practices further reinforce the learning process. When employees feel well-prepared and supported, they are far more likely to embrace change rather than resist it.

Learning from High-Profile Failures

The landscape of digital transformation is littered with expensive failures that offer valuable lessons for organizations embarking on their own change journeys. These failures often share common characteristics: inadequate change management, unrealistic timelines, and insufficient attention to the human element of transformation.

One of the most instructive failures comes from the retail sector, where J.C. Penney's attempt at transformation under CEO Ron Johnson demonstrates the catastrophic consequences of ignoring change management principles. Johnson's vision of transforming the century-old retailer into a modern, boutique-style shopping destination was bold, but his approach was disastrous. He eliminated sales and coupons without preparing customers for the change, redesigned stores without testing customer reactions, and dismissed long-tenured employees who understood the company's traditional customer base. The result was a 25% decline in revenue in just one year and Johnson's termination after 17 months. The failure wasn't in the vision itself but in the complete absence of change management strategy that considered the human elements—both employees and customers.

The technology sector provides equally instructive examples. Hewlett-Packard's massive restructuring and technology overhaul in the early 2010s serves as a cautionary tale about the importance of maintaining organizational stability during transformation. The company's attempt to split into two entities while simultaneously implementing new ERP systems and downsizing created a perfect storm of change fatigue. Employees were dealing with job insecurity, new systems, and unclear reporting structures simultaneously. The transformation, which was supposed to position HP for future growth, instead led to years of declining performance and market share losses.

In the public sector, the troubled rollout of Healthcare.gov demonstrates how technical failures can be compounded by poor change management. While much attention focused on the website's technical problems, the underlying issue was the failure to prepare healthcare navigators, insurance companies, and consumers for the massive change in how health insurance would be purchased and managed. The lack of comprehensive training programs and support systems meant that even when technical issues were resolved, the human systems were unprepared to handle the transformation.

The financial services industry offers particularly relevant lessons as banks increasingly integrate AI into their operations. Wells Fargo's account fraud scandal, while not strictly a digital transformation failure, illustrates how organizational culture and change management failures can undermine even well-intentioned initiatives. The bank's aggressive sales culture and lack of ethical guardrails created an environment where employees felt pressured to open unauthorized accounts. When the bank later attempted to implement AI-powered monitoring systems to prevent such behaviors, employees were skeptical and resistant, viewing the technology as punitive rather than supportive.

The AI Implementation Challenge

As artificial intelligence becomes increasingly central to digital transformation initiatives, organizations face new and complex change management challenges. AI implementations often fail not because of technical limitations but because of inadequate attention to the human aspects of working alongside intelligent systems.

The retail giant Amazon provides an illuminating case study in both AI success and failure. While the company has successfully implemented AI in areas like recommendation engines and supply chain optimization, their attempt to use AI for resume screening had to be abandoned after it was discovered the system was biased against women. The technical failure was compounded by inadequate change management—HR professionals weren't adequately trained to understand the AI system's limitations, leading to over-reliance on automated recommendations. This experience highlights how AI implementations require not just technical expertise but also comprehensive change management that helps employees understand both the capabilities and limitations of AI systems.

In the healthcare sector, IBM's Watson for Oncology represents one of the most high-profile AI implementation failures. Despite massive investment and marketing, the system failed to gain widespread adoption among oncologists. The primary reasons weren't technical but related to change management: doctors didn't trust recommendations they couldn't understand, the system wasn't integrated into existing workflows, and there was insufficient training on how to effectively use AI as a decision-support tool rather than a replacement for clinical judgment.

These failures underscore a critical principle: AI implementations require a fundamentally different approach to change management than traditional technology deployments. Employees need to understand not just how to use AI tools but how to work collaboratively with intelligent systems. This requires new skills in areas like prompt engineering, AI literacy, and human-AI collaboration.

Conversely, organizations that successfully implement AI often follow a different playbook. They start with clear communication about AI's role as an augmentation rather than replacement tool. They provide extensive training not just on how to use AI systems but on how to interpret and validate AI outputs. Most importantly, they involve employees in the design and testing of AI systems, ensuring that the technology enhances rather than disrupts existing workflows.

Leveraging Change Champions to Drive Transformation

In any digital transformation initiative, having the right advocates in place can significantly impact the success of adoption across an organization. Identifying early adopters who are naturally tech-savvy, adaptable, and enthusiastic about change is a crucial strategy for fostering a culture of innovation. These individuals, known as change champions, serve as catalysts in driving enthusiasm and engagement among their colleagues. Their ability to lead by example, mentor peers, and provide real-time feedback to leadership helps ensure that transformation efforts are met with positivity and proactive adoption rather than resistance.

The success of change champions becomes even more critical in AI implementations, where employees may feel particularly anxious about working with unfamiliar technology. Champions who can demonstrate practical applications of AI and share positive experiences help demystify the technology and reduce fears about job displacement.

One of the most effective ways to leverage change champions is to provide them with specialized training tailored to the transformation initiative. By equipping them with deep knowledge of new technologies, systems, and workflows, they become credible sources of information and support for their peers. Additionally, giving these employees leadership roles within the initiative, such as serving on advisory committees or participating in decision-making processes, helps reinforce their influence and ensures that their insights are valued by the organization.

The global technology company Siemens exemplifies this approach in their digital factory initiative. Rather than imposing new AI-powered manufacturing systems from the top down, they identified and trained champions within each factory who could demonstrate the benefits of predictive maintenance and intelligent automation. These champions became local experts who could address concerns, provide training, and adapt the technology to local needs. This approach was instrumental in achieving adoption rates exceeding 85% across their global manufacturing network.

Change champions are instrumental in addressing resistance within the workforce. Employees who are hesitant to adopt new tools or processes may be more receptive to guidance from a peer rather than from senior management. When employees witness their colleagues successfully navigating the transformation, it builds confidence and reduces apprehension. This peer-driven approach fosters a sense of community and shared purpose, making the transition smoother for all involved.

Furthermore, these champions provide invaluable feedback to leadership, helping to identify pain points, usability issues, or workflow inefficiencies that may not be immediately apparent. Their insights allow organizations to fine-tune implementation strategies in real-time, ensuring that adjustments can be made to improve adoption rates and overall success. Without such feedback loops, digital transformation efforts risk stagnation or disengagement.

To maximize the impact of change champions, organizations should recognize and reward their contributions. This can be achieved through incentives, public acknowledgment, career development opportunities, or financial bonuses. Demonstrating appreciation for their efforts not only motivates the champions themselves but also encourages other employees to step up and take an active role in the transformation process.

By fostering a grassroots approach to digital transformation, organizations create a ripple effect of engagement and motivation throughout the workforce. When change champions are empowered and supported, they help establish a positive and resilient organizational culture, where innovation is embraced rather than resisted. Ultimately, their influence plays a critical role in ensuring that transformation efforts are not only successful but also sustainable in the long term.

Preventing Change Fatigue and Maintaining Momentum

Digital transformation initiatives often involve significant shifts in technology, processes, and organizational culture. While change is necessary for growth, too much change introduced too quickly can lead to change fatigue—an overwhelming sense of exhaustion and disengagement among employees. Organizations must recognize the risks associated with change fatigue and take proactive steps to prevent it, ensuring that momentum is sustained throughout the transformation journey.

The phenomenon of change fatigue has become increasingly prevalent as organizations attempt to keep pace with rapid technological advancement. A prime example comes from the aerospace industry, where Boeing's attempts to simultaneously modernize manufacturing processes, implement new design software, and integrate AI-powered quality control systems led to widespread employee burnout and ultimately contributed to production delays and quality issues. The company's experience illustrates how even well-intentioned transformation efforts can backfire when they overwhelm an organization's capacity for change.

One of the primary strategies for mitigating change fatigue is to pace transformation efforts in a manageable way. Instead of introducing multiple initiatives simultaneously, organizations should prioritize key changes and roll them out in phases. A phased approach allows employees to adapt gradually, reducing feelings of anxiety and resistance. Breaking down the transformation into digestible steps also provides opportunities for continuous feedback and improvement, ensuring that each phase is implemented effectively before moving on to the next.

The pharmaceutical company Merck successfully employed this approach during their global digital transformation. Rather than attempting to implement new AI-powered drug discovery tools, modernize manufacturing systems, and overhaul customer relationship management simultaneously, they created a carefully sequenced roadmap that allowed employees to master each new system before introducing the next. This approach not only reduced change fatigue but also enabled the company to apply lessons learned from early phases to subsequent implementations.

Clear and transparent communication plays a crucial role in maintaining momentum without overwhelming employees. Leadership should provide regular updates on the progress of the transformation, explaining the rationale behind each change and how it aligns with the organization's long-term goals.

Addressing concerns proactively and creating open channels for feedback fosters trust and engagement, making employees feel included in the process rather than subjected to it.

This communication challenge becomes particularly complex when implementing AI systems, where employees may have fundamental misconceptions about the technology's capabilities and intentions. Organizations that successfully manage AI transformations often invest heavily in AI literacy programs that help employees understand not just how AI works but why it's being implemented and how it will affect their specific roles.

Another key factor in preventing change fatigue is allowing employees adequate time to adjust before introducing further changes. Organizations should be mindful of the cognitive load associated with learning new systems and processes. Implementing change management strategies that include training sessions, hands-on workshops, and continuous support ensures that employees feel prepared and confident rather than stressed and uncertain. Investing in ongoing education and professional development opportunities helps employees view transformation as a learning experience rather than a disruption.

Additionally, leadership must acknowledge that adapting to new ways of working can be mentally and emotionally taxing. Providing resources for mental health and well-being support is essential in helping employees navigate change in a healthy way. Initiatives such as stress management workshops, access to counseling services, or even flexible work arrangements can make a significant difference in maintaining morale and productivity.

The consulting firm McKinsey & Company faced this challenge during their own digital transformation when they implemented AI-powered analytics tools across all practice areas. Recognizing the potential for overwhelm, they established "digital wellness" programs that included stress management resources, flexible learning schedules, and peer support networks. These initiatives helped maintain high engagement levels throughout the transformation process.

Recognizing and celebrating milestones is another effective way to sustain momentum. Acknowledging employee efforts and successes, whether through formal recognition programs or casual team celebrations, reinforces a positive culture around transformation. When employees feel that their hard work is valued, they are more likely to remain engaged and committed to the overall vision of change.

Ultimately, preventing change fatigue requires a balanced approach that prioritizes employee well-being alongside organizational progress. By implementing change at a sustainable pace, providing strong communication and support, and fostering a culture of appreciation, organizations can ensure that their transformation efforts remain effective and well-received. A workforce that feels supported and empowered is far more likely to embrace change rather than resist it, leading to a smoother and more successful digital transformation journey.

Celebrating Progress and Creating a Culture of Continuous Change

Recognizing and celebrating small wins is crucial for maintaining motivation and momentum throughout the digital transformation process. These milestones serve as proof points that the organization is moving in the right direction, reinforcing the collective belief in the transformation's success. By acknowledging the teams and individuals who have successfully adopted new tools and processes, companies can create a culture that rewards adaptability and innovation. This reinforcement encourages further engagement, helping to sustain enthusiasm even when challenges arise.

One of the most effective ways to celebrate progress is through storytelling. Leaders can share success stories that highlight how digital transformation efforts have improved efficiency, streamlined workflows, or enhanced customer experiences. These stories can be presented in company-wide meetings, internal newsletters, or dedicated digital transformation forums. Employees who see their colleagues being recognized for their efforts may feel more inspired to embrace change themselves.

The technology company Salesforce has mastered this approach through their "Trailblazer" program, which celebrates employees who successfully adopt new technologies and processes. By sharing these success stories across the organization and recognizing individuals who exemplify successful change adoption, they've created a culture where transformation is viewed as an opportunity for recognition and career advancement rather than a burden.

Beyond verbal recognition, organizations can implement structured incentive programs that reward employees for their contributions to digital transformation. Incentives can range from financial bonuses and public recognition to additional training opportunities or career advancement prospects. Gamification, such as digital badges or leaderboards that track progress in adopting new systems, can also be an effective tool for fostering a sense of achievement. The goal is to make change a rewarding and engaging experience rather than something imposed upon employees.

However, celebrating early wins is only one piece of the puzzle. Organizations must recognize that digital transformation is not a finite project but an ongoing journey. Successfully managing change requires a shift in mindset—from viewing transformation as a one-time event to embracing it as a continuous process of improvement. As new technologies emerge and business landscapes evolve, companies must remain agile, ready to adapt their strategies and workflows to stay competitive.

The rapid advancement of AI technologies exemplifies this need for continuous adaptation. Organizations that successfully implemented basic automation systems five years ago now find themselves needing to integrate more sophisticated AI capabilities. Those that view this as a continuation of their transformation journey rather than a new disruption are better positioned to succeed.

To cultivate this culture of continuous change, leaders must take a proactive approach in addressing resistance. Change is often met with skepticism or fear, particularly when employees feel uncertain about how new processes will impact their roles. Transparent and consistent communication is essential to alleviating these concerns. Leaders should clearly articulate the vision behind digital transformation, explaining why it is necessary and how it benefits both the organization and its employees.

Engagement at all levels is another critical factor. Employees should feel like active participants in the transformation rather than passive recipients of top-down decisions. Organizations can encourage involvement by soliciting feedback, hosting interactive workshops, and creating cross-functional transformation teams. When employees have a voice in shaping the process, they are more likely to take ownership of change rather than resist it.

Training and support should not end after the initial rollout of new systems. Organizations must invest in ongoing learning and development to ensure that employees continue to build their digital capabilities. Providing access to on-demand training resources, mentorship programs, and peer learning networks can help employees adapt to new technologies at their own pace. Additionally, organizations should regularly assess skill gaps and offer targeted training to address evolving needs.

The global bank JPMorgan Chase demonstrates this commitment to continuous learning through their massive investment in employee reskilling programs. Recognizing that AI and automation would fundamentally change many job roles, they created comprehensive training programs that help employees develop new skills while technology evolves. This proactive approach has helped maintain high employee engagement even as the nature of work continues to change.

Another key component of sustaining digital transformation is the willingness to evolve based on feedback.

Organizations should establish mechanisms for continuously gathering input from employees, customers, and stakeholders to refine their strategies. Regular check-ins, pulse surveys, and data-driven insights can help identify areas that require improvement. Rather than sticking rigidly to initial plans, companies should remain flexible, making iterative adjustments that optimize transformation efforts over time.

Addressing Digital Transformation Change Management Failures

While success stories provide valuable guidance, understanding common change management failures in digital transformation offers equally important insights. Many organizations underestimate the complexity of change management for digital initiatives, leading to resistance, poor adoption, and ultimately project failure.

Revlon's ERP implementation failure provides a sobering example of inadequate change management in digital transformation. In 2020, the company embarked on an ambitious project to consolidate systems from two separate business units into a single SAP S/4HANA platform. The initiative was intended to streamline operations and reduce costs, but it encountered significant resistance and implementation challenges.

Early in the implementation, Revlon leadership realized the project was likely to fail due to poor system design, inadequate process mapping, and insufficient change management. However, these technical issues were compounded by communication failures that left employees unprepared for the complexity and scope of the transformation.

The company failed to adequately communicate how employees' roles would change, what new skills they would need to develop, and how the organization would support them through the transition. Training programs were insufficient for the complexity of the new system, and feedback mechanisms were inadequate for identifying and addressing user concerns.

The change management failures amplified technical problems and made recovery much more difficult. Employees who were already struggling with system complexity became increasingly frustrated with lack of support and unclear communication about expectations and timelines. The combination of technical and change management problems ultimately contributed to the company's bankruptcy filing in 2022.

Revlon's experience demonstrates that change management failures can have catastrophic business consequences, particularly when they occur during mission-critical system implementations. The case illustrates the importance of investing adequately in change management capabilities and treating them as essential to project success rather than optional additions.

Nike's supply chain system failure in the early 2000s provides another example of change management deficiencies in digital transformation. The company implemented demand planning software from i2 Technologies intended to optimize inventory management, but the implementation encountered significant problems that led to $100 million in lost sales.

While technical issues contributed to the failure, change management problems amplified the impact. Employees were not adequately trained to use the new system effectively, and backup processes were not in place when the system failed to perform as expected. The lack of change management planning meant that employees were unprepared to adapt when the system behaved differently than anticipated.

The Nike failure illustrates how change management problems can turn technical issues into business disasters. Better change management might not have prevented the technical problems, but it could have reduced their impact and accelerated recovery by ensuring employees were better prepared to respond to unexpected situations.

Pacific Gas & Electric's data breach during an Oracle ERP implementation demonstrates how change management failures can create security risks. A third-party vendor hired to create a new asset management platform copied live PG&E data to its own network without implementing necessary security measures, exposing over 30,000 customer records for nearly 70 days.

The breach occurred partly because change management processes didn't adequately address security responsibilities and data handling procedures for external vendors. While technical security measures were important, the incident also reflected failures to communicate security requirements clearly and ensure that all project participants understood their responsibilities for protecting sensitive data.

The PG&E case shows how change management failures can have regulatory and legal consequences beyond operational impacts. The company faced significant fines and reputational damage that could have been avoided with more comprehensive change management processes that addressed security and compliance requirements.

Managing AI-Specific Change Management Challenges

Artificial intelligence implementations present unique change management challenges that go beyond traditional digital transformation initiatives. AI systems can make decisions, identify patterns, and recommend actions that humans might not understand or anticipate, requiring new approaches to training, oversight, and collaboration between humans and intelligent systems.

The failure rate for AI projects—over 80% according to RAND Corporation research—stems partly from organizations underestimating the change management complexity of these implementations. Unlike traditional software that automates existing processes in predictable ways, AI systems learn and adapt, potentially changing their behavior over time in ways that weren't anticipated during initial implementation.

IBM's Watson for Oncology project provides a compelling example of AI-specific change management challenges. Despite substantial investment and technical sophistication, the project was discontinued in 2023 after failing to gain widespread adoption in the medical community. The failure stemmed partly from inadequate change management that didn't address the unique requirements of AI implementation in healthcare settings.The Watson project encountered resistance from oncologists who found the system's recommendations inconsistent with their clinical experience and judgment. The AI system had been trained primarily on data from Memorial Sloan Kettering Cancer Center, leading to recommendations that often didn't align with local treatment protocols or available resources in other healthcare settings.More significantly, the change management approach failed to address the fundamental differences between AI-assisted decision-making and traditional clinical decision-making. Oncologists needed training not just on how to use the system, but on how to interpret AI recommendations, when to trust them, and how to maintain appropriate clinical oversight. The system's "black box" nature made it difficult for physicians to understand why specific recommendations were made, creating uncertainty about when to follow AI guidance versus relying on their own expertise.

The Watson case illustrates several critical AI-specific change management requirements. First, training must address not just system operation but also AI interpretation and oversight skills. Second, change management must account for the iterative nature of AI systems that may improve or change behavior over time. Third, organizations must address transparency and explainability concerns that are unique to AI implementations.

Amazon's abandoned AI recruiting system provides another example of AI-specific change management challenges. The system developed bias against female candidates because it was trained on historical hiring data that predominantly reflected male hires. While the technical bias was the immediate problem, the incident also revealed change management failures in how AI systems are monitored and governed.

The Amazon case demonstrates that AI change management must include ongoing monitoring and bias detection capabilities. Employees must be trained to recognize when AI systems are producing inappropriate results and have clear escalation procedures for addressing these issues. Change management processes must also address the ethical dimensions of AI decision-making, which don't exist in traditional software implementations.

Organizations implementing AI systems must develop change management approaches that address several unique factors:

Explainability and Trust: Employees must understand how AI systems make decisions and when to trust their recommendations. This requires training that goes beyond system operation to include AI interpretation skills and judgment about when human oversight is necessary.

Continuous Learning and Adaptation: AI systems change and improve over time, requiring ongoing training and adaptation rather than one-time change management efforts. Organizations must establish processes for updating training materials, communication strategies, and performance expectations as AI capabilities evolve.

Ethical and Bias Considerations: AI implementations raise ethical questions and potential bias issues that don't exist in traditional technology implementations. Change management must address these concerns proactively and establish clear governance procedures for handling ethical dilemmas.

Human-AI Collaboration: Employees must learn new ways of working that combine human judgment with AI capabilities. This requires developing new skills around interpreting AI outputs, maintaining appropriate oversight, and knowing when to override AI recommendations.

Regulatory and Compliance Requirements: AI implementations often involve evolving regulatory requirements that affect how systems can be used and monitored. Change management must ensure that employees understand these requirements and can adapt to regulatory changes over time.

Building Sustainable Change Management Capabilities

Successful change management for digital transformation requires building organizational capabilities that support continuous adaptation rather than just managing discrete change events. The pace of technological change means that organizations must develop the ability to manage ongoing transformation rather than returning to stable states after implementing new systems.

Organizations that excel at change management develop several key capabilities that enable them to navigate multiple transformations successfully. These capabilities include structured change processes that can be applied across different types of initiatives, change management expertise distributed throughout the organization rather than concentrated in specialized teams, and cultural attributes that support adaptation and continuous learning.

Developing these capabilities requires investment in both formal change management training and experiential learning opportunities. Organizations should establish change management centers of excellence that can provide guidance and support for transformation initiatives while also building internal expertise and best practices.

However, building sustainable change management capabilities also requires recognizing that different types of changes require different approaches. The change management strategies that work for traditional process improvements may be inadequate for AI implementations or other emerging technology deployments. Organizations must develop flexible change management frameworks that can be adapted to different technological and organizational contexts.

Leadership development is particularly important for building sustainable change management capabilities. Leaders at all levels must understand change management principles and be able to apply them in their specific contexts. This includes understanding how to communicate about complex technologies, how to address employee concerns about job security and skill requirements, and how to maintain momentum during extended transformation initiatives.

Organizations should also establish measurement and feedback systems that help them learn from each change initiative and continuously improve their change management capabilities. These systems should track both immediate outcomes (such as user adoption rates and productivity measures) and longer-term impacts (such as employee engagement and organizational adaptability).

Sustaining Change for Long-Term Success

For change initiatives to succeed in the long run, organizations must foster cultures that embrace continuous learning and adaptability rather than viewing change as a temporary disruption to normal operations. Change management is not a one-time process—it is an ongoing capability that enables businesses to remain responsive to technological advancements, market shifts, and evolving customer expectations.

Research shows that organizations with strong change management practices experience 264% greater revenue growth than those with below-average change effectiveness. This success stems from their ability to adapt quickly to new opportunities and challenges rather than being constrained by legacy processes and resistance to change.

Leadership plays a central role in sustaining change by actively modeling adaptability and demonstrating commitment to innovation and continuous improvement. When leaders show willingness to learn new skills, admit when approaches aren't working, and adapt strategies based on feedback, employees are more likely to embrace similar behaviors.

Organizations that prioritize employee engagement, provide opportunities for professional growth, and encourage experimentation and learning from failure create environments where change is seen as an opportunity rather than a threat. This requires establishing reward systems that recognize adaptation and learning rather than just adherence to existing procedures.

However, sustaining change also requires balancing stability with adaptation. Organizations cannot be in constant flux without experiencing change fatigue and decreased performance. Effective change management includes identifying which elements of the organization should remain stable to provide foundation and continuity while other elements adapt to new requirements and opportunities.

The most successful organizations develop change management capabilities that enable them to pursue multiple transformation initiatives simultaneously without overwhelming employees or compromising operational effectiveness. This requires sophisticated planning and coordination to ensure that changes complement rather than conflict with each other.

Organizations must also recognize that change management extends beyond internal operations to include customers, suppliers, and other external stakeholders who may be affected by digital transformation initiatives. Comprehensive change management strategies address these external relationships and help manage the broader ecosystem impacts of organizational transformation.

Ultimately, change management is about guiding people through transformation with clarity, empathy, and support while building organizational capabilities that enable continuous adaptation and innovation. Organizations that invest in comprehensive change management strategies will be better equipped to navigate digital transformation, minimize resistance, and unlock long-term value from their initiatives.

Whether implementing new enterprise systems, transitioning to remote work, adopting artificial intelligence-driven processes, or pursuing other digital transformation initiatives, companies that focus on the human element of change will be the ones that thrive in an increasingly digital world. The organizations that master change management will not just survive digital transformation—they will use it to create competitive advantages and drive sustainable growth in rapidly evolving markets.

The future belongs to organizations that can manage change as effectively as they manage technology, treating change management as a core organizational capability rather than an optional addition to technology projects. These organizations will be the ones that successfully navigate the ongoing digital transformation wave and emerge stronger, more adaptable, and better positioned for future success.

Chapter 12

User Adoption and Engagement in Digital Transformation

Implementing new systems within an organization is a complex process that extends far beyond the mere deployment of technology. While businesses often focus on the technical aspects of implementation—system configuration, data migration, and integration testing—the real challenge lies in ensuring that employees embrace and effectively use these new systems. User adoption and engagement are critical to the success of digital transformation initiatives, yet they remain among the most underestimated and poorly managed aspects of organizational change.

Without proper engagement, even the most advanced technologies can become underutilized, leading to inefficiencies, frustration, and potential project failure. Research consistently shows that only 33% of companies are very satisfied or satisfied with their ERP systems, while 40% to 50% of sales employees don't use their CRM systems effectively. These statistics reveal a fundamental disconnect between technology implementation and user adoption that undermines the business value of digital transformation investments.

The challenge becomes even more complex when considering that 65% of organizations struggle with inadequate project planning and resource allocation, while 39% experience challenges with insufficient user training and support during rollouts. These statistics paint a picture of organizations that invest heavily in technology while underinvesting in the human factors that determine whether these technologies will actually be used effectively.

Maximizing user adoption requires a strategic approach that involves comprehensive planning, clear communication, extensive training, and continuous support throughout the transformation process. Employees must feel that change is not being imposed on them but rather represents an opportunity to improve their work processes and career prospects. When organizations prioritize engagement, they foster cultures where employees become active participants in the transformation process rather than passive recipients of new technology.

Understanding the User Adoption Challenge

The user adoption challenge has evolved significantly as digital technologies have become more sophisticated and pervasive. Traditional software implementations required users to learn new interfaces and workflows, but modern digital transformation often involves artificial intelligence, automation, and other technologies that fundamentally change how work gets done.

AI implementations present particularly complex adoption challenges because these systems can make decisions, identify patterns, and recommend actions that users might not understand or anticipate. Unlike traditional software where users control all system actions, AI systems can exhibit behaviors that surprise or concern users, creating resistance and reluctance to rely on these tools.

The high failure rate of AI projects—over 80% according to RAND Corporation research—stems partly from organizations underestimating the user adoption challenges of these implementations. Technical teams may successfully deploy AI systems that perform well in testing environments, but these systems fail to deliver business value because users don't trust them, don't understand how to use them effectively, or actively avoid using them.

Amazon's abandoned AI recruiting system illustrates how user adoption challenges can derail AI projects. While the system's bias against female candidates was the immediate technical problem, the incident also revealed deeper issues with user acceptance and oversight. Recruiters who used the system didn't have adequate training to recognize bias in AI recommendations, and there were no clear procedures for escalating concerns about system behavior.

The Amazon case demonstrates that AI adoption requires not just training on system operation, but also education about AI limitations, bias detection, and appropriate human oversight. Users must understand when to trust AI recommendations, how to identify potential problems, and how to maintain appropriate control over AI-assisted processes.

IBM's Watson for Oncology project provides another example of user adoption challenges in AI implementation. Despite substantial investment and technical sophistication, the system failed to gain widespread adoption in the medical community. Oncologists found the system's recommendations inconsistent with their clinical experience and were uncomfortable relying on AI guidance they couldn't fully understand or explain to patients.The Watson case illustrates that user adoption for AI systems requires addressing professional and ethical concerns that don't exist in traditional software implementations. Healthcare professionals needed to understand not just how to operate the system, but how to integrate AI recommendations with their clinical judgment, how to explain AI-driven decisions to patients, and how to maintain professional responsibility for treatment decisions.

These examples highlight that user adoption for modern digital transformation involves more than learning new procedures—it requires developing new ways of thinking about work, decision-making, and the relationship between human judgment and technological capabilities.

Addressing the Human Side of Digital Transformation

Digital transformation affects people in profound ways that extend beyond learning new software interfaces. Employees may experience anxiety about job security, concerns about their ability to master new skills, uncertainty about changing role requirements, and resistance to abandoning familiar processes and tools.

Research shows that 39% of employee resistance to digital transformation stems from fear of job displacement, while additional resistance comes from concerns about skill adequacy and uncertainty about future career paths. These concerns are particularly acute for AI implementations, where employees may worry that intelligent systems will replace their roles entirely.

Addressing these human factors requires comprehensive change management approaches that acknowledge employee concerns, provide realistic information about how roles will evolve, and offer concrete support for skill development and career transition. Organizations cannot simply announce that new technologies will make work more interesting and expect employees to embrace change enthusiastically.

The retail industry provides instructive examples of both successful and unsuccessful approaches to managing the human side of digital transformation. Some major retailers have successfully implemented AI-powered inventory management and customer service systems by involving employees in system design, providing extensive training on human-AI collaboration, and clearly communicating how these technologies enhance rather than replace human capabilities.

However, other retailers have encountered significant resistance when implementing similar technologies because they failed to address employee concerns about job security and didn't provide adequate training on working with AI systems. These implementations often result in poor system utilization, workarounds that undermine system effectiveness, and ongoing conflicts between technology and human processes.

The key difference between successful and unsuccessful approaches is the extent to which organizations invest in understanding and addressing the human impact of technological change. Successful implementations treat user adoption as a strategic priority that requires the same level of planning and investment as technical implementation.

Techniques to Maximize User Adoption of New Systems

Understanding the "Why" Behind the Change

Before rolling out any new technology, leaders must clearly articulate the reasons for change in terms that resonate with employees' daily experiences and career aspirations. Employees are more likely to embrace new systems when they understand how these tools will alleviate existing frustrations, enhance their productivity, or create new opportunities for professional growth.

Simply stating that a system will improve efficiency is insufficient; employees need to see tangible examples of how it will make their daily tasks easier and more effective. This communication becomes more complex for AI implementations, where the benefits may not be immediately apparent and where employees may have concerns about the implications of AI-assisted decision-making.

Organizations should communicate the business case for change through multiple channels and formats, including company-wide meetings, departmental discussions, internal newsletters, and one-on-one conversations between managers and their direct reports. Leadership must highlight how new systems align with broader organizational goals while also demonstrating clear benefits for individual employees.

For AI implementations, this communication must address common misconceptions about artificial intelligence while providing realistic information about system capabilities and limitations. Employees need to understand that AI systems are tools that enhance human capabilities rather than replacements for human judgment and expertise.

The communication strategy must also acknowledge that change involves both opportunities and challenges. Employees appreciate honesty about potential difficulties and are more likely to support change initiatives when leaders demonstrate understanding of their concerns and provide concrete plans for addressing them.

Engaging Employees in the Selection Process

A common reason employees resist new technology is that they feel it has been imposed on them without their input or consideration of their actual needs. To maximize adoption, organizations should involve employees in the decision-making process through surveys, focus groups, pilot testing phases, and other mechanisms that allow them to influence technology selection and implementation approaches.

This involvement creates a sense of ownership and investment in new systems, making employees more likely to support adoption rather than resist it. When employees feel they have played a role in shaping change, they develop more positive attitudes toward transformation and are more willing to help others adapt to new systems.

However, employee involvement must be meaningful rather than symbolic. Organizations should be prepared to adjust their technology selections and implementation approaches based on employee feedback, even when this requires additional time or resources. Employees can quickly identify when consultation processes are designed to create buy-in for predetermined decisions rather than genuinely seeking input.

For AI implementations, employee involvement is particularly important because these systems may affect work in ways that aren't immediately apparent to technology selection teams. Employees who will use AI tools daily often have insights about potential applications, limitations, and concerns that technical evaluation teams might miss.

Employee involvement should also extend to ongoing system refinement and improvement. Users often identify opportunities for enhancement or discover new applications for technologies after they begin using them in their daily work. Organizations that create mechanisms for capturing and acting on this feedback are more likely to achieve high levels of user satisfaction and system utilization.

Ensuring User-Friendly Design and Compatibility

No matter how powerful a new system is, it will struggle with adoption if employees find it cumbersome to use or if it conflicts with their existing workflows and tools. Businesses should prioritize selecting user-friendly technologies that require minimal effort to learn and integrate seamlessly with other frequently used applications.

User experience testing should be part of the selection process, with real employees evaluating system usability under realistic conditions. If possible, businesses should choose customizable solutions that allow for role-specific configurations so that employees only interact with features relevant to their responsibilities.

For AI implementations, user-friendly design involves more than intuitive interfaces—it also requires systems that provide appropriate levels of transparency and explainability. Users need to understand why AI systems make specific recommendations and have confidence that they can identify when systems are performing inappropriately.

Eliminating unnecessary complexity increases the likelihood of smooth transitions and minimizes frustration during the learning process. However, simplification must be balanced against functionality—systems that are too simplified may not provide the capabilities users need to accomplish their work effectively.

Organizations should also consider how new systems will integrate with existing tools and workflows. Systems that require users to abandon familiar processes entirely are more likely to encounter resistance than those that enhance existing workflows while maintaining some continuity with established practices.

Providing Comprehensive and Tailored Training

Lack of adequate training is one of the most common reasons employees struggle to adopt new technology effectively. Training programs should not be one-size-fits-all but rather customized to meet the varying needs of different user groups, accounting for different skill levels, learning preferences, and job requirements.

Some employees may prefer instructor-led training that allows for immediate questions and clarification, while others might benefit more from self-paced online modules that they can complete at their convenience. Many employees learn best through hands-on workshops that allow them to practice with real data and scenarios relevant to their actual work.

Organizations should develop training programs that include real-world use cases relevant to employees' daily tasks rather than generic system demonstrations. Instead of showing employees how systems work in theory, training should demonstrate exactly how new technologies will affect their specific workflows and responsibilities.

For AI implementations, training must go beyond system operation to include AI interpretation skills, bias recognition, and appropriate human oversight procedures. Employees need to understand how to evaluate AI recommendations, when to trust system outputs, and how to maintain appropriate control over AI-assisted processes.

Training should also be ongoing rather than a one-time event. As employees become more comfortable with basic system operation, they often want to learn advanced features and capabilities. As systems are updated with new functionality, users need additional training to take advantage of these enhancements.

Organizations should establish multiple training resources, including formal training sessions, online documentation, peer support networks, and expert help desk services. Different employees will prefer different support mechanisms, and providing multiple options increases the likelihood that everyone can get the help they need when they need it.

Establishing Internal Champions

Internal champions—employees who are early adopters and advocates of new systems—play crucial roles in driving user adoption throughout the organization. These champions should be selected from different departments and receive advanced training that enables them to provide peer support, answer questions, and encourage adoption among their colleagues.

Employees are often more comfortable seeking help from peers than from IT support staff or external consultants. Internal champions who understand both the technology and the specific challenges their colleagues face can provide more relevant and accessible assistance than formal support channels.

Organizations can create ambassador programs where champions receive additional training, recognition, and sometimes compensation for their role in supporting change initiatives. These programs should provide champions with the resources and authority necessary to help their colleagues effectively while also recognizing their contributions to organizational success.

For AI implementations, internal champions play particularly important roles because they can help colleagues understand how to interpret AI outputs, recognize potential problems, and develop confidence in working with intelligent systems. Champions who have successfully integrated AI tools into their workflows can provide practical guidance that formal training programs might not cover.

However, champion programs must be carefully managed to ensure that champions don't become overwhelmed with support requests or develop negative attitudes toward the technologies they're supposed to promote. Organizations should provide champions with adequate resources and support while also establishing clear boundaries around their responsibilities.

Offering Incentives and Recognizing Achievements

Incentivizing adoption can accelerate transitions and encourage employees to engage actively with new systems rather than avoiding them or using workarounds that undermine system effectiveness. Recognition programs that reward employees for successfully using technology can boost morale and reinforce the importance of change initiatives.

Incentives can take various forms, including monetary bonuses, additional paid time off, professional development opportunities, or public recognition in company meetings and communications. The key is choosing incentives that resonate with different employee groups and align with organizational values and culture.

Gamification techniques, such as leaderboards, challenges, and progress tracking, can make learning new systems more engaging while creating positive peer pressure for adoption. Encouraging friendly competition and rewarding employees for mastering new tools helps reinforce positive perceptions of change while building momentum for broader adoption.

However, incentive programs must be designed carefully to avoid creating perverse incentives or undermining intrinsic motivation. Programs that reward quantity of system usage without regard to quality or appropriateness may encourage employees to use systems ineffectively just to earn rewards.

For AI implementations, incentive programs should reward not just system usage but also appropriate oversight, bias detection, and continuous learning about AI capabilities and limitations. Recognition programs should highlight employees who demonstrate excellent judgment in human-AI collaboration rather than simply those who use AI tools most frequently.

Organizations should also establish incentives for employees who contribute to system improvement through feedback, suggestion, and problem identification. Users who help identify issues or suggest enhancements should be recognized for their contributions to organizational learning and improvement.

Maintaining Ongoing Support and Open Communication

Adoption does not end once systems are implemented and initial training is completed. Continuous support mechanisms are necessary to address ongoing challenges, answer questions that arise during actual usage, and ensure employees remain confident in using new technologies as their skills and responsibilities evolve.

Organizations should establish multiple support channels, including help desks, knowledge bases, online forums, and on-demand support through chatbots or dedicated IT personnel. Different employees will prefer different support mechanisms, and providing multiple options ensures that everyone can get assistance in ways that work for them.

Fostering an open feedback culture is equally important for maintaining high levels of user engagement and system effectiveness. Employees should feel comfortable sharing concerns, asking questions, and suggesting improvements without fear of criticism or negative consequences. Regular check-ins, surveys, town halls, and informal feedback sessions allow leadership to gauge user sentiment, address roadblocks, and make necessary adjustments to systems and processes.

The feedback culture becomes particularly important for AI implementations, where system behavior may change over time as models learn and adapt. Users may notice changes in AI performance or discover new applications for AI tools that weren't anticipated during initial implementation. Organizations need mechanisms for capturing and acting on this feedback to ensure systems continue to meet user needs effectively.

Communication about system performance, updates, and improvements should be ongoing rather than limited to initial implementation periods. Users want to know how systems are performing, what enhancements are planned, and how their feedback is being incorporated into system development and refinement efforts.

Organizations should also establish clear escalation procedures for addressing user concerns and system problems. When employees encounter issues they cannot resolve through normal support channels, they need to know how to escalate these problems and can expect timely resolution and communication about solutions.

Learning from User Adoption Failures

Understanding why user adoption initiatives fail provides valuable insights for improving implementation approaches and avoiding common pitfalls. Many adoption failures stem from predictable causes that can be prevented through better planning and execution.

Hershey's ERP implementation disaster in 1999 provides a compelling example of user adoption failure with catastrophic business consequences. The company attempted to implement comprehensive ERP, advanced planning, and warehouse management systems simultaneously during their peak shipping season leading up to Halloween.

The implementation encountered significant technical problems, but these were amplified by user adoption failures. Employees were not adequately trained on the new systems, backup procedures were insufficient when systems failed, and support resources were overwhelmed by the volume of user problems and questions.

The combination of technical issues and adoption failures led to massive operational disruptions. Orders were delayed, shipments were incorrect, and customer service deteriorated dramatically. The company lost approximately $100 million in sales during the critical Halloween season, and it took months to fully resolve the operational issues.

Hershey's failure illustrates how user adoption problems can transform technical issues into business disasters. Better user preparation, more comprehensive training, and stronger support systems might not have prevented the technical problems, but they could have reduced their impact and accelerated recovery.

Mission Produce's ERP implementation provides another example of user adoption challenges in digital transformation. In 2022, the company implemented a new ERP system across its entire operation simultaneously, despite extensive planning and preparation. The implementation encountered significant problems that forced the company to revert to manual processes to maintain customer service.

The company's CEO later admitted that "the extent and magnitude was greater than we anticipated," highlighting the gap between planning expectations and implementation reality. While technical complexity was a significant factor, user adoption challenges amplified the impact of technical problems.

Employees struggled to use the new system effectively under operational pressure, leading to errors, delays, and workarounds that undermined system effectiveness. The lack of adequate user preparation for handling complex scenarios meant that technical problems quickly cascaded into operational failures.

Mission Produce's experience demonstrates the importance of realistic user preparation that accounts for the stress and complexity of real operational environments. Training that works well in controlled settings may be inadequate when users must apply new skills under pressure while maintaining service quality and operational effectiveness.

Pacific Gas & Electric's data breach during an Oracle ERP implementation illustrates how user adoption failures can create security risks and regulatory violations. A third-party vendor hired to support the implementation copied live customer data to its own network without implementing necessary security measures, exposing over 30,000 customer records for nearly 70 days.

The breach occurred partly because user adoption processes didn't adequately address security responsibilities and data handling procedures. While technical security measures were important, the incident also reflected failures to ensure that all users understood their security obligations and had the knowledge and tools necessary to handle sensitive data appropriately.

The PG&E case shows how user adoption failures can have legal and regulatory consequences beyond operational impacts. The company faced significant fines and reputational damage that could have been avoided through more comprehensive user education and oversight processes.

These failures highlight common themes in user adoption challenges: inadequate preparation for real-world complexity, insufficient training for handling unexpected situations, poor communication about user responsibilities and expectations, and lack of adequate support during critical operational periods.

Engaging Employees Throughout the Transformation Process

Maximizing user adoption requires keeping employees engaged throughout the entire transformation process rather than just during initial training and implementation phases.

Organizations that maintain strong engagement strategies see higher success rates in their digital initiatives and better long-term outcomes from technology investments.

Transparent and consistent communication is the foundation of successful engagement, but this communication must evolve as transformation initiatives progress. Employees need different types of information at different stages of implementation—strategic context during planning phases, practical guidance during training periods, performance feedback during initial usage, and ongoing updates about system improvements and organizational impacts.

During planning phases, employees need to understand the business rationale for change, how new technologies will affect their work, what support they will receive during transition periods, and what success will look like both for the organization and for them personally. This communication must be honest about challenges and realistic about timelines while maintaining confidence in the overall direction and approach.

During implementation phases, communication should focus on practical guidance for using new systems effectively, addressing common problems and questions, and providing regular updates about progress and any changes to timelines or expectations. Employees also need clear channels for providing feedback and raising concerns during this critical period.

After initial implementation, communication should emphasize performance results, system improvements, and ongoing learning opportunities. Employees want to know whether systems are delivering expected benefits, how their feedback is being used to improve systems and processes, and what new capabilities or applications are being developed.

Engaging employees in planning and implementation builds trust and fosters commitment to transformation initiatives. Instead of presenting change as a top-down directive, organizations should create opportunities for employees to contribute ideas, voice concerns, and influence implementation approaches. When employees feel like partners in transformation rather than subjects of change, they are more likely to approach new technologies with positive attitudes and genuine commitment to success.

This engagement must be meaningful rather than token consultation. Organizations should be prepared to adjust their approaches based on employee input, even when this requires additional time or resources. Employees can quickly identify when participation opportunities are designed to create buy-in for predetermined decisions rather than genuinely seeking input and influence.

For AI implementations, employee engagement becomes even more critical because these systems may affect work in ways that aren't immediately apparent to technology planning teams. Employees who will work with AI tools daily often have insights about potential applications, limitations, and concerns that technical teams might miss during system selection and configuration.

Providing continuous learning opportunities beyond initial training reinforces confidence and skill development while demonstrating organizational commitment to employee success. Organizations should encourage employees to deepen their expertise through advanced training, certification programs, mentorship opportunities, and participation in technology user communities.

A learning-oriented culture ensures that employees view digital transformation as an opportunity for professional growth rather than an imposed challenge or threat to job security. This culture must be supported by concrete investments in education and development as well as recognition and reward systems that value continuous learning and adaptation.

Fostering a supportive workplace culture makes transitions smoother and more successful. Employees should feel that they have access to leadership support, IT assistance, and peer help whenever they encounter difficulties or have questions. Open forums, discussion groups, mentorship networks, and informal support systems create environments where employees can share experiences and help each other navigate change.

Support systems become particularly important for AI implementations, where employees may encounter unexpected system behaviors or ethical dilemmas that aren't covered in formal training programs. Peer support networks allow employees to share experiences, develop best practices, and collectively learn how to work effectively with intelligent systems.Recognizing and celebrating milestones keeps momentum alive throughout extended transformation initiatives. Whether it's reaching significant adoption rates, successfully completing training modules, achieving productivity improvements, or discovering new applications for technology, every achievement should be acknowledged and celebrated.

Celebrating progress creates sense of accomplishment and reinforces the long-term value of transformation initiatives. It also provides opportunities to share success stories, highlight effective practices, and build enthusiasm for continued learning and improvement.However, recognition programs must be carefully designed to highlight genuine achievements rather than simply participation. Employees respond better to recognition that acknowledges real contributions to organizational success rather than participation awards that don't reflect meaningful accomplishment.

XYZ Corporation Case Study: Comprehensive User Adoption Strategy

XYZ Corporation, a multinational manufacturing company with over 20,000 employees across different regions, provides an instructive example of comprehensive user adoption strategy in digital transformation. In 2019, the company embarked on a digital transformation initiative to modernize operations, improve productivity, and enhance customer engagement through ERP implementation, supply chain automation, and AI integration for predictive maintenance.

Initial Challenges and Assessment

Early assessments revealed significant challenges that could undermine user adoption efforts. Many employees were accustomed to legacy systems and processes, creating natural resistance to change. A significant portion of the workforce had limited experience with digital tools, which could hinder their ability to adapt to new systems effectively.

Initial training programs were generic and didn't cater to the specific needs of different user groups, leading to low engagement and adoption rates during pilot testing. Communication about transformation benefits was inadequate, creating skepticism and reluctance to embrace new technologies.

The complexity of new systems, particularly AI-powered predictive maintenance tools, discouraged adoption among employees who were comfortable with existing manual processes and concerned about their ability to master sophisticated new technologies.

Comprehensive Strategy Implementation

To address these challenges, XYZ Corporation implemented a multi-faceted approach that addressed both technical and human factors in digital transformation:

Structured Change Management: The company introduced a comprehensive change management program that included strong leadership involvement, extensive stakeholder engagement, and clear communication about transformation benefits and requirements. Leadership demonstrated commitment by participating in training programs, using new systems themselves, and consistently communicating about the importance of transformation success.

Personalized Training Programs: XYZ Corporation developed customized training modules based on specific user roles and responsibilities, ensuring that employees received relevant and practical hands-on training. Training programs included multiple formats—instructor-led sessions, online modules, hands-on workshops, and peer mentoring—to accommodate different learning preferences and schedules.

Digital Ambassadors Program: The company appointed a group of digitally-savvy employees as 'Digital Ambassadors' to mentor their colleagues and provide on-the-ground support during transition periods. Ambassadors received advanced training and were given time and resources to help their colleagues adapt to new systems and processes.

Gamification and Incentives: XYZ integrated gamification elements, such as rewards and recognition programs, to encourage employees to engage with new systems actively rather than avoiding them. The program included individual achievements, team challenges, and organization-wide competitions that made learning new technologies more engaging and rewarding.

User-Centric Design Approach: The IT team worked closely with employees and customers to refine user interfaces and enhance system usability based on real-world feedback and usage patterns. This iterative approach ensured that systems met actual user needs rather than just technical specifications.

Continuous Feedback and Improvement: The company established comprehensive feedback mechanisms where employees and customers could provide input on system performance and usability, leading to ongoing improvements and refinements. Feedback was actively solicited, genuinely considered, and used to make concrete improvements to systems and processes.

Results and Business Impact

After implementing these strategies, XYZ Corporation observed significant improvements in user adoption and business outcomes:

Employee adoption of the ERP system rose from 45% in the first three months to 85% within a year, demonstrating the effectiveness of comprehensive user engagement strategies. The automation of supply chain processes reduced manual errors by 30% and increased overall efficiency by 20%, showing that higher adoption rates led to better business results.

Employees reported a 40% improvement in their confidence in using digital tools, as measured through internal surveys and performance evaluations. This increased confidence led to more effective system utilization and willingness to explore advanced features and capabilities.

Customer satisfaction scores increased by 25% due to improved service delivery enabled by AI-driven predictive maintenance and more efficient operational processes. The organization successfully cultivated a culture of continuous learning and innovation, which made future digital initiatives easier to implement and more likely to succeed.

Critical Success Factors and Lessons Learned

The XYZ Corporation case provides several important insights about effective user adoption strategies:

Stakeholder Involvement is Crucial: Engaging employees and customers early in the transformation process helps build trust, reduce resistance, and identify potential issues before they become major problems.

This involvement must be meaningful and influential rather than token consultation.

Customization Matters: Tailored training programs and user-friendly systems that address specific user needs and preferences play significant roles in driving adoption and ensuring effective system utilization. One-size-fits-all approaches are inadequate for complex digital transformations.

Continuous Support is Key: Ongoing mentorship, feedback mechanisms, and responsive support services ensure sustained engagement throughout transformation initiatives rather than just during initial implementation periods.

Communication and Transparency: Clear messaging about transformation benefits, realistic expectations about challenges, and honest communication about progress and setbacks foster positive attitudes and sustained commitment to change initiatives.

Cultural Transformation: Digital transformation requires cultural changes that support continuous learning, adaptation, and innovation rather than just technical system implementations.

The XYZ Corporation case demonstrates that successful user adoption requires comprehensive strategies that address technical, human, and organizational factors simultaneously. Organizations that invest adequately in user adoption see better business results from their technology investments and build capabilities that support future transformation initiatives.

Building Sustainable User Engagement

User adoption and engagement are not just checkboxes in digital transformation initiatives—they are the key drivers of long-term success and sustainable business value. Organizations that invest in comprehensive user engagement strategies create competitive advantages that extend far beyond individual technology implementations.

Research consistently shows that organizations with high user engagement achieve significantly better business outcomes from their technology investments. These organizations see higher productivity improvements, better return on investment, and greater agility in responding to market changes and competitive pressures.

However, building sustainable user engagement requires more than successful initial implementations. Organizations must create cultures and capabilities that support continuous adaptation as technologies evolve, business requirements change, and new opportunities emerge.

Developing Organizational User Engagement Capabilities

The most successful organizations develop systematic approaches to user engagement that can be applied across multiple transformation initiatives rather than treating each implementation as a unique challenge. These organizations build internal expertise in user psychology, change management, training design, and continuous improvement that enables them to achieve consistently high adoption rates.

Developing these capabilities requires investment in both formal training and experiential learning opportunities. Organizations should establish user engagement centers of excellence that can provide guidance and support for transformation initiatives while also building internal best practices and institutional knowledge.

These centers of excellence should include expertise in multiple disciplines: behavioral psychology to understand how people respond to technological change, instructional design to create effective training programs, communication strategy to develop compelling change narratives, and data analytics to measure and improve engagement outcomes.

However, user engagement capabilities must also be distributed throughout the organization rather than concentrated in specialized teams. Managers at all levels need to understand user engagement principles and be able to apply them in their specific contexts. This includes understanding how to communicate about complex technologies, how to address employee concerns about skill requirements and job security, and how to maintain motivation during extended transformation initiatives.

Creating Sustainable Engagement Through Continuous Value Delivery

Sustainable user engagement requires demonstrating continuous value rather than just initial benefits. Users who see ongoing improvements in their work experience, new capabilities that enhance their effectiveness, and recognition for their contributions to organizational success are more likely to remain engaged and supportive of future transformation initiatives.

This continuous value delivery requires organizations to view digital transformation as an ongoing process rather than a series of discrete projects. Systems should be designed for continuous improvement, with regular updates, feature enhancements, and capability expansions that keep users interested and engaged.

For AI implementations, continuous value delivery is particularly important because these systems can improve significantly over time through additional training data and algorithm refinements. Organizations that help users understand and benefit from these improvements build stronger engagement and trust in AI-assisted processes.

User engagement also requires recognition that different employees find value in different aspects of digital transformation. Some employees may be motivated by productivity improvements, others by opportunities to learn new skills, and still others by the ability to focus on more strategic work rather than routine tasks. Engagement strategies must address these diverse value propositions.

Organizations should establish regular communication about the business and individual benefits being achieved through digital transformation initiatives. This communication should include specific examples of how systems are improving work processes, enhancing customer service, or creating new opportunities for professional growth and development.

Managing the Evolution of User Needs and Expectations

User engagement strategies must evolve as employees become more sophisticated in their use of digital technologies and as their expectations change based on their experiences. Early adopters may be satisfied with basic functionality and obvious productivity improvements, but experienced users expect more advanced capabilities and greater integration between systems.

This evolution requires organizations to continuously assess user needs and expectations rather than assuming that initial engagement strategies will remain effective indefinitely. Regular surveys, focus groups, and usage analytics can help organizations understand how user requirements are changing and what new capabilities or support services are needed.

For AI implementations, managing evolving user needs is particularly challenging because these systems can develop new capabilities over time that users may not be aware of or know how to utilize effectively. Organizations need ongoing education and communication strategies that help users understand new possibilities and applications for AI tools.

The evolution of user needs also requires flexibility in system design and implementation approaches. Systems that are too rigid or difficult to modify may become obstacles to user engagement as requirements change and new opportunities emerge.

Organizations should design their technology architectures and governance processes to support continuous adaptation based on user feedback and changing business requirements. This includes establishing clear procedures for evaluating and implementing user suggestions, upgrading system capabilities, and modifying workflows based on operational experience.

Building User Communities and Peer Support Networks

Some of the most effective user engagement strategies leverage peer-to-peer learning and support rather than relying exclusively on formal training and support programs. Users often learn more effectively from colleagues who have similar responsibilities and challenges than from generic training materials or external consultants.

Organizations should actively foster user communities that bring together employees with similar roles, interests, or challenges to share experiences, solve problems collaboratively, and develop best practices for using digital tools effectively. These communities can be formal user groups with regular meetings and structured activities, or informal networks that connect through digital platforms and social channels.

For AI implementations, user communities play particularly important roles because they allow employees to share experiences with unexpected system behaviors, discuss ethical considerations, and collectively develop approaches for maintaining appropriate human oversight of AI-assisted processes.

User communities also serve as valuable feedback mechanisms for identifying system improvements, training needs, and emerging applications that weren't anticipated during initial implementation planning. Organizations that actively listen to and act on community feedback demonstrate commitment to user success while also improving their systems and processes.

However, user communities require careful cultivation and support to remain active and valuable. Organizations should provide resources, recognition, and leadership support for community activities while also ensuring that communities don't become venues for complaints and negativity that undermine transformation efforts.

Measuring and Improving User Engagement

Sustainable user engagement requires continuous measurement and improvement rather than one-time assessments during initial implementation periods. Organizations should establish comprehensive metrics that track both behavioral indicators (such as system usage and feature adoption) and attitudinal measures (such as user satisfaction and confidence levels).

These metrics should be tracked over time to identify trends, detect emerging problems, and evaluate the effectiveness of engagement strategies and interventions. Regular measurement also allows organizations to benchmark their performance against industry standards and identify opportunities for improvement.

However, measurement systems must be designed carefully to avoid creating perverse incentives or undermining intrinsic motivation. Metrics that focus exclusively on system usage without regard to quality or appropriateness may encourage employees to use systems ineffectively just to meet performance targets.

For AI implementations, measurement becomes more complex because traditional usage metrics may not capture whether employees are using AI tools appropriately or effectively. Organizations need metrics that assess the quality of human-AI collaboration, the appropriateness of AI oversight, and the business outcomes achieved through AI-assisted processes.

The most effective measurement approaches combine quantitative data with qualitative feedback to provide comprehensive understanding of user engagement and system effectiveness. Regular surveys, focus groups, and individual interviews can provide insights that usage analytics alone cannot capture.

Organizations should also establish clear processes for acting on measurement results rather than simply collecting data. Measurement systems are only valuable if they lead to concrete improvements in user experience, system functionality, and business outcomes.

Preparing for Future Technology Adoption

Organizations that excel at user engagement for current technologies are better positioned to successfully adopt future technologies as they emerge. The capabilities, processes, and cultural attributes that support effective user engagement are transferable across different types of technological change.

However, preparing for future adoption also requires anticipating how technological evolution might change user engagement requirements. Emerging technologies like advanced AI, quantum computing, and brain-computer interfaces may require fundamentally different approaches to training, support, and human-technology collaboration.

Organizations should invest in developing adaptive user engagement capabilities that can evolve as technologies and user requirements change. This includes building internal expertise in emerging technologies, establishing flexible training and support infrastructures, and cultivating cultures that embrace continuous learning and adaptation.

The most successful organizations also maintain awareness of technological trends and begin preparing for future adoptions before new technologies become critical to business success. This preparation includes assessing potential impacts on user engagement, developing preliminary training materials, and building relationships with technology vendors and research institutions.

Creating Competitive Advantage Through User Engagement Excellence

Organizations that consistently achieve high user engagement create sustainable competitive advantages that extend beyond individual technology implementations. These organizations are more agile in responding to market changes, more effective at leveraging new technologies, and more attractive to talented employees who want to work with cutting-edge tools and systems.

User engagement excellence also creates positive feedback loops that make future transformation initiatives more likely to succeed. Employees who have positive experiences with digital transformation become advocates for future changes rather than sources of resistance, and organizations build institutional knowledge and capabilities that improve with each implementation.

However, achieving user engagement excellence requires sustained investment and commitment from leadership at all levels. It cannot be treated as a secondary consideration or delegated entirely to training and support teams. User engagement must be recognized as a strategic capability that requires the same level of attention and investment as technical implementation.

The organizations that master user engagement will be those that recognize it as an ongoing competitive differentiator rather than a temporary implementation requirement. They will build cultures where technological adaptation is viewed as an opportunity for growth and innovation rather than a disruptive threat to established ways of working.

In an increasingly digital world where technological change is accelerating, the ability to engage users effectively in transformation initiatives will become even more critical to organizational success. The companies that develop superior user engagement capabilities today will be the ones that thrive in the digital economy of tomorrow, continuously adapting to new technologies while maintaining high levels of employee satisfaction and business performance.

Ultimately, user adoption and engagement represent the bridge between technological possibility and business value. Organizations that invest in building this bridge effectively will not only achieve better outcomes from their current transformation initiatives but will also position themselves for sustained success in an era of continuous technological evolution and change.

Chapter 13

Data Migration and Integration: Learning from the World's Costliest Failures

Data migration and integration represent the most technically complex and risk-laden aspects of digital transformation initiatives. As organizations transition from legacy systems to modern platforms, the process of transferring data efficiently while ensuring different systems work harmoniously becomes not just a necessity, but a make-or-break determinant of project success. When executed correctly, these processes preserve data integrity, minimize operational disruptions, and optimize business functions. However, as demonstrated by some of the world's most spectacular digital transformation failures, inadequate planning and execution can result in lost or corrupted data, system downtime, and inefficiencies that not only undermine the transformation effort but can cost organizations billions of dollars and, in some cases, human lives.

The sobering reality is that data migration failures have plagued organizations across every sector and geography. From the UK's National Health Service losing over £10 billion on a failed digitization attempt to Queensland Health's payroll disaster that left thousands of healthcare workers unpaid, the consequences of poor data migration extend far beyond IT departments into the heart of organizational operations. These failures share common characteristics: underestimation of data complexity, inadequate stakeholder engagement, rushed timelines, and a fundamental misunderstanding of the interdependencies between legacy and target systems.

Consider the case of NHS England's National Programme for IT, launched in 2002 with the ambitious goal of creating the world's largest civilian electronic health record system. Despite contracts worth £6.2 billion awarded to industry giants including Accenture, Fujitsu, and CSC, the program was dismantled in 2011 after achieving virtually none of its objectives. The core failure centered on data migration challenges that were never adequately addressed. The NHS had accumulated decades of patient data across thousands of systems, each with unique data structures, coding schemes, and business rules. The migration strategy failed to account for the sheer complexity of harmonizing this data landscape, resulting in a system that could neither accept existing data nor provide the integrated patient records that were the program's primary objective.

The Queensland Health payroll system implementation presents another cautionary tale of data migration gone catastrophically wrong. What began as a straightforward replacement of an aging payroll system evolved into a $1.25 billion disaster that left over 35,000 healthcare workers either unpaid, underpaid, or overpaid. The root cause traced back to fundamental data migration failures. Queensland Health's existing payroll data contained over 24,000 different combinations of wage payments and withholdings across multiple industrial agreements and contractor types. The migration team failed to adequately map these complex data relationships to the new system, resulting in payroll calculations that bore no resemblance to actual employment conditions. The system went live without proper data validation, immediately generating thousands of payroll anomalies that took years to resolve.

Best Practices for Data Migration: Lessons from Failure

The path to successful data migration begins with acknowledging that most organizations dramatically underestimate the complexity of their existing data landscape. A comprehensive assessment of existing data must go far beyond simple data profiling to include deep analysis of data lineage, business rules, exception handling, and the informal processes that have evolved around data inconsistencies. Organizations must evaluate their current data environment by identifying not just the obvious sources, but the shadow systems, spreadsheet-based processes, and manual workarounds that have developed over time.

The NHS failure illustrates the critical importance of this comprehensive assessment. The program's initial data assessment identified the major clinical systems but failed to account for the thousands of departmental databases, specialty applications, and local innovations that had been developed to fill gaps in the official systems. When migration began, these systems contained critical patient data that could not be accommodated by the new platform, leading to data loss and system fragmentation that ultimately doomed the project.

Not all data merits migration to new systems. Organizations must make difficult decisions about data cleansing, transformation, and archival. However, these decisions cannot be made in isolation by technical teams. The

Queensland Health disaster demonstrates the consequences of inadequate business involvement in data migration decisions. Critical payroll calculation rules were embedded in legacy data structures, but the migration team lacked sufficient domain expertise to recognize and preserve these relationships. Business stakeholders must be deeply involved in evaluating which data sets are essential and defining the business rules that govern data transformation.

Once a clear understanding of the existing data environment is established, organizations must define specific objectives for data migration that extend beyond simple system replacement. The migration process should be viewed as an opportunity to enhance data quality, improve business intelligence capabilities, and establish governance frameworks that will serve the organization for years to come. Organizations must determine which data sets are essential and outline expected outcomes, including enhanced reporting capabilities, better compliance with industry regulations, and improved decision-making support.

The US Air Force's Expeditionary Combat Support System provides a masterclass in how not to approach data migration objectives. The Air Force attempted to consolidate 240 legacy systems into a single Enterprise Resource Planning platform without establishing clear data migration success criteria. After spending over $1 billion across seven years, the program was terminated without achieving any significant military capability. The fundamental issue was that the Air Force never clearly defined what success looked like from a data perspective. Legacy systems contained decades of logistics data with complex interdependencies that were never fully understood or documented. Without clear objectives for how this data should be transformed and integrated, the migration effort became an expensive exercise in system replacement rather than organizational transformation.

A detailed migration plan must be developed to guide the transition, incorporating lessons learned from high-profile failures. This plan should outline each phase of the migration, including realistic timelines, adequate resource allocation, comprehensive risk assessment, and robust contingency measures. The absence of structured roadmaps has been a common factor in major migration failures. Organizations cannot afford to treat data migration as a technical afterthought to system implementation.

The Extract, Transform, Load process remains the foundation of effective data migration, but its implementation must be far more sophisticated than many organizations realize. The ETL methodology begins with extracting data from existing sources, but this extraction must account for the full complexity of legacy systems, including embedded business logic, data validation rules, and exception handling procedures. The transformation phase requires deep understanding of both source and target systems, along with comprehensive business rule mapping that preserves the intent of original data while adapting it to new system requirements.

Modern digital transformation initiatives must also account for artificial intelligence and machine learning capabilities in their data migration strategies. AI-powered data migration tools can help identify patterns in legacy data, suggest transformation rules, and detect anomalies that might indicate data quality issues. However, organizations must be cautious about over-relying on AI without proper human oversight and domain expertise. The most sophisticated AI tools cannot replace the deep business knowledge required to understand data relationships and business rules.

Risk mitigation through pilot testing has proven essential in preventing large-scale migration disasters. By testing the migration process with representative data subsets, organizations can identify and resolve potential issues before they affect entire systems. Pilot testing must go beyond technical validation to include business process testing and user acceptance validation. The Queensland Health disaster might have been prevented if adequate pilot testing had revealed the payroll calculation errors before system go-live.

Data validation and quality assurance must be embedded throughout the migration process, not treated as final checkpoints. Even after loading data into new systems, rigorous validation procedures must verify accuracy, completeness, and consistency. Organizations must implement both automated validation tools and manual audit procedures to detect discrepancies and address them before they escalate into operational crises. The scale of modern data migration efforts requires sophisticated validation approaches that can handle millions of records while maintaining precision in error detection.

Ensuring Seamless Integration with Existing Systems

Data migration represents only one component of the broader integration challenge. Ensuring that new systems integrate seamlessly with existing business applications requires strategic thinking that extends beyond technical connectivity to encompass business process alignment, user experience optimization, and long-term maintainability. The failures of major digital transformation initiatives demonstrate that poor integration can undermine even technically successful migrations.

The integration challenge has been compounded by the rise of artificial intelligence and machine learning capabilities within enterprise systems. Modern ERP platforms increasingly incorporate AI-powered features for predictive analytics, automated decision-making, and intelligent process optimization. However, these AI capabilities are only as effective as the data and integrations that support them. Organizations implementing AI-enhanced systems must ensure that their integration strategies can support the data flows and real-time processing requirements that AI features demand.

Consider how AI is transforming supply chain management within integrated ERP environments. Modern systems can predict demand fluctuations, optimize inventory levels, and automatically adjust procurement schedules based on market conditions and historical patterns. However, these capabilities require seamless integration between ERP systems, external data sources, and real-time analytics platforms. Organizations that fail to plan for these integration requirements may find themselves with AI features that cannot access the data needed to function effectively.

The first step in seamless integration involves focusing on delivering direct value to end-users rather than implementing features for their own sake. Integration should be designed to support ongoing business processes without overcomplicating workflows or creating additional burden for users. This principle becomes particularly important when integrating AI capabilities, as users may be skeptical of automated decision-making systems that they don't understand or trust.

Continuous improvement must be built into integration efforts from the beginning. The digital landscape evolves rapidly, and integration processes must be adaptable to future changes. Organizations must foster a culture of ongoing assessment and refinement to ensure that their systems remain efficient and aligned with business needs. This includes staying current with AI and machine learning developments that may offer new opportunities for process optimization.

Cross-functional collaboration proves crucial in integration efforts, particularly when implementing AI-enhanced systems that may impact multiple business functions simultaneously. IT teams, business leaders, and end-users must work together to ensure that integration meets the needs of all stakeholders while taking advantage of AI capabilities where appropriate. Empowering cross-functional teams to make decisions fosters innovation and streamlines the integration process.

Integration efforts must align with overall business objectives rather than being treated as purely technical initiatives. Organizations should consider how integration impacts broader business goals, including customer experience, operational efficiency, and competitive advantage. The integration of AI capabilities should be evaluated based on their potential to support strategic initiatives rather than their technical sophistication.

Planning for future changes requires particular attention in the age of AI. As artificial intelligence capabilities continue to evolve rapidly, integration solutions must be flexible enough to accommodate new technologies and operational shifts. Designing adaptable integration frameworks ensures that organizations can take advantage of emerging AI capabilities without requiring complete system overhauls.

Automation plays an increasingly crucial role in reducing integration complexity and improving efficiency. Automating data transfers, system updates, and workflow synchronization minimizes the risk of human error while ensuring that data remains accurate and up-to-date. However, organizations must balance automation with appropriate human oversight, particularly when AI systems are making decisions that affect business operations.

AI-powered integration monitoring represents an emerging best practice that can help organizations maintain system performance and detect issues before they impact operations. Machine learning algorithms can analyze integration patterns, predict potential failures, and recommend optimization strategies. These capabilities become particularly valuable in complex integration environments where traditional monitoring approaches may miss subtle performance degradations.

Quality assurance must be embedded throughout the integration process, with particular attention to AI system validation. Regular testing and validation ensure that integrated systems function as intended and that data flows seamlessly between applications. Organizations must implement monitoring tools that can detect integration issues in real-time while also validating that AI-powered features are producing accurate and reliable results.

Middleware solutions continue to facilitate smoother integration by acting as bridges between different systems, but modern middleware increasingly incorporates AI capabilities for intelligent routing, data transformation, and error handling. These AI-enhanced middleware platforms can adapt to changing data patterns, optimize performance based on usage patterns, and provide predictive insights about integration health.

Standardization of data formats and communication protocols becomes even more critical when integrating AI-enhanced systems that may have specific requirements for data structure and quality. Establishing common standards simplifies data exchange while ensuring that AI systems can access the high-quality data they need to function effectively.

The integration of AI capabilities also requires attention to ethical considerations and regulatory compliance. Organizations must ensure that their integrated systems can provide transparency into AI decision-making processes, maintain audit trails for compliance purposes, and protect sensitive data throughout the integration environment.

Training and support strategies must evolve to address the complexity of AI-enhanced integrated systems. Employees need training not only on how to use new systems but also on how to work effectively with AI-powered features, understand system recommendations, and override automated decisions when appropriate. Comprehensive training programs should address both technical skills and the critical thinking needed to work effectively with AI systems.

By learning from the failures of major digital transformation initiatives and incorporating modern AI capabilities thoughtfully, organizations can navigate the complexities of data migration and integration with minimal disruption. The key lies in comprehensive planning, realistic timeline development, adequate resource allocation, and a deep understanding of both current and future system requirements.

Chapter 14

Testing and Quality Assurance in Digital Transformation: When Good Systems Go Bad

In the high-stakes arena of digital transformation, the implementation of new systems represents far more than a technical upgrade—it constitutes a fundamental reimagining of how organizations operate, compete, and serve their stakeholders. The complexity of these endeavors demands rigorous testing and quality assurance processes that go far beyond traditional software validation to encompass organizational readiness, change management effectiveness, and long-term sustainability. Yet as demonstrated by some of the most spectacular system failures in history, even well-funded projects backed by industry leaders can collapse when testing and quality assurance are treated as afterthoughts rather than integral components of the transformation journey.

The sobering reality facing executives is that digital transformation failures have become so commonplace that they represent a distinct category of organizational risk. From healthcare systems that endanger patient safety to financial platforms that lose billions in transactions, the consequences of inadequate testing extend far beyond project budgets into the realm of organizational survival. These failures share disturbing commonalities: rushed implementation timelines, insufficient user testing, inadequate performance validation, and a fundamental disconnect between system capabilities and real-world operational requirements.

The National Health Service's £10 billion National Programme for IT stands as perhaps the most expensive testament to the consequences of inadequate testing in digital transformation. Despite involving some of the world's most sophisticated technology companies and consuming nearly a decade of development effort, the program was ultimately dismantled without delivering a single significant capability. The core failure centered on the absence of comprehensive testing strategies that could validate not just technical functionality, but organizational readiness and user acceptance across one of the world's largest healthcare systems.

The NHS program's testing failures were multifaceted and systemic. Technical testing focused primarily on individual system components rather than end-to-end integration scenarios that reflected real clinical workflows. User acceptance testing was limited in scope and failed to account for the diversity of clinical practices across different healthcare settings. Performance testing never adequately simulated the transaction volumes and concurrent user loads that would be experienced in live deployment. Most critically, the program never implemented comprehensive change management testing that could validate whether healthcare workers would actually adopt and effectively use the new systems.

Queensland Health's payroll disaster provides another stark illustration of how testing failures can cascade into operational catastrophe. The system that was intended to simplify payroll processing for over 80,000 healthcare workers instead generated more than

35,000 payroll anomalies within months of deployment. The Queensland Health Payroll System Commission of Inquiry revealed that critical testing phases were abbreviated or bypassed entirely due to timeline pressures and budget constraints. During the final acceptance testing phases, over 2,000 system defects were identified, including 14 critical "showstopper" defects that should have prevented system deployment. However, project leadership made the decision to proceed with go-live despite these unresolved issues, prioritizing schedule adherence over system quality.

The inquiry's findings were particularly damning regarding the testing culture within the project. When defects were identified during testing, project managers frequently downgraded their severity ratings to circumvent quality gates and maintain project momentum. This manipulation of testing results created an artificial picture of system readiness that bore no resemblance to actual system quality. The lack of independent testing oversight meant that these practices continued unchecked until system deployment revealed their catastrophic consequences.

The Critical Role of Testing in Digital Transformation Success

Testing serves as the final validation checkpoint in digital transformation initiatives, but its role extends far beyond defect identification to encompass organizational readiness assessment, user experience validation, and performance verification under real-world conditions. In the context of digital transformations, where organizations are fundamentally reimagining their operational models, the stakes for effective testing have never been higher. The integration of artificial intelligence and machine learning capabilities into enterprise systems adds additional layers of complexity that traditional testing approaches struggle to address.

Modern enterprise systems increasingly incorporate AI-powered features for predictive analytics, automated decision-making, and intelligent process optimization. These capabilities offer tremendous potential for organizational efficiency and competitive advantage, but they also introduce new categories of testing requirements that many organizations are not prepared to address. AI systems must be tested not only for functional correctness but also for bias detection, decision transparency, and adaptability to changing conditions.

Consider the testing challenges presented by an AI-enhanced supply chain management system. Traditional testing would validate that the system can process purchase orders, update inventory levels, and generate reports. However, AI-powered features require testing of predictive algorithms, demand forecasting accuracy, and automated reordering decisions. Organizations must validate that AI recommendations are based on appropriate data, that decision-making logic is transparent and auditable, and that the system can adapt to changing market conditions without human intervention.

The failure to adequately test AI capabilities can have consequences that extend far beyond system performance issues. Biased algorithms can perpetuate discrimination in hiring, lending, or service delivery. Poorly trained machine learning models can make decisions based on correlations rather than causation, leading to inappropriate automated actions. AI systems that lack proper testing may be vulnerable to adversarial attacks or may fail catastrophically when confronted with data patterns they haven't been trained to handle.

Software assurance, which encompasses activities designed to ensure that software processes and products conform to requirements, standards, and procedures, becomes even more critical when AI capabilities are involved. This includes requirements analysis that accounts for AI behavior, design reviews that validate machine learning model architectures, code inspections that examine algorithm implementations, testing that validates AI decision-making, and formal verification of system behavior under various conditions.

The rise of AI in enterprise systems also necessitates new approaches to user acceptance testing. Users must not only validate that systems perform required functions but also that AI-powered features provide valuable insights, that automated decisions align with business objectives, and that human-AI collaboration enhances rather than hinders productivity. This requires testing scenarios that go beyond traditional use cases to explore how humans and AI systems work together in complex, real-world situations.

Strategies for Ensuring Quality and Performance in AI-Enhanced Systems

Ensuring the quality and performance of modern digital transformation initiatives requires a multi-faceted approach that addresses both traditional system validation and the emerging challenges of AI-enhanced platforms. Organizations must implement structured testing methodologies, adopt performance-focused engineering principles, leverage continuous testing techniques, and develop new approaches for validating AI capabilities. Each of these strategies contributes to minimizing risk, improving system reliability, and ensuring that new technologies drive business value rather than operational disruption.

Adopting a Structured Testing Framework for AI Systems

The DMAIC framework (Define, Measure, Analyze, Improve, Control) provides a systematic approach to process improvement that can be adapted for AI-enhanced system testing. However, traditional DMAIC implementation must be extended to address the unique characteristics of artificial intelligence and machine learning systems.

The Define phase for AI systems must identify not only functional testing objectives and key performance indicators but also AI-specific success criteria such as prediction accuracy, decision transparency, and bias detection. Organizations must define acceptable thresholds for AI performance while establishing metrics for measuring AI system behavior across different scenarios and data conditions.

The Measure phase requires sophisticated approaches to assess AI system performance against predefined criteria. This includes not only traditional performance metrics like response time and throughput but also AI-specific measurements such as model accuracy, false positive and false negative rates, and decision confidence levels. Organizations must establish baselines for AI behavior while implementing monitoring systems that can detect drift in AI performance over time.

The Analyze phase becomes particularly complex when dealing with AI systems, as it must investigate not only traditional system defects and performance bottlenecks but also AI-specific issues such as model bias, overfitting, and decision explainability. This requires expertise in both traditional software testing and machine learning validation techniques.

The Improve phase must address both traditional system optimization and AI-specific enhancements such as model retraining, algorithm tuning, and bias mitigation. Organizations must develop processes for continuous AI improvement that can adapt to changing data patterns and business requirements.

The Control phase ensures that AI systems continue to meet quality standards post-deployment through ongoing monitoring, performance validation, and model governance. This includes implementing AI model versioning, establishing retraining schedules, and maintaining audit trails for AI decision-making.

Implementing Continuous Testing for AI-Enhanced Platforms

Traditional testing methodologies that treat testing as a final phase before deployment are inadequate for AI-enhanced systems that must adapt and learn from new data continuously. Continuous testing for AI systems involves ongoing validation of not only system functionality but also AI model performance, decision quality, and adaptation to changing conditions.

AI systems require continuous monitoring of model performance to detect drift, bias, or degradation in decision quality. This monitoring must be integrated into the development and deployment pipeline to enable rapid response to AI system issues. Automated testing tools must be capable of validating AI behavior across different scenarios while detecting anomalies that might indicate model problems.

The integration of AI capabilities into continuous testing pipelines requires sophisticated approaches to test data management. AI systems need diverse, representative datasets for training and validation, but these datasets must be carefully managed to avoid bias introduction or data leakage. Organizations must implement data governance frameworks that ensure AI testing uses appropriate data while maintaining privacy and security requirements.

Continuous testing of AI systems also requires new approaches to test automation that can validate not only functional behavior but also AI decision quality. This includes automated bias testing, fairness validation, and explainability verification. These automated tests must be capable of running continuously to detect issues as AI systems learn and adapt.

Performance Engineering for AI-Enhanced Systems

Performance engineering for AI-enhanced systems extends beyond traditional concerns with response time and throughput to encompass AI-specific performance requirements such as inference speed, model accuracy, and resource utilization for machine learning workloads. Organizations must consider AI performance requirements from the system design phase to prevent issues that might arise from inadequate AI infrastructure or poorly optimized algorithms.

AI-enhanced systems often have unique performance characteristics that differ significantly from traditional enterprise applications. Machine learning inference may require significant computational resources, particularly for complex models or real-time decision-making scenarios. Organizations must implement performance testing that validates AI system behavior under various load conditions while ensuring that AI features don't degrade overall system performance.

Performance testing for AI systems must also account for the dynamic nature of machine learning models. As AI systems learn and adapt, their performance characteristics may change, requiring ongoing performance validation and optimization. This includes testing how AI performance scales with data volume, user concurrency, and model complexity.

The integration of AI capabilities also requires attention to performance testing of human-AI collaboration scenarios.

Organizations must validate that AI-enhanced interfaces provide responsive user experiences while ensuring that AI recommendations and automated actions don't create bottlenecks in human workflows.

Reliability Engineering for AI Systems

Reliability engineering for AI-enhanced systems must address both traditional system reliability concerns and AI-specific failure modes such as model degradation, bias introduction, and adversarial attacks. Organizations must implement comprehensive approaches to AI system reliability that can detect and mitigate these unique risks.

AI systems can fail in ways that traditional software systems cannot. Model performance may degrade gradually as data patterns change, making failures difficult to detect until they significantly impact business operations. Organizations must implement monitoring and alerting systems that can detect subtle changes in AI behavior before they become critical issues.

Reliability engineering for AI systems also requires attention to explainability and transparency. When AI systems make incorrect decisions, organizations must be able to understand why the failure occurred and implement corrective measures. This requires comprehensive logging of AI decision-making processes and the ability to trace decisions back to their underlying data and algorithms.

The integration of AI capabilities also introduces new categories of security risks that must be addressed through reliability engineering. AI systems may be vulnerable to adversarial attacks designed to manipulate their decision-making, or they may inadvertently learn patterns from training data that could be exploited by malicious actors.

Design for Six Sigma in AI-Enhanced Systems

Design for Six Sigma methodologies can be adapted for AI-enhanced systems to ensure that AI capabilities meet high-quality standards from the design phase. However, traditional DFSS approaches must be extended to address the unique characteristics of artificial intelligence and machine learning systems.

DFSS for AI systems must emphasize prevention of AI-specific quality issues such as bias, overfitting, and poor generalization. This requires careful attention to training data quality, algorithm selection, and validation methodologies during the design phase. Organizations must implement design processes that can prevent AI quality issues before they occur rather than detecting them during testing.

The customer-focused approach of DFSS becomes particularly important for AI-enhanced systems, as AI capabilities are only valuable if they provide meaningful benefits to users. Organizations must implement design processes that ensure AI features align with user needs and business objectives while providing transparent and understandable decision-making.

The Critical Role of End-User Testing in AI Adoption

User acceptance testing for AI-enhanced systems extends far beyond traditional functional validation to encompass user trust, decision transparency, and human-AI collaboration effectiveness. Organizations must implement comprehensive UAT processes that validate not only system functionality but also user comfort with AI-powered features and their ability to work effectively with automated decision-making systems.

The integration of AI capabilities fundamentally changes the nature of user acceptance testing. Users must validate not only that systems perform required functions but also that AI recommendations are valuable, that automated decisions are appropriate, and that they can effectively override AI systems when necessary. This requires testing scenarios that explore the full range of human-AI interaction patterns.

User acceptance testing for AI systems must also address trust and transparency concerns. Users need to understand how AI systems make decisions, when they should rely on AI recommendations, and how to identify when AI systems may be providing inappropriate guidance. UAT processes must validate that AI systems provide adequate transparency while building user confidence in AI capabilities.

The failure to adequately involve users in AI system testing can result in systems that meet technical specifications but fail to deliver meaningful business value. Users who don't trust AI recommendations will ignore them, while users who over-rely on AI systems may make poor decisions when AI guidance is inappropriate.

Organizations must also implement ongoing user feedback processes that can detect changes in user satisfaction with AI capabilities. As AI systems learn and adapt, their behavior may change in ways that affect user experience. Continuous user feedback helps organizations identify when AI changes are improving or degrading user effectiveness.

Post-Implementation Monitoring and Quality Assurance for AI Systems

Even after successful deployment, AI-enhanced systems require ongoing monitoring and quality assurance that extends beyond traditional system maintenance. Organizations must implement comprehensive approaches to post-deployment AI governance that can detect model drift, bias introduction, and performance degradation while ensuring continued alignment with business objectives.

AI systems require continuous monitoring of decision quality, not just system performance. Organizations must implement processes that can detect when AI recommendations become less accurate, when bias is introduced into decision-making, or when AI systems begin behaving in unexpected ways. This monitoring must be integrated with business processes to enable rapid response to AI quality issues.

Post-implementation quality assurance for AI systems also requires attention to regulatory compliance and ethical considerations. As AI regulations continue to evolve, organizations must ensure that their AI systems remain compliant with changing requirements while maintaining ethical decision-making standards.

The dynamic nature of AI systems means that post-implementation quality assurance must be treated as an ongoing process rather than a periodic review. AI systems that perform well initially may degrade over time as data patterns change or as business requirements evolve. Organizations must implement governance frameworks that can adapt to these changes while maintaining system quality.

Through comprehensive testing strategies that address both traditional system validation and emerging AI-specific requirements, organizations can enhance the quality and performance of their digital transformation initiatives. The key lies in recognizing that AI-enhanced systems require fundamentally different approaches to testing and quality assurance while learning from the failures of organizations that underestimated these requirements.

Chapter 15

Post-Implementation Reviews: Transforming Failure into Strategic Advantage

Post-implementation reviews represent the most underutilized yet potentially transformative component of digital transformation initiatives. While organizations typically celebrate system go-live as project completion, the reality is that true success can only be measured months or years after implementation, when the full impact of technology changes becomes apparent through operational performance, user adoption, and business outcome achievement. The systematic analysis of what worked, what failed, and why provides organizations with invaluable intelligence that can transform future digital initiatives from expensive gambles into strategic investments with predictable returns.

The evidence from major digital transformation failures demonstrates that organizations consistently repeat the same mistakes across projects, sectors, and decades. The UK's National Health Service spent over £10 billion on failed digital initiatives spanning nearly two decades, yet continued to make the same fundamental errors in program management, stakeholder engagement, and technology selection. Queensland Health's payroll disaster followed patterns identical to previous ERP failures in other jurisdictions, suggesting that lessons learned were never captured or applied. The US Air Force's $1 billion Expeditionary Combat Support System failure repeated mistakes documented in numerous prior military IT projects, indicating that institutional learning was not occurring despite massive financial losses.

This pattern of repeated failure across organizations suggests a fundamental gap in organizational learning processes. Post-implementation reviews, when conducted effectively, can break this cycle by creating institutional knowledge that prevents future mistakes while amplifying successful practices. However, the majority of organizations either skip post-implementation reviews entirely or conduct superficial assessments that focus on blame assignment rather than systemic learning.

The integration of artificial intelligence into enterprise systems adds new dimensions to post-implementation review requirements. AI-enhanced systems behave differently than traditional software applications, learning and adapting over time in ways that may not be apparent during initial deployment. Organizations must develop new approaches to post-implementation assessment that can evaluate AI system performance, decision quality, and business impact over extended periods.

Consider the challenges of evaluating an AI-powered supply chain optimization system six months after implementation. Traditional post-implementation reviews would assess whether the system is functioning technically and whether users have adopted the new processes. However, AI system evaluation requires analysis of prediction accuracy, decision quality, adaptation to changing market conditions, and the business impact of automated recommendations. The system may be technically successful while providing poor business value, or it may be delivering significant benefits that are not immediately apparent through traditional metrics.

Conducting Effective Post-Implementation Reviews in the Age of AI

Effective post-implementation reviews in the modern digital landscape must address both traditional system assessment criteria and the emerging challenges of AI-enhanced platforms. Organizations must develop comprehensive evaluation frameworks that can assess technical performance, user adoption, business impact, and AI-specific success factors while creating actionable insights for future initiatives.

The scope of modern post-implementation reviews must extend beyond traditional project boundaries to encompass the full ecosystem of organizational change. This includes evaluation of change management effectiveness, training program impact, process reengineering success, and cultural transformation outcomes. AI-enhanced systems often require more significant organizational changes than traditional software implementations, making comprehensive scope definition even more critical.

The NHS National Programme for IT failure illustrates the consequences of inadequate post-implementation review scope. Early assessments focused primarily on technical system functionality rather than clinical workflow integration, user adoption patterns, or patient care impact. By the time comprehensive evaluations revealed fundamental design flaws and user resistance, the program had consumed billions of pounds and was too politically and financially committed to cancel despite obvious failure indicators.

Assembling diverse review teams becomes even more critical when evaluating AI-enhanced systems. Traditional review teams including IT professionals, business executives, project managers, and end-users must be supplemented with AI specialists, data scientists, and ethics experts who can evaluate AI-specific performance criteria. The complexity of modern digital transformation initiatives requires review teams with deep expertise across multiple domains.

Queensland Health's payroll disaster demonstrates the importance of independent review team composition. Internal reviews conducted by project stakeholders consistently reported progress and minimized issues, while independent external reviews revealed fundamental system flaws and project management failures. The Commission of Inquiry found that internal project reviews had been systematically biased toward positive reporting, preventing early identification and correction of critical issues.

Data collection for AI-enhanced system reviews requires sophisticated approaches that can capture both quantitative performance metrics and qualitative user experience indicators. Traditional system performance data must be supplemented with AI-specific metrics such as prediction accuracy, decision confidence levels, bias detection results, and adaptation effectiveness. Organizations must implement comprehensive data collection frameworks that can provide both real-time AI performance monitoring and historical trend analysis.

The dynamic nature of AI systems means that post-implementation data collection must be ongoing rather than point-in-time assessment. AI system performance may vary significantly over time as models learn and adapt, requiring longitudinal analysis to understand true system effectiveness. Organizations must implement data collection processes that can detect gradual changes in AI behavior while identifying sudden performance shifts that might indicate system problems.

Stakeholder interviews for AI-enhanced systems must explore not only traditional user satisfaction and adoption metrics but also user trust in AI recommendations, understanding of AI decision-making processes, and effectiveness of human-AI collaboration. Users may be satisfied with system functionality while lacking confidence in AI capabilities, or they may be over-relying on AI recommendations without understanding their limitations.

The US Air Force ECSS failure reveals the importance of honest stakeholder feedback in post-implementation reviews. Military culture and hierarchical reporting structures created environments where negative feedback was suppressed or minimized, preventing accurate assessment of system problems. Post-implementation reviews must create safe environments for honest feedback while ensuring that political or organizational pressures don't bias assessment results.

Analysis of post-implementation findings must account for the unique characteristics of AI systems, including their ability to learn and improve over time. Traditional analysis approaches that focus on fixed system capabilities may miss the dynamic aspects of AI performance that could indicate future success or failure. Organizations must develop analytical frameworks that can evaluate AI system trajectory rather than just current performance.

The development of actionable recommendations from post-implementation reviews requires deep understanding of both traditional system optimization techniques and AI-specific improvement strategies. Recommendations might include AI model retraining, algorithm optimization, bias mitigation measures, or human-AI interaction improvements. The complexity of these recommendations requires review teams with sufficient expertise to provide meaningful guidance.

Documentation and knowledge sharing from AI-enhanced system reviews must capture not only traditional lessons learned but also AI-specific insights about model performance, data requirements, and implementation challenges. This documentation must be accessible and actionable for future project teams while protecting sensitive information about AI capabilities and performance.

Learning from Implementation Failures to Drive Continuous Improvement

The analysis of major digital transformation failures reveals consistent patterns that organizations can use to improve future initiatives. Post-implementation reviews that focus on systemic learning rather than individual blame assignment create the foundation for organizational transformation that extends far beyond technology implementation. The most valuable insights often emerge from comprehensive analysis of failure patterns, stakeholder behavior, and organizational responses to implementation challenges.

The NHS National Programme for IT provides a masterclass in how not to learn from implementation failures. Despite consuming over £10 billion across nearly a decade, the program's post-implementation reviews focused primarily on political blame assignment and vendor accountability rather than systemic organizational learning. Subsequent NHS digital initiatives repeated many of the same fundamental errors, including unrealistic timeline expectations, inadequate stakeholder engagement, and insufficient attention to change management requirements. The pattern of repeated failure suggests that institutional learning processes were inadequate despite massive financial losses and public scrutiny.

In contrast, organizations that successfully learn from implementation failures develop comprehensive knowledge management systems that capture both explicit lessons and tacit organizational knowledge. These systems must be designed to survive personnel changes, organizational restructuring, and shifting strategic priorities. The most effective approaches combine formal documentation with mentoring programs, cross-project knowledge sharing, and systematic application of lessons learned to new initiatives.

The integration of artificial intelligence into post-implementation learning processes offers new opportunities for pattern recognition and insight generation. AI-powered analysis of project data can identify subtle correlations between implementation approaches and outcomes that might not be apparent through traditional analysis methods. Machine learning algorithms can analyze project documentation, stakeholder feedback, and performance metrics to identify success factors and failure predictors that inform future project planning.

Consider how AI can enhance learning from the Queensland Health payroll disaster. Traditional analysis identified obvious failure factors such as inadequate testing, poor project management, and unrealistic timelines. However, AI analysis of project communications, decision-making patterns, and stakeholder interactions might reveal more subtle indicators of project distress that could serve as early warning signals for future initiatives. Natural language processing of project documents could identify communication patterns that correlate with project success or failure, while predictive analytics could help organizations assess the likelihood of project success based on early implementation indicators.

Transforming Project Management Through Failure Analysis

The systematic analysis of digital transformation failures reveals fundamental flaws in traditional project management approaches that must be addressed through post-implementation learning. The most common failure patterns include scope creep, unrealistic timeline expectations, inadequate resource allocation, poor stakeholder communication, and insufficient risk management. However, the root causes of these symptoms often lie in deeper organizational dynamics that traditional project management methodologies fail to address.

The US Air Force ECSS failure exemplifies how organizational culture can undermine even well-intentioned project management efforts. The military's hierarchical structure and "can-do" attitude created an environment where project managers were reluctant to report problems or request assistance. Post-implementation analysis revealed that project status reporting was systematically biased toward positive outcomes, preventing senior leadership from making informed decisions about project continuation or cancellation. The Air Force spent over $1 billion on a system that never delivered meaningful capability because organizational culture prevented honest assessment of project viability.

Organizations that successfully learn from project management failures implement cultural changes that encourage honest reporting, reward early problem identification, and support data-driven decision-making. This requires fundamental shifts in performance measurement, incentive systems, and leadership behavior. Post-implementation reviews must evaluate not only project outcomes but also the organizational dynamics that influenced project execution.

AI-enhanced project management tools offer new opportunities for objective project assessment that can overcome traditional reporting biases. Machine learning algorithms can analyze project metrics, communication patterns, and resource utilization to provide independent assessments of project health. These tools can identify discrepancies between reported project status and actual project indicators, enabling early intervention before problems become critical.

Process Improvement Through Comprehensive Analysis

Digital transformation failures often expose fundamental inefficiencies in existing organizational processes that extend far beyond the scope of the original technology implementation. Post-implementation reviews provide opportunities to identify and address these broader process improvement opportunities while ensuring that future initiatives benefit from enhanced operational foundations.

The Queensland Health payroll failure revealed systematic problems with procurement processes, vendor management, change management, and governance structures that extended throughout the organization. Traditional post-implementation reviews might have focused only on payroll system issues, missing the broader organizational improvement opportunities. Comprehensive analysis identified process improvements that could prevent similar failures across all technology initiatives while enhancing overall organizational effectiveness.

Organizations must develop post-implementation review processes that can identify process improvement opportunities across multiple organizational domains. This requires review teams with broad expertise and analytical frameworks that can trace failure root causes to their organizational origins. The most valuable insights often emerge from understanding how organizational processes interact with technology implementations rather than treating technology as an isolated domain.

AI-powered process mining techniques can enhance post-implementation analysis by providing objective views of how processes actually functioned during implementation rather than how they were supposed to function. Process mining algorithms can analyze system logs, transaction records, and user behavior patterns to identify bottlenecks, inefficiencies, and deviations from planned processes. This analysis can reveal process improvement opportunities that might not be apparent through traditional interview-based assessments.

Building Institutional Knowledge Through Systematic Learning

The most successful organizations treat post-implementation reviews as components of broader knowledge management strategies that capture, organize, and apply learning across multiple initiatives. This requires systematic approaches to knowledge capture that can preserve insights across personnel changes, organizational restructuring, and strategic shifts.

Effective institutional knowledge systems must balance formal documentation with tacit knowledge preservation through mentoring, communities of practice, and cross-functional collaboration. The most valuable implementation knowledge often exists in the form of contextual understanding, relationship insights, and situational judgment that cannot be easily documented but must be transferred through human interaction.

The integration of AI into knowledge management systems offers new opportunities for intelligent knowledge discovery and application. Natural language processing can analyze post-implementation reports, project documentation, and stakeholder feedback to identify patterns and insights that inform future initiatives. Machine learning algorithms can recommend relevant lessons learned based on project characteristics, stakeholder profiles, and implementation approaches.

AI-powered knowledge systems can also provide proactive guidance during project execution by identifying similarities between current initiatives and previous projects. These systems can alert project managers to potential risks based on historical patterns while recommending proven solutions for common implementation challenges.

Stakeholder Engagement Enhancement

Post-implementation reviews consistently reveal that stakeholder engagement failures are among the most common causes of digital transformation disappointment. These failures manifest in various forms, including inadequate user training, poor communication strategies, resistance to change, and misaligned expectations. However, the root causes often trace to fundamental misunderstandings about stakeholder needs, motivations, and constraints.

The NHS programme failure illustrates how inadequate stakeholder engagement can doom even technically sophisticated initiatives. Healthcare workers were never adequately consulted about system requirements, workflow impacts, or implementation preferences. When systems were deployed, they failed to integrate with actual clinical practices, leading to widespread user resistance and system abandonment. Post-implementation analysis revealed that meaningful stakeholder engagement could have identified these issues early in the development process when they could have been addressed cost-effectively.

Organizations that learn effectively from stakeholder engagement failures implement fundamental changes in their approach to user involvement, communication strategies, and change management processes. This includes earlier stakeholder involvement, more comprehensive needs assessment, continuous feedback mechanisms, and adaptive implementation approaches that can respond to stakeholder concerns.

AI-enhanced stakeholder engagement tools can provide more sophisticated approaches to understanding and responding to stakeholder needs. Sentiment analysis of stakeholder communications can identify emerging concerns or resistance patterns before they become critical issues. Predictive analytics can help organizations anticipate stakeholder reactions to planned changes while recommending engagement strategies based on stakeholder characteristics and preferences.

Strategic Decision-Making Improvement

The aggregation of insights from multiple post-implementation reviews enables organizations to identify strategic patterns that inform digital transformation strategy, technology selection, and resource allocation decisions. Organizations that systematically analyze implementation outcomes across multiple initiatives can identify which approaches consistently deliver value and which consistently fail to meet expectations.

The pattern of repeated ERP failures across government organizations suggests fundamental problems with strategic decision-making processes that extend beyond individual project management issues. Organizations continue to select inappropriate technology solutions, underestimate implementation complexity, and fail to adequately prepare for organizational change despite extensive documentation of previous failures in similar contexts.

Post-implementation reviews must be designed to inform strategic decision-making rather than just project management improvement. This requires analytical frameworks that can identify strategic success factors, technology selection criteria, and organizational readiness indicators that correlate with implementation success.

AI-powered strategic analysis can enhance post-implementation learning by identifying complex relationships between strategic choices and implementation outcomes that might not be apparent through traditional analysis. Machine learning algorithms can analyze multiple dimensions of implementation data to identify success factors, risk indicators, and optimal implementation approaches for different organizational contexts.

Compliance and Risk Management Enhancement

Post-implementation reviews often reveal compliance gaps and risk management failures that extend beyond the immediate scope of technology implementations. Digital transformation initiatives frequently involve handling sensitive data, integrating with regulatory systems, and implementing controls that must meet various compliance requirements. Failures in these areas can have legal, financial, and reputational consequences that far exceed the original project investment.

The Queensland Health payroll disaster exposed fundamental weaknesses in procurement processes, contract management, and vendor oversight that violated multiple governance requirements. The Commission of Inquiry found that proper procurement processes were not followed, that vendor performance was not adequately monitored, and that governance structures were insufficient to provide effective project oversight.

Organizations must use post-implementation reviews to assess compliance effectiveness and identify risk management improvements that apply across all digital initiatives. This requires review processes that can evaluate legal compliance, regulatory adherence, security effectiveness, and governance adequacy while recommending systematic improvements.

AI-enhanced compliance monitoring can provide more sophisticated approaches to identifying and addressing compliance risks. Machine learning algorithms can analyze implementation patterns, process deviations, and outcome variations to identify potential compliance issues before they become critical. These systems can also recommend compliance improvement measures based on analysis of successful implementations in similar regulatory environments.

Customer Experience Optimization

Digital transformation initiatives inevitably impact customer-facing processes, whether through new service delivery channels, automated interaction systems, or enhanced data analytics capabilities. Post-implementation reviews must evaluate these customer impacts while identifying opportunities for experience improvement that extend beyond the original project scope.

The integration of AI into customer-facing systems creates additional complexity for post-implementation assessment. AI-powered chatbots, recommendation engines, and automated service systems behave differently than traditional software applications, requiring specialized evaluation approaches that can assess AI effectiveness from customer perspectives.

Organizations must develop post-implementation review processes that can evaluate customer experience impacts across multiple touchpoints and interaction channels. This requires comprehensive data collection that combines traditional customer satisfaction metrics with behavioral analysis, sentiment monitoring, and outcome measurement.

AI-powered customer experience analysis can provide deeper insights into how digital transformation initiatives impact customer relationships. Natural language processing of customer feedback can identify specific improvement opportunities while predictive analytics can anticipate customer behavior changes resulting from system implementations.

Technology Evolution and Future Readiness

The rapid evolution of artificial intelligence and other emerging technologies means that post-implementation reviews must assess not only current system performance but also future readiness and adaptation potential. Organizations must evaluate whether their digital transformation investments position them to take advantage of emerging technologies or whether they have created technical debt that will hinder future innovation.

The integration of AI capabilities into existing systems requires ongoing evaluation of model performance, data quality, and algorithm effectiveness. Post-implementation reviews must assess whether AI implementations are delivering expected business value while identifying opportunities for AI enhancement or optimization.

Organizations must develop post-implementation assessment processes that can evaluate technology evolution readiness across multiple dimensions, including technical architecture flexibility, data infrastructure adequacy, skill availability, and organizational change capacity. This assessment must inform strategic planning for future technology investments while ensuring that current implementations don't constrain future opportunities.

AI-powered technology evolution analysis can help organizations anticipate future technology trends and assess their readiness to adopt emerging capabilities. Machine learning algorithms can analyze technology adoption patterns, performance trends, and capability evolution to predict future requirements while recommending preparation strategies.

Transforming Post-Implementation Reviews into Strategic Advantage

Post-implementation reviews represent the most underutilized opportunity for organizational learning and strategic advantage development in digital transformation initiatives. Organizations that treat these reviews as bureaucratic requirements rather than strategic learning opportunities forfeit valuable insights that could transform future initiatives from expensive risks into predictable investments.

The evidence from major digital transformation failures demonstrates that organizations consistently repeat the same mistakes across projects, sectors, and time periods. This pattern suggests fundamental gaps in organizational learning processes that effective post-implementation reviews can address. By systematically analyzing implementation outcomes, organizations can develop institutional knowledge that prevents future failures while amplifying successful practices.

The integration of artificial intelligence into post-implementation review processes offers new opportunities for insight generation, pattern recognition, and strategic guidance that can enhance organizational learning capabilities. However, AI tools must be implemented thoughtfully to supplement rather than replace human judgment and contextual understanding.

Organizations that master post-implementation review processes gain sustainable competitive advantages through superior implementation capabilities, reduced project risks, and enhanced strategic decision-making. These advantages compound over time as organizational learning accumulates and institutional capabilities mature.

The future of digital transformation success lies not in perfect initial implementations but in organizational abilities to learn, adapt, and improve continuously. Post-implementation reviews provide the foundation for this continuous improvement while ensuring that each digital transformation initiative contributes to organizational capability development rather than just technology deployment.

Through comprehensive post-implementation review processes that address traditional assessment requirements and emerging AI-specific challenges, organizations can transform digital transformation from a series of isolated projects into a strategic capability that drives sustained competitive advantage. The key lies in treating post-implementation reviews as investments in organizational learning rather than project closure activities, while leveraging AI capabilities to enhance rather than replace human insight and judgment.

The organizations that will thrive in an increasingly digital future are those that learn most effectively from their implementation experiences, both successes and failures. Post-implementation reviews provide the mechanism for this learning while ensuring that digital transformation investments compound over time to create sustainable organizational advantages.

Part IV: THE PATH FORWARD

Chapter 16

Achieving Operational Excellence: The Role of Digital Transformation in Enhancing Efficiency

Operational excellence is the foundation of sustainable business success. It is not merely about improving efficiency but about creating a system of continuous improvement, agility, and innovation that allows an organization to maximize its resources, enhance customer satisfaction, and maintain a competitive edge. Businesses are increasingly leveraging technology to streamline operations, reduce costs, and improve performance. From automation and artificial intelligence to advanced analytics and cloud computing, digital transformation is redefining what it means to achieve operational excellence.

However, the path to operational excellence through digital transformation is fraught with challenges. The technology landscape is littered with expensive failures that serve as sobering reminders of what can go wrong when organizations fail to properly plan, execute, or manage their digital initiatives. Understanding these failures is just as important as celebrating the successes, as they provide invaluable lessons for executives navigating their own transformation journeys.

The Promise and Peril of Digital Tools in Operational Efficiency

The adoption of digital tools has become a game-changer for organizations striving for operational excellence. Digital transformation initiatives focus on improving processes, increasing accuracy, and reducing manual inefficiencies that slow down productivity. Yet for every success story, there are cautionary tales of organizations that invested heavily in digital solutions only to see their operations disrupted, costs balloon, and performance decline.

One of the primary ways businesses enhance operational efficiency is through Enterprise Resource Planning (ERP) systems. ERP solutions integrate various business functions—such as finance, supply chain management, human resources, and customer service—into a centralized system. This eliminates data silos, improves decision-making, and enhances collaboration across departments. Companies that successfully implement ERP systems can optimize resource allocation, track real-time performance metrics, and minimize operational redundancies.

However, ERP implementations are notoriously difficult to execute successfully. Consider the case of Lidl, the German retail giant that spent seven years and over $500 million attempting to implement SAP before ultimately abandoning the project in 2018. The failure was so significant that it forced the company to completely rethink its digital strategy and ultimately led to leadership changes at the highest levels. The project failed primarily due to a fundamental mismatch between Lidl's unique business processes and SAP's standardized approach, complicated by inadequate change management and unrealistic timelines.

Similarly, Nike's $400 million ERP implementation in the early 2000s resulted in approximately $100 million in lost sales and a 20% drop in stock price. The company's attempt to implement a comprehensive supply chain management system was rushed to market without adequate testing, leading to massive inventory shortages and fulfillment delays during critical selling periods. Nike's experience demonstrates how even well-resourced organizations with strong technology capabilities can stumble when they fail to properly align technology implementation with business processes and market timing.

The Double-Edged Sword of Automation and AI

Another transformative technology driving operational efficiency is automation and robotic process automation (RPA). By automating repetitive and manual tasks, businesses can free up employees to focus on higher-value activities. RPA can be applied to functions such as invoice processing, customer service inquiries, and supply chain logistics. The benefits extend beyond cost savings—automation reduces errors, improves speed, and enhances compliance by ensuring standardized processes.

Artificial intelligence and machine learning are also playing an integral role in operational excellence. AI-driven predictive analytics help businesses anticipate demand, optimize inventory, and improve forecasting accuracy. In manufacturing, AI-powered quality control systems can detect defects in products faster and more accurately than human inspectors. In customer service, AI chatbots and virtual assistants streamline interactions by providing real-time responses to inquiries, reducing the burden on human agents and improving response times.

However, the integration of AI into business operations is not without risk. The technology is still maturing, and many organizations rush to implement AI solutions without fully understanding their limitations or properly preparing their workforce for the change. As highlighted in industry research, many AI initiatives fail because organizations lack the data quality, governance structures, and cultural readiness necessary for successful implementation.

The key to successful AI integration lies in understanding that artificial intelligence is not a magic solution but a tool that requires careful implementation, proper data management, and ongoing refinement. Organizations must invest in data infrastructure, establish clear governance protocols, and ensure their workforce is equipped with the skills necessary to work alongside AI systems effectively.

Infrastructure Foundations: Cloud Computing and IoT

Cloud computing and Software-as-a-Service (SaaS) solutions are enabling organizations to achieve greater flexibility and scalability. Cloud-based platforms allow businesses to store, manage, and analyze vast amounts of data in real time, ensuring that critical insights are always accessible. The ability to access cloud-based applications from anywhere also improves remote work productivity, facilitates collaboration, and reduces IT infrastructure costs.

Additionally, the Internet of Things (IoT) is transforming operational efficiency across industries. IoT-enabled sensors collect and transmit data in real time, allowing businesses to monitor equipment performance, track shipments, and optimize maintenance schedules. For example, in the logistics sector, IoT sensors help track fleet movements, fuel efficiency, and cargo conditions, ensuring that deliveries are completed on time and with minimal waste.

Yet the promise of cloud and IoT technologies comes with significant implementation challenges. Organizations must navigate complex integration requirements, security concerns, and the need for new operational models. The failure to properly plan for these challenges can result in expensive missteps and operational disruptions.

Learning from High-Profile Failures

Many organizations have struggled with digital transformation initiatives that promised operational excellence but delivered operational chaos instead. The US Air Force's $5 billion Oracle ERP implementation stands as one of the most expensive digital transformation failures in government history. Despite massive investment and years of effort, the system failed to deliver basic functionality, leading to widespread operational disruptions and ultimately requiring a complete restart with a new systems integrator.

The failure stemmed from multiple factors including unrealistic scope and timelines, inadequate change management, and a fundamental misunderstanding of the complexity involved in modernizing decades-old legacy systems. The Air Force's experience demonstrates that even organizations with substantial resources and technical expertise can fail when they underestimate the organizational and cultural challenges inherent in large-scale digital transformation.

Similarly, the UK's National Health Service experienced one of the most expensive public sector IT failures in history with its National Programme for IT (NPfIT). Despite an initial budget of £6.2 billion and involvement from major systems integrators including Accenture, Fujitsu, and CSC, the project was ultimately abandoned in 2011 after nearly a decade of delays, cost overruns, and stakeholder resistance. The program's failure cost British taxpayers over £10 billion and delivered minimal tangible benefits.

The NHS failure was particularly instructive because it highlighted the dangers of top-down digital transformation initiatives that fail to engage end users and stakeholders effectively. Healthcare professionals, including doctors and nurses, expressed concerns early in the project that the system didn't meet their accessibility or usability requirements. However, these concerns were largely ignored, leading to widespread resistance and ultimately project failure.

Queensland Health in Australia provides another sobering example of digital transformation gone wrong. What began as a $6.19 million payroll system replacement project with IBM ultimately cost taxpayers $1.25 billion and led to over 35,000 payroll errors affecting healthcare workers. The system failure was so severe that many doctors and nurses were either incorrectly paid or not paid at all, leading to strikes, staff departures, and significant operational disruption.

The Queensland Health failure was particularly damaging because it affected critical healthcare services and employee livelihoods. The project suffered from inadequate requirements gathering, insufficient testing, and unrealistic timelines that compressed complex system integration work into impossibly short timeframes.

Success Stories and Best Practices

Despite these high-profile failures, many organizations have successfully leveraged digital transformation to achieve operational excellence. Amazon has revolutionized supply chain management through automation, AI-driven logistics, and robotics. Amazon's warehouses use robotic systems to pick, pack, and sort inventory, dramatically reducing fulfillment times. The company's AI-powered recommendation engine personalizes customer experiences, leading to increased sales and customer satisfaction. By integrating digital tools into every aspect of its operations, Amazon has set the benchmark for efficiency and scalability.

General Electric has embraced predictive maintenance through IoT and AI. GE's industrial IoT platform, Predix, enables businesses to monitor machinery performance in real time. By analyzing data from sensors installed on equipment, GE can predict potential failures before they occur, reducing downtime and maintenance costs. This has significantly improved operational reliability in industries such as aviation, healthcare, and manufacturing.

In the healthcare sector, Mayo Clinic has leveraged digital transformation to enhance patient care and operational efficiency. The hospital uses AI and data analytics to optimize scheduling, reducing patient wait times and improving resource allocation. Additionally, Mayo Clinic's telemedicine platform allows patients to consult with doctors remotely, increasing accessibility to healthcare services while reducing the strain on in-person facilities.

Walmart has benefited significantly from digital transformation through its advanced inventory management system that uses AI and machine learning to forecast demand, adjust stock levels, and optimize supply chain logistics. By analyzing customer purchasing patterns, Walmart can ensure that popular products remain in stock while minimizing overstock of slow-moving items. This data-driven approach reduces waste, improves profitability, and enhances the shopping experience for customers.

The Critical Role of Artificial Intelligence in Modern Operations

The integration of artificial intelligence into operational systems represents perhaps the most significant opportunity for achieving operational excellence in the digital age. AI technologies are transforming how organizations process information, make decisions, and interact with customers. Machine learning algorithms can analyze vast datasets to identify patterns, predict outcomes, and recommend actions that would be impossible for human analysts to discover independently.

In manufacturing environments, AI-powered predictive maintenance systems analyze equipment sensor data to predict failures before they occur, reducing unplanned downtime and maintenance costs. Quality control systems use computer vision and machine learning to identify defects with greater accuracy and speed than human inspectors. Supply chain optimization uses AI to balance inventory levels, predict demand fluctuations, and optimize logistics routing in real time.

Customer service operations are being revolutionized by AI-powered chatbots and virtual assistants that can handle routine inquiries, escalate complex issues to human agents, and learn from each interaction to improve future responses. These systems not only reduce operational costs but also improve customer satisfaction by providing 24/7 availability and consistent service quality.

However, successful AI implementation requires more than just deploying advanced algorithms. Organizations must invest in data infrastructure, establish governance frameworks, and develop workforce capabilities to effectively leverage AI technologies. Many AI initiatives fail because organizations underestimate the importance of data quality, change management, and the cultural shifts required to work effectively with intelligent systems.

Building a Roadmap to Sustained Operational Excellence

While digital tools provide the foundation for operational improvements, achieving sustained excellence requires a strategic approach that goes beyond technology implementation. Organizations must first define clear objectives for their digital transformation initiatives, ensuring that technological investments align with business goals. Implementing new technology without a well-defined purpose can lead to wasted resources and inefficiencies. Employee engagement is another critical factor in achieving operational excellence. Training and upskilling programs should be implemented to ensure that employees are proficient in using new digital tools. Resistance to change can hinder adoption, so businesses must foster a culture of continuous learning and innovation. This is particularly important when implementing AI systems, as employees need to understand how to work effectively alongside intelligent technologies.

Data-driven decision-making should be at the core of operational strategies. Businesses must invest in advanced analytics to measure performance, identify areas for improvement, and optimize processes in real time. Organizations that leverage data effectively can make informed decisions that enhance efficiency, reduce costs, and improve customer experiences.

The lessons from both successful implementations and spectacular failures make clear that technology alone is insufficient to sustain operational excellence. Businesses must integrate digital tools into their broader strategic vision, invest in workforce training, and embrace data-driven decision-making. Change management, stakeholder engagement, and realistic timeline planning are equally critical to success.

Managing Risk and Expectations

One of the most important lessons from digital transformation failures is the need for realistic expectations and robust risk management. Many organizations set overly ambitious timelines, underestimate implementation complexity, and fail to plan for contingencies when systems don't perform as expected.

Successful digital transformation requires a phased approach that allows for testing, refinement, and course correction. Organizations should start with pilot projects that can demonstrate value and build confidence before scaling to enterprise-wide implementations. This approach reduces risk and allows organizations to learn and adapt their strategies based on real-world experience.

Risk management should also include contingency planning for system failures, data breaches, and other potential disruptions. Organizations need backup systems, recovery procedures, and communication plans to manage crises when they occur. The most successful digital transformations are those that plan for failure and build resilience into their operational systems.

Operational excellence in the digital age is driven by the strategic use of technology, but success requires more than just implementing the latest digital tools. Organizations that leverage ERP systems, automation, AI, cloud computing, IoT, and data analytics can streamline processes, reduce costs, and enhance customer experiences when these technologies are properly planned, implemented, and managed.

The real-world examples from both industry leaders and spectacular failures demonstrate how digital transformation can reshape operations for better or worse. Success depends on integrating digital tools into broader strategic vision, investing in workforce training, embracing data-driven decision-making, and maintaining realistic expectations about timelines and complexity.

By fostering a culture of continuous improvement and innovation, while learning from the failures of others, organizations can achieve long-term operational success and position themselves as industry leaders in an increasingly digital world. The key is to approach digital transformation with both ambition and humility, recognizing that technology is a powerful tool that must be wielded wisely to achieve lasting operational excellence.

Chapter 17

Sustaining Change: Ensuring Long-Term Success in Digital Transformations

The success of a digital transformation is not determined solely by its initial implementation but by an organization's ability to sustain and evolve these changes over time. Many companies invest significant resources into digital initiatives only to see their efforts stall or regress due to a lack of long-term commitment. Sustaining change requires continuous leadership support, strategic alignment, adaptability, and a culture that embraces ongoing innovation. Without these elements, digital transformations can lose momentum, leading to stagnation, employee disengagement, and inefficiencies that ultimately undermine the intended benefits of modernization.

The challenge of sustaining digital transformation is perhaps more difficult than the initial implementation itself. While the excitement and urgency of a new initiative can drive initial success, maintaining that momentum over months and years requires different skills, approaches, and organizational capabilities. The technology landscape is littered with examples of organizations that achieved initial digital transformation success only to see their competitive advantage erode as they failed to sustain and evolve their digital capabilities over time.

The Hidden Dangers of Digital Transformation Decay

Understanding the factors that lead to digital transformation decay is critical for executives who want to ensure long-term success. Research indicates that many digital transformation initiatives experience significant performance degradation within two to three years of implementation, not due to technical failures but due to organizational failures to sustain change.

One of the most instructive examples of failed sustainability comes from General Electric's ambitious digital transformation initiative. Under CEO Jeff Immelt, GE invested billions of dollars in creating GE Digital and developing the Predix industrial IoT platform. The initiative showed initial promise, with GE Digital generating significant revenue and market excitement. However, when leadership changed and new priorities emerged, the organization failed to sustain its commitment to digital transformation. The lack of sustained leadership support, combined with cultural resistance and changing strategic priorities, ultimately led to the dismantling of GE Digital and massive write-downs of the company's digital investments.

The GE experience highlights several critical factors that contribute to digital transformation decay. First, digital transformation must be embedded deeply enough in the organization's DNA that it can survive leadership changes and shifting priorities. Second, the financial and operational benefits of digital transformation must be clearly measurable and communicated to maintain organizational support. Third, the organization must develop internal capabilities to sustain and evolve digital initiatives without relying entirely on external consultants or temporary project teams.

Another cautionary example comes from the retail sector, where many traditional retailers invested heavily in digital transformation initiatives during the early 2000s only to see these efforts stagnate as leadership attention shifted to other priorities. Companies like Sears and JCPenney launched ambitious e-commerce and digital customer experience initiatives that showed initial promise but failed to sustain the investment and attention necessary for long-term success. As these companies faced financial pressures, digital transformation budgets were cut, technical teams were reduced, and the momentum of change was lost.

Building Sustainable Digital Transformation Through Strategic Integration

Sustaining change begins with embedding digital transformation within the company's strategic framework. Organizations that treat digital initiatives as temporary projects rather than as integral to their long-term vision struggle to maintain their impact. Instead, businesses must align their digital strategies with broader organizational goals, ensuring that digital transformation remains a driving force behind decision-making, operational efficiency, and customer engagement.

This strategic integration requires digital transformation to be woven into core business processes, performance metrics, and organizational structures. Companies that successfully sustain digital change integrate digital capabilities into their fundamental value propositions, making them inseparable from how the organization operates and competes in the marketplace.

Leadership plays a critical role in sustaining change, but this leadership must extend beyond senior executives to include middle management and frontline supervisors. The enthusiasm and commitment of executives and managers must extend beyond the initial rollout of new systems and processes. Leaders must continually reinforce the value of digital transformation, ensuring that employees remain engaged and aligned with evolving business objectives.

This requires ongoing communication that highlights progress, acknowledges challenges, and provides a clear roadmap for future improvements. Without visible and consistent leadership support, employees may revert to old ways of working, undermining the transformation's effectiveness. However, leadership support must be backed by concrete actions, including continued investment in digital capabilities, recognition and rewards for digital adoption, and consequences for resistance to change.

The Critical Role of Governance and Accountability

Another essential factor in sustaining digital change is strong governance and accountability. Organizations must establish governance structures that oversee digital initiatives, ensuring that changes are consistently evaluated, refined, and aligned with strategic goals. This includes defining clear ownership for various aspects of digital transformation, from technology management to employee training and performance measurement.

Effective governance requires both strategic oversight and operational accountability. At the strategic level, organizations need senior executive committees or boards that regularly review digital transformation progress, allocate resources, and make critical decisions about future directions. At the operational level, they need dedicated roles and teams responsible for day-to-day management of digital systems and continuous improvement initiatives.

By holding teams accountable for maintaining and improving digital initiatives, businesses can prevent stagnation and ensure long-term value creation. This accountability must be supported by clear performance metrics, regular reporting, and consequences for both success and failure. Organizations that successfully sustain digital transformation create cultures where maintaining and improving digital capabilities is viewed as a core responsibility rather than an optional activity.

Creating a Culture of Adaptability and Learning

An organization's culture plays a fundamental role in sustaining digital transformation. Companies that cultivate a culture of adaptability and continuous learning are better positioned to sustain change than those that resist new ways of working. Employees must feel encouraged to embrace new technologies, experiment with digital tools, and contribute to process improvements.

Creating an environment where innovation is rewarded and failures are seen as learning opportunities fosters a mindset of continuous progress, preventing digital transformation from becoming a one-time event. This cultural transformation often requires changes to hiring practices, performance evaluation systems, training programs, and organizational structures.

Organizations must also address the natural human tendency to revert to familiar processes and systems when under pressure. Sustaining digital transformation requires creating systems and incentives that make it easier and more rewarding to use new digital processes than to fall back on old ways of working.

The Power of Data-Driven Performance Management

Sustaining change requires a proactive approach to monitoring performance and measuring success. Organizations must track key performance indicators (KPIs) to assess the impact of digital transformation efforts and identify areas for improvement. Data-driven insights allow businesses to make informed decisions, address inefficiencies, and refine their strategies to optimize results.

However, many organizations struggle with establishing effective measurement systems for digital transformation. Traditional performance metrics may not capture the full value of digital initiatives, particularly in areas like employee satisfaction, customer experience, and organizational agility. Organizations must develop new measurement frameworks that can accurately assess the ongoing value of digital transformation investments.

Regular performance reviews help ensure that digital initiatives continue to evolve alongside business needs, rather than becoming obsolete over time. These reviews should include both quantitative metrics and qualitative assessments of user satisfaction, system effectiveness, and strategic alignment.

Learning from Artificial Intelligence Integration Challenges

The integration of artificial intelligence technologies provides particularly instructive examples of both successful and failed efforts to sustain digital transformation. AI systems require continuous training, monitoring, and refinement to maintain their effectiveness over time. Organizations that treat AI implementation as a one-time project often see system performance degrade as data patterns change and business requirements evolve.

Successful AI sustainability requires ongoing investment in data quality, model training, and system optimization. Organizations must develop internal capabilities to manage and improve AI systems rather than relying entirely on external vendors or consultants. This requires sustained investment in training, infrastructure, and organizational capabilities.

Companies like Netflix and Amazon have successfully sustained their AI initiatives by treating them as core business capabilities that require continuous investment and improvement. In contrast, many organizations have seen their AI initiatives stagnate due to lack of sustained attention and investment after initial implementation.

Maintaining Momentum Through Strategic Evolution

One of the biggest challenges organizations face after implementing digital transformation is maintaining momentum.

Many digital initiatives start strong but lose traction due to competing priorities, lack of resources, or employee fatigue. To prevent this, companies must establish mechanisms that keep digital transformation efforts active and relevant.

One key strategy for maintaining momentum is embedding digital transformation into everyday operations. Rather than treating digital initiatives as separate projects, organizations should integrate them into standard business processes. This ensures that digital tools and strategies become part of the company's DNA, making it easier to sustain change over the long term.

Additionally, organizations must foster a mindset of continuous improvement. Digital transformation is not a destination but an ongoing journey that requires businesses to adapt to emerging technologies, industry trends, and evolving customer expectations. Companies that remain flexible and open to change are more likely to sustain their digital initiatives and capitalize on new opportunities.

Implementing frameworks such as agile methodologies allows organizations to make incremental improvements, iterate based on real-world feedback, and remain responsive to shifting business needs. These frameworks help maintain momentum by creating regular opportunities for evaluation, improvement, and celebration of progress.

The Importance of Continuous Learning and Development

Regular training and upskilling efforts are also critical to sustaining digital change. Technology evolves rapidly, and employees must continuously develop new skills to keep pace with innovations. Organizations should invest in ongoing professional development programs that equip their workforce with the knowledge and confidence to leverage digital tools effectively.

Providing access to training resources, workshops, and mentorship opportunities helps employees stay engaged and motivated, reducing resistance to future technological advancements. This investment in human capital is often the difference between sustained success and gradual decline in digital transformation initiatives.

Organizations must also develop internal training capabilities rather than relying entirely on external providers. Internal training programs can be customized to specific organizational needs and can evolve alongside the organization's digital transformation journey.

Leveraging Employee Engagement and Feedback

Another important factor in maintaining digital transformation momentum is leveraging employee feedback and engagement. Employees are on the front lines of digital change, and their insights can provide valuable perspectives on what is working and what needs improvement. Organizations should create open communication channels that encourage employees to share their experiences, report challenges, and suggest enhancements.

This two-way dialogue ensures that digital initiatives are continuously refined to better meet the needs of the workforce.

Employee feedback can identify usability issues, training gaps, and process inefficiencies that might not be apparent to management. More importantly, involving employees in the continuous improvement process helps maintain their engagement and commitment to digital transformation initiatives.

Organizations should also recognize and celebrate successes in digital transformation, both large and small. Recognition programs that highlight successful adoption of digital tools, innovative uses of technology, or process improvements help maintain momentum and encourage continued engagement.

Preparing for Future Technological Shifts

To sustain change, businesses must also prepare for future technological shifts. The digital landscape is constantly evolving, and organizations that fail to anticipate change risk falling behind. Companies should actively monitor industry trends, evaluate emerging technologies, and experiment with new digital solutions to stay ahead of competitors.

This proactive approach ensures that digital transformation efforts remain relevant and aligned with market demands. Organizations should establish innovation labs, technology scouting programs, or partnerships with technology vendors to stay current with emerging trends and opportunities.

However, organizations must balance innovation with stability. The pursuit of new technologies should not undermine existing systems and processes that are working effectively. Successful organizations develop capabilities to selectively adopt new technologies while maintaining the stability and performance of their core digital systems.

Case Study: FinTech Solutions - A Comprehensive Approach to Sustaining Digital Transformation

This case study explores how a global financial services company, FinTech Solutions, successfully ensured the long-term success of its digital transformation initiatives by implementing comprehensive sustaining change strategies.

FinTech Solutions, a multinational financial services provider, embarked on a large-scale digital transformation to modernize its operations, improve customer experiences, and enhance data-driven decision-making. The initiative included cloud migration, artificial intelligence adoption, automation of manual processes, and the implementation of a unified digital customer platform. However, after the initial success of the digital rollout, the company faced significant challenges in sustaining these changes over time.

The organization encountered several critical challenges that threatened the sustainability of their digital transformation:

Employee Resistance and Adaptation Issues: Many employees were hesitant to adopt new technologies, citing concerns over job security and lack of digital proficiency. Without proper reassurance and support, employees feared automation would render their roles obsolete. This resistance manifested in low system utilization rates, workarounds that bypassed new processes, and passive resistance to training programs.

Inadequate Ongoing Training Programs: The absence of continuous upskilling programs led to stagnation in digital adoption. Employees who initially engaged with new systems struggled with advanced functionalities, causing inefficiencies and frustration. Many users reverted to familiar processes when facing challenging tasks, undermining the benefits of digital transformation.

Process Inertia and Legacy Mindsets: Some legacy processes persisted despite new digital tools, leading to inefficiencies and confusion. Employees continued to rely on outdated workflows due to familiarity and resistance to altering established routines. This created parallel systems where both old and new processes coexisted, reducing overall efficiency.

Leadership Commitment Sustainability: While leadership was enthusiastic during the transformation phase, sustaining engagement over time proved difficult. Initial excitement waned as other priorities emerged, leading to gaps in strategic alignment and reduced reinforcement of digital transformation goals.

Customer Adaptation Challenges: Customers, especially in traditional banking segments, were slow to embrace digital interactions. Many found digital services overwhelming, preferring in-person assistance, which limited the realization of digital transformation benefits.

To address these challenges, FinTech Solutions implemented a comprehensive sustaining change framework, focusing on five key areas:

Change Management and Cultural Transformation: The organization developed a Change Champions Network, consisting of influential employees who advocated for digital adoption. These champions received specialized training to act as peer mentors and facilitators within their teams. The company conducted awareness campaigns to highlight the benefits of digital transformation, using internal newsletters, town halls, and digital storytelling to demonstrate success stories and tangible benefits. Additionally, they created feedback loops to continuously address employee concerns through monthly surveys, focus groups, and digital forums that provided employees with a voice in shaping the transformation journey.

Continuous Learning and Skill Development: FinTech Solutions introduced comprehensive Digital Upskilling Programs in collaboration with technology partners. Employees attended workshops, earned certifications, and participated in interactive e-learning modules tailored to their roles. The company provided on-demand learning platforms for employees to improve their digital proficiency, integrating AI-driven learning management systems that personalized training based on user performance and engagement. They also conducted periodic workshops and hackathons to encourage innovation and hands-on experience, fostering creativity and allowing employees to experiment with new tools while building a culture of continuous learning.

Process Optimization and Integration: The organization established Digital Process Audits to identify redundant legacy processes and integrate them with digital solutions. A dedicated team reviewed workflows, identified bottlenecks, and streamlined operations. They implemented AI-driven analytics to monitor operational efficiency and optimize workflows, using real-time dashboards to provide insights into system performance, employee adoption rates, and productivity levels. A Digital Transformation Governance Board was created to ensure continuous improvement, with this cross-functional team assessing new technologies, measuring key performance indicators, and recommending process refinements.

Sustained Leadership Commitment: Executive performance metrics were mandated to include digital adoption goals, with leaders held accountable for digital KPIs that aligned corporate objectives with transformation efforts. Leaders were encouraged to act as role models, demonstrating the use of digital tools by actively participating in training programs and using digital platforms in their daily operations. Quarterly progress reviews were conducted to maintain leadership engagement, providing visibility into progress, addressing challenges, and reinforcing strategic alignment.

Customer Engagement and Support: The company launched customer education programs to ease the transition to digital platforms, providing tutorials, webinars, and personalized support to help customers navigate new services. They provided multi-channel support including chatbots, video tutorials, and customer service hotlines for users navigating new technologies, with AI-driven chatbots and 24/7 helplines ensuring continuous assistance. Customer feedback was collected through digital surveys and used to adjust platforms accordingly, with data-driven insights informing user experience enhancements that led to more intuitive and accessible digital services.

Within two years of implementing sustaining change strategies, FinTech Solutions achieved remarkable results that demonstrated the value of comprehensive change sustainability efforts:

The organization achieved a 90% employee adoption rate of new digital tools, with increased confidence and proficiency across departments. This represented a significant improvement from the initial 45% adoption rate observed six months after implementation.

Operational inefficiencies were reduced by 35% due to process automation, leading to faster turnaround times and improved service delivery. The company was able to process customer requests 50% faster while maintaining higher accuracy rates.

Customer engagement increased significantly, with 75% of users migrating to digital banking services, reducing in-person dependency and enhancing convenience. Customer satisfaction scores for digital services improved by 40% over the two-year period.

Leadership support remained consistent, ensuring the continuous evolution of digital initiatives. Executives actively championed further innovations and integration, with digital transformation becoming a standard agenda item in all strategic planning sessions.

Workforce satisfaction increased substantially, with employees citing better career growth opportunities due to digital upskilling. Employee attrition rates decreased by 25% as workers felt more empowered and valued in their enhanced roles.

The FinTech Solutions case study reveals several critical lessons for sustaining digital transformation:

Comprehensive Approach: Successful sustainability requires addressing multiple dimensions simultaneously including technology, people, processes, and culture. Organizations cannot focus on just one area and expect lasting change.

Continuous Investment: Sustaining digital transformation requires ongoing investment in training, technology updates, and organizational development. The initial implementation budget should include provisions for long-term sustainability activities.

Employee Centricity: Employees are the ultimate determiners of digital transformation success. Organizations must prioritize employee experience, development, and engagement throughout the transformation journey.

Leadership Consistency: Leadership commitment must be institutionalized through performance metrics, governance structures, and accountability mechanisms that survive changes in personnel and priorities.

Customer Integration: Digital transformation sustainability requires customers to adopt and value new digital capabilities. Organizations must invest in customer education and support to ensure sustained adoption.

Building Resilience Against External Disruptions

Organizations must also build resilience into their digital transformation initiatives to withstand external disruptions such as economic downturns, regulatory changes, or global crises like the COVID-19 pandemic. Companies that build agility into their transformation efforts—such as by leveraging cloud-based solutions, automation, and AI-driven analytics—are better equipped to navigate uncertainty and sustain their competitive edge.

Resilience requires organizations to design digital systems and processes that can adapt to changing circumstances without requiring complete overhauls. This includes building redundancy into critical systems, developing flexible operational models, and maintaining financial reserves to support continued digital investment during challenging periods.

The Role of Continuous Innovation

Finally, sustaining digital transformation requires organizations to maintain a commitment to continuous innovation. Digital transformation is not a one-time event but an ongoing process of adaptation and improvement. Organizations must establish innovation processes, allocate resources for experimentation, and create cultures that encourage creative problem-solving and technological exploration.

This commitment to innovation should be balanced with operational stability. Organizations need to maintain reliable core systems while simultaneously exploring new technologies and approaches. The ability to manage this balance between innovation and stability is often what separates organizations that sustain digital transformation success from those that experience decline over time.

Sustaining digital transformation requires a long-term commitment to continuous improvement, adaptability, and cultural change. Organizations that successfully sustain digital initiatives do so by embedding transformation into their strategic framework, fostering a culture of innovation, and maintaining strong leadership support. Governance structures, performance tracking, and proactive change management ensure that digital transformation remains an ongoing priority rather than a short-lived initiative.

To maintain momentum, businesses must integrate digital strategies into daily operations, invest in employee training, and remain agile in the face of evolving technological advancements. Leveraging feedback from employees and monitoring key performance metrics allows organizations to refine their digital efforts, ensuring that they continue to drive value over time.

The FinTech Solutions case study demonstrates that sustaining change is possible when organizations take a comprehensive approach that addresses technology, people, processes, and culture simultaneously. By embracing a mindset of continuous progress and learning from both successes and failures, organizations can sustain digital transformation efforts and remain competitive in an ever-changing business environment.

Rather than viewing digital transformation as a one-time effort, companies must recognize it as an evolving journey—one that requires ongoing investment, adaptation, and a commitment to innovation. The businesses that succeed in sustaining change will be those that remain flexible, future-focused, and dedicated to harnessing technology as a long-term driver of success while building the organizational capabilities necessary to adapt and thrive in an increasingly digital world.

Chapter 18

Emerging Technologies: Preparing for the Future of Digital Transformation

As businesses evolve in the digital age, emerging technologies are reshaping enterprise operations, customer engagement, and decision-making processes. Staying ahead of technological advancements is crucial for maintaining competitiveness, driving efficiency, and leveraging innovation to create new business opportunities. From artificial intelligence and machine learning to blockchain, next-generation enterprise resource planning systems, and edge computing, organizations must anticipate and prepare for the future by understanding which technologies will have the most significant impact and how to integrate them effectively.

However, the rapid pace of technological change also creates significant risks for organizations that fail to carefully evaluate and implement emerging technologies. The business landscape is littered with examples of companies that invested heavily in promising new technologies only to see these investments fail to deliver expected returns. Understanding both the opportunities and risks associated with emerging technologies is essential for executives who must make strategic decisions about technology investments in an increasingly complex and rapidly evolving digital landscape.

The Double-Edged Nature of Emerging Technology Adoption

The rapid pace of technological innovation presents both opportunities and challenges for organizations seeking to optimize their digital strategies. While emerging technologies offer the potential for significant competitive advantages, they also carry inherent risks including implementation complexity, uncertain returns on investment, and the potential for disruptive failures that can damage operations and organizational credibility.

Consider the case of many organizations that rushed to implement blockchain technologies during the cryptocurrency boom of 2017-2018. Companies across various industries announced blockchain initiatives and made significant investments in distributed ledger technologies, often without clear use cases or understanding of the technology's limitations. Many of these initiatives failed to deliver tangible business value, resulting in wasted resources and damaged credibility for both the organizations and the blockchain technology itself.

Similarly, the early adoption of virtual and augmented reality technologies by many retailers and training organizations has produced mixed results. While some organizations have found valuable applications for these technologies in product visualization and employee training, many others have struggled to justify the significant investments required for VR/AR implementations. The technology's limitations, including user adoption challenges, technical complexity, and high implementation costs, have led to numerous failed initiatives.

These examples highlight the importance of approaching emerging technologies with both enthusiasm and skepticism. Organizations must carefully evaluate new technologies not just for their potential benefits, but also for their readiness, implementation complexity, and alignment with specific business needs and capabilities.

The AI Revolution: Promise and Peril in Equal Measure

Among the most transformative emerging technologies, artificial intelligence stands out as both the most promising and the most challenging for organizations to implement successfully. AI technologies are revolutionizing how businesses manage data, automate processes, and enhance customer experiences. AI-driven analytics enable companies to gain deeper insights into market trends, predict customer behavior, and make data-driven decisions with greater accuracy. AI-powered automation is streamlining repetitive tasks, improving operational efficiency, and reducing human error.

The growing influence of AI in digital transformation is undeniable. AI-driven predictive analytics allow businesses to forecast trends, optimize operations, and improve decision-making by analyzing vast amounts of data in real time and identifying patterns, detecting anomalies, and generating actionable insights that drive business strategy. For instance, AI-powered predictive analytics in supply chain management helps businesses optimize inventory levels, reduce waste, and anticipate demand fluctuations.

AI is also playing a crucial role in process automation, particularly through robotic process automation (RPA). RPA uses AI-driven bots to automate repetitive and rule-based tasks, such as invoice processing, customer inquiries, and compliance reporting. This reduces human workload, minimizes errors, and improves operational efficiency. Companies that leverage AI-driven automation can redirect human resources toward more strategic and creative tasks, fostering innovation and growth.

AI-driven customer experiences represent another area of significant transformation. Chatbots, virtual assistants, and natural language processing technologies are improving how businesses interact with customers. AI-powered chatbots can provide 24/7 customer support, resolve queries faster, and personalize interactions based on historical data. Advanced sentiment analysis allows businesses to gauge customer satisfaction and tailor responses accordingly.

However, the implementation of AI technologies is fraught with challenges and potential pitfalls. Many organizations have discovered that successful AI implementation requires much more than simply deploying advanced algorithms. AI systems require high-quality data, sophisticated infrastructure, specialized skills, and careful change management to deliver meaningful business value.

The failure of IBM's Watson for Oncology provides a sobering example of AI implementation gone wrong. Despite massive investment and marketing hype, Watson for Oncology failed to deliver on its promise of revolutionizing cancer treatment recommendations. The system struggled with data quality issues, couldn't effectively interpret complex medical information, and failed to gain acceptance from healthcare professionals. The failure highlighted the challenges of implementing AI in complex domains where human expertise, judgment, and contextual understanding remain critical.

Similarly, many organizations have struggled with AI chatbot implementations that were rushed to market without adequate training data or understanding of customer needs. These chatbots often provide frustrating user experiences, leading to customer dissatisfaction and abandonment of AI-powered customer service channels.

The Reality of AI in ERP Systems

The integration of AI into ERP systems represents one of the most significant opportunities for operational improvement, but also one of the most complex implementation challenges. All major ERP software vendors are focusing on integrating AI into their offerings, sometimes marketing future visions for AI integration even before the capabilities are fully developed.

AI enables organizations to leverage the massive amounts of data accumulated over decades of ERP usage. This includes not just internal data, but external data sources like macroeconomic indicators, weather patterns, and market trends. AI-powered ERP systems can provide predictive analytics and machine learning capabilities that help organizations anticipate problems, optimize processes, and make more informed decisions.

However, the reality of AI in ERP is more complex than vendor marketing materials suggest. Many AI features in current

ERP systems are relatively basic, focusing on areas like automated data entry, simple pattern recognition, and basic predictive analytics. More sophisticated AI capabilities like natural language processing, complex decision-making, and autonomous process optimization are still in early development stages.

Organizations must approach AI-enabled ERP systems with realistic expectations and careful implementation planning. The most successful AI implementations in ERP focus on specific, well-defined use cases where AI can provide clear business value, such as demand forecasting, fraud detection, or automated invoice processing. Organizations should avoid the temptation to implement AI capabilities simply because they are available, instead focusing on areas where AI can solve real business problems and deliver measurable results.

Blockchain: Beyond the Hype

Blockchain technology represents another emerging technology with significant potential but also substantial implementation challenges. The decentralized and immutable nature of blockchain allows organizations to create more secure digital transactions, protect sensitive data, and establish trust in multi-party collaborations.

For industries such as supply chain management, healthcare, and finance, blockchain can provide enhanced security measures and improve operational transparency. Smart contracts—self-executing contracts with predefined rules—are streamlining operations by reducing the need for intermediaries and automating transactions securely.

However, blockchain implementations have proven more challenging than initially anticipated. Many organizations that invested heavily in blockchain technologies during the peak of the cryptocurrency boom found that the technology's limitations—including scalability issues, energy consumption concerns, and integration complexity—made it unsuitable for their specific use cases.

The failure of Walmart's early blockchain supply chain initiatives provides an instructive example. While the concept of using blockchain to track food products through the supply chain seemed promising, the implementation proved complex and expensive, with limited benefits compared to simpler tracking technologies. Walmart eventually scaled back its blockchain ambitions and focused on more practical digital tracking solutions.

Organizations considering blockchain implementations should carefully evaluate whether the technology's benefits justify its complexity and costs. In many cases, traditional database technologies or simpler digital solutions can provide similar benefits with less implementation risk and lower costs.

The Evolution of Next-Generation ERP Systems

The evolution of enterprise resource planning systems is playing a significant role in digital transformation, but this evolution is also creating new challenges and risks for organizations. Traditional ERP solutions are being replaced by next-generation, cloud-based platforms that offer greater scalability, flexibility, and AI-driven insights.

Modern ERP solutions integrate advanced technologies such as IoT, AI, and predictive analytics, enabling organizations to make real-time decisions and optimize resource planning. Businesses that adopt modern ERP systems can gain competitive advantages through improved process automation, reduced operational silos, and enhanced data-driven decision-making.

Cloud-based ERP platforms provide greater accessibility and cost savings, allowing businesses to scale operations without the burden of maintaining expensive on-premise infrastructure. These systems offer real-time data synchronization across departments, leading to improved collaboration and more informed decision-making.

However, the transition to next-generation ERP systems is not without risk. Many organizations have experienced significant challenges and failures when attempting to migrate from legacy ERP systems to modern cloud-based platforms. The complexity of data migration, process reengineering, and user training can overwhelm organizations that underestimate the scope and difficulty of ERP modernization.

The failure of Lidl's SAP implementation, which cost the company over $500 million before being abandoned, demonstrates the risks associated with next-generation ERP implementations. Despite working with experienced system integrators and investing substantial resources, Lidl was unable to successfully implement the new ERP system due to fundamental misalignments between the system's capabilities and the company's business requirements.

Edge Computing and Real-Time Processing Challenges

As businesses generate and rely on vast amounts of data, edge computing is emerging as a critical technology for reducing latency and bringing computation closer to data sources. This is particularly critical for industries leveraging Internet of Things devices, where real-time data processing is essential for decision-making.

By implementing edge computing strategies, businesses can improve response times, enhance security, and reduce dependency on centralized cloud infrastructure. This is particularly beneficial in industries such as manufacturing, where real-time machine monitoring can prevent equipment failures and improve operational efficiency.

However, edge computing implementations introduce new complexity in terms of system management, security, and data governance. Organizations must manage distributed computing resources across multiple locations while maintaining security, performance, and reliability standards. The failure to properly plan and implement edge computing solutions can result in fragmented systems that are difficult to manage and secure.

The Metaverse and Virtual Reality: Promise vs. Reality

The expansion of metaverse and virtual reality applications is generating significant excitement, but organizations must carefully evaluate the practical applications and limitations of these technologies. Companies across various industries are exploring the use of immersive digital experiences for employee training, customer engagement, and remote collaboration.

Organizations that successfully integrate VR and augmented reality into their digital strategies can create new ways to interact with customers, streamline onboarding and training programs, and enhance productivity through virtual workspaces. For example, some retail businesses are experimenting with virtual showrooms, while healthcare organizations are using VR for surgical simulations and remote patient consultations.

However, many VR and metaverse initiatives have failed to deliver expected business value due to technology limitations, user adoption challenges, and implementation costs that exceed benefits. The failure of many corporate metaverse initiatives launched during 2021-2022 demonstrates the importance of carefully evaluating emerging technologies before making significant investments.

Organizations should approach VR and metaverse technologies with specific use cases and clear success metrics rather than implementing these technologies simply to appear innovative. The most successful implementations focus on solving specific business problems rather than exploring technology for its own sake.

Preparing for Technological Disruption

To capitalize on emerging technologies while avoiding common pitfalls, organizations must develop a proactive strategy that incorporates ongoing learning, investment in digital infrastructure, and agile adaptation to market changes. This requires establishing a culture of continuous innovation while maintaining disciplined evaluation processes for new technologies.

The first step in preparing for technological advancements is establishing a culture of continuous innovation. Businesses that foster an environment where employees are encouraged to experiment with new technologies and contribute to digital initiatives are better positioned to adapt to change. However, this culture must be balanced with rigorous evaluation processes that assess technologies based on their potential business value rather than their novelty or hype.

Leadership must set the tone by investing in emerging technologies strategically rather than reactively. This means developing technology adoption roadmaps that align with business objectives and conducting thorough evaluations of new technologies before making significant investments.

Developing a Strategic Technology Adoption Framework

Another key approach is developing a technology adoption roadmap that aligns with business objectives. Instead of adopting new technologies reactively, organizations should evaluate how specific innovations align with their industry needs, customer expectations, and operational goals. Conducting pilot projects to test emerging technologies before full-scale implementation helps companies assess potential risks, refine use cases, and optimize strategies for adoption.

This framework should include clear criteria for evaluating emerging technologies, including:

Business Value Assessment: Does the technology solve a specific business problem or create new opportunities for value creation? Organizations should avoid implementing technologies without clear business cases.

Implementation Readiness: Does the organization have the skills, infrastructure, and resources necessary to successfully implement the technology? Many technology failures occur because organizations underestimate implementation requirements.

Risk Evaluation: What are the potential risks associated with the technology, including technical risks, financial risks, and operational risks? Organizations should develop comprehensive risk mitigation strategies before implementing new technologies.

Scalability Potential: Can the technology be successfully scaled across the organization if initial implementations are successful? Technologies that work in pilot environments may not scale effectively to enterprise deployments.

Building Internal Capabilities for Technology Adoption

Investing in employee training and skill development is crucial for ensuring smooth transitions to new technologies. Organizations must equip their workforce with the necessary skills to leverage AI, blockchain, ERP advancements, and other innovations effectively. Providing ongoing education, certification programs, and hands-on training opportunities will help employees adapt to new tools and drive digital transformation initiatives forward.

However, training programs must be carefully designed to address both technical skills and change management challenges. Many technology implementations fail not because of technical issues but because employees resist adopting new tools and processes. Effective training programs address both the "how" and the "why" of new technology adoption.

Organizations should also develop internal capabilities for evaluating and managing emerging technologies rather than relying entirely on external consultants or vendors. This includes building teams with expertise in technology evaluation, implementation planning, and change management.

Strategic Partnerships and Ecosystem Development

Collaboration with technology partners and industry experts is another effective way to stay ahead of emerging trends. Partnering with technology providers, attending industry conferences, and engaging with digital transformation consultants can provide valuable insights into the latest innovations and best practices for implementation.

However, organizations must carefully manage these partnerships to avoid being oversold on technologies that may not be appropriate for their specific needs. The most effective partnerships are those where both parties have aligned incentives for successful technology implementation rather than just technology sales.

Building Scalable and Flexible Digital Infrastructure

A critical aspect of leveraging emerging technologies is ensuring scalability and flexibility in digital transformation strategies. As new technologies continue to evolve, businesses must design digital systems that are adaptable and capable of integrating future advancements. Cloud-based solutions, modular software architectures, and API-driven integrations allow organizations to scale their digital infrastructure while remaining agile in response to technological developments.

This infrastructure must also be secure and compliant with relevant regulations. As new technologies create new security risks and regulatory requirements, organizations must ensure their infrastructure can adapt to changing security and compliance needs.

Learning from Emerging Technology Failures

Understanding common failure patterns in emerging technology adoption can help organizations avoid similar mistakes. Research indicates that most emerging technology failures occur due to:

Unrealistic Expectations: Organizations often expect emerging technologies to deliver transformational results immediately, without accounting for implementation complexity and learning curves.

Inadequate Preparation: Many organizations attempt to implement emerging technologies without adequate preparation in terms of infrastructure, skills, or change management.

Poor Use Case Definition: Organizations sometimes implement technologies without clear use cases or success criteria, making it difficult to evaluate success or optimize implementations.

Insufficient Investment: Emerging technologies often require sustained investment over time to deliver value, but organizations may underestimate these ongoing costs.

Lack of Integration Planning: New technologies must integrate with existing systems and processes, but organizations often underestimate integration complexity and costs.

The Future of AI in Business Operations

Looking ahead, artificial intelligence will likely become increasingly integrated into all aspects of business operations. AI technologies will become more sophisticated, more accessible, and more integrated into standard business applications. However, successful AI adoption will require organizations to develop new capabilities in data management, algorithmic governance, and human-AI collaboration.

The most successful organizations will be those that view AI as a tool for augmenting human capabilities rather than replacing human workers. This requires developing new approaches to job design, skill development, and organizational structure that leverage the complementary strengths of humans and AI systems.

Managing the Pace of Technology Change

One of the biggest challenges facing organizations is managing the pace of technological change. The rapid evolution of emerging technologies creates pressure to constantly adopt new tools and approaches, but this can lead to technology fragmentation and reduced organizational effectiveness.

Organizations must develop disciplined approaches to technology adoption that balance innovation with stability. This includes establishing clear criteria for technology evaluation, maintaining focus on core business objectives, and avoiding the temptation to adopt every new technology that emerges.

Preparing for Quantum Computing and Advanced Technologies

As we look further into the future, even more advanced technologies like quantum computing, advanced robotics, and biotechnology will begin to impact business operations. While these technologies are still in early development stages, organizations should begin preparing for their eventual adoption by developing the foundational capabilities necessary for advanced technology implementation.

This preparation includes building strong data and analytics capabilities, developing expertise in emerging technology evaluation, and creating organizational cultures that can adapt to radical technological change.

Building Organizational Resilience

Perhaps most importantly, organizations must build resilience into their technology strategies to handle both successful adoption and implementation failures. This includes maintaining diversified technology portfolios, developing contingency plans for technology failures, and building organizational learning capabilities that can extract value from both successes and failures.

Resilient organizations view emerging technology adoption as a portfolio of experiments rather than betting everything on single technologies. They invest in multiple promising technologies while maintaining the flexibility to pivot when specific technologies prove unsuccessful.

The rapid advancement of emerging technologies presents both unprecedented opportunities and significant risks for businesses undergoing digital transformation. Organizations that anticipate technological trends, invest in continuous innovation, and develop adaptive strategies will be well-positioned to stay ahead of the competition. AI, blockchain, next-generation ERP systems, edge computing, and the metaverse are among the key technologies shaping the future of digital business.

However, success in emerging technology adoption requires more than just investment in new tools. Organizations must foster cultures of innovation while maintaining disciplined evaluation processes, invest in workforce training and development, collaborate strategically with industry leaders, and implement scalable, secure, and data-driven digital strategies.

The lessons from both successful implementations and spectacular failures make clear that emerging technology adoption is not just about technology—it's about organizational capability, strategic planning, and change management. Organizations that master these fundamentals while staying current with technological advances will be best positioned for sustained success in the digital future.

By staying informed and proactive, organizations can leverage emerging technologies to enhance operational efficiency, improve customer engagement, and drive long-term growth in an increasingly digital world. The key is to approach emerging technologies with both optimism and realism, recognizing that technological capability must be matched with organizational readiness and strategic clarity to achieve lasting success.

Digital transformation is indeed an ongoing journey, and businesses that continuously evolve alongside technological advancements will be best equipped for sustained success in the future. Those who fail to adapt risk falling behind, while those who embrace change thoughtfully and strategically will thrive in an ever-evolving technological landscape. The organizations that succeed will be those that can balance the excitement of technological possibility with the discipline of strategic implementation, creating sustainable competitive advantages through the intelligent application of emerging technologies.

Chapter 19

The Future of ERP and Digital Platforms: Navigating the Next Evolution of Business Technology

Enterprise Resource Planning systems and digital platforms have long served as the backbone of business operations, enabling organizations to streamline processes, manage data, and facilitate decision-making across various departments. However, as digital transformation accelerates, these systems are evolving at an unprecedented pace. The future of ERP and digital platforms will be shaped by emerging technologies such as artificial intelligence, automation, cloud computing, and data analytics. Businesses that proactively prepare for these changes will gain a competitive advantage, improve operational efficiency, and drive innovation.

Yet the path forward is littered with cautionary tales. The spectacular failure of the UK's NHS National Programme for IT serves as a stark reminder of what happens when organizations rush into digital transformation without proper planning. After spending over £10 billion over nearly a decade, the NHS was forced to abandon the world's largest civil IT program in 2011. The project failed not because of technological limitations, but due to fundamental organizational and strategic shortcomings that continue to plague ERP implementations today.

The NHS failure began with top-down political mandates rather than genuine business needs assessment. Prime Minister Tony Blair announced the project in 2002 with great fanfare, but the program suffered from a complete lack of stakeholder buy-in from the outset. Doctors and general practitioners expressed concerns early on that the system didn't meet accessibility or use requirements, yet their feedback was largely ignored. This resistance from end-users created an insurmountable barrier to adoption, demonstrating that even the most sophisticated technology is worthless without user acceptance.

Predictions for the Evolution of ERP Systems and Digital Platforms

ERP systems have undergone significant transformations over the years, transitioning from monolithic, on-premise solutions to cloud-based, modular platforms that offer greater flexibility. Looking ahead, ERP systems will continue evolving to become more intelligent, automated, and interconnected with emerging technologies. However, the evolution must be guided by lessons learned from past failures.

AI-Driven ERP: The Next Frontier

Artificial intelligence will play a central role in shaping the future of ERP. Traditional ERP systems require extensive manual input, making data management, workflow automation, and decision-making time-consuming and prone to human error. AI-powered ERP solutions will revolutionize these processes by introducing advanced automation, predictive analytics, and intelligent decision-making.

The promise of AI in ERP is substantial, but executives must approach it with realistic expectations. Too often, organizations fall victim to what can be called "AI theater" – implementing artificial intelligence solutions for the sake of appearing innovative rather than addressing genuine business problems. The reality is that most AI implementations in ERP today are focused on narrow, specific use cases rather than the transformational capabilities that vendors often promise.

Machine learning algorithms will continuously analyze business data to identify trends, forecast demand, and provide recommendations for optimizing operations. AI-driven chatbots and virtual assistants will enhance user interactions, allowing employees to retrieve information, generate reports, and resolve queries through natural language processing. However, the key to success lies not in the sophistication of the AI itself, but in the quality of the data feeding these systems and the organizational readiness to act on AI-generated insights.

The Queensland Health payroll disaster offers a sobering perspective on what happens when organizations fail to understand their underlying data complexity before implementing new systems. When Queensland Health attempted to replace its aging payroll system in 2010, the project quickly spiraled into what became known as the most spectacular technology failure in the Southern Hemisphere. The AU$1.25 billion disaster resulted in over 35,000 payroll errors, leaving thousands of healthcare workers either unpaid or incorrectly paid.

The Queensland failure demonstrates why AI implementations require exceptional data quality and process understanding. The health system's payroll comprised 24,000 different combinations of wage payments and withholdings for over 80,000 workers across multiple industrial agreements. When IBM attempted to implement an interim solution in just seven months, the complexity overwhelmed the system. AI algorithms are only as good as the data they process, and if organizations don't understand their current state processes and data quality, AI will simply amplify existing problems at scale.

Additionally, AI-driven automation will reduce manual workloads, streamline supply chain management, and improve financial forecasting. Organizations that integrate AI-powered ERP solutions will benefit from real-time insights, proactive problem-solving, and increased agility. The challenge lies in ensuring that these AI systems are transparent, explainable, and aligned with business objectives rather than becoming black boxes that make decisions without clear rationale.

Composable ERP and Modular Architectures

The era of one-size-fits-all ERP systems is fading, making way for composable ERP architectures that allow businesses to select and integrate best-in-class applications tailored to their unique needs. Composable ERP enables organizations to build a flexible technology stack, adding or replacing components without overhauling the entire system.

This shift toward modular systems represents both an opportunity and a risk. While composable architectures offer greater flexibility, they also introduce integration complexity that can derail implementations if not properly managed. The US Air Force's Expeditionary Combat Support System failure provides a cautionary tale about the dangers of scope creep in modular implementations.

The Air Force began its Oracle ERP implementation in 2005 with the goal of replacing hundreds of legacy systems with a single, unified platform. However, what started as a straightforward ERP implementation gradually expanded into a multi-system, multi-vendor effort that consumed eight years and over $5 billion before being canceled in 2012. The project suffered from what Senator John McCain's investigation described as an "organizational disaster" characterized by poor project governance and constant scope expansion.

The Air Force failure illustrates why composable ERP success requires disciplined governance and clear boundaries. When organizations attempt to solve every problem with their ERP implementation, they create a level of complexity that becomes unmanageable. The key to successful composable ERP lies in maintaining focus on core business processes while resisting the temptation to expand scope without proper analysis and planning.

By leveraging modular ERP solutions, companies can avoid vendor lock-in, scale their systems based on business needs, and integrate emerging technologies seamlessly. This shift aligns with the broader trend of API-driven ecosystems, where ERP platforms act as central hubs that connect various specialized applications, from human resources and finance to customer relationship management and supply chain management.

Cloud-Native and Edge Computing ERP

Cloud-based ERP solutions have already become the industry standard, offering greater scalability, accessibility, and cost efficiency than on-premise systems. However, the next phase of ERP evolution will see deeper integration with edge computing, enabling real-time data processing closer to its source.

Edge computing allows organizations to process critical data locally rather than relying on centralized cloud servers. This will be particularly beneficial for industries that require instantaneous decision-making, such as manufacturing, logistics, and healthcare. By combining cloud-native ERP with edge computing, businesses can enhance their ability to manage distributed operations, reduce latency, and optimize resource allocation.

Blockchain Integration for Secure and Transparent Transactions

Blockchain technology is expected to enhance ERP security, transparency, and trust in digital transactions. As supply chains become increasingly globalized and complex, blockchain will provide an immutable ledger for tracking transactions, verifying authenticity, and ensuring compliance with regulatory standards.

ERP platforms integrated with blockchain will enable secure data sharing, fraud prevention, and automated smart contracts. This will be particularly useful for industries such as finance, healthcare, and logistics, where data integrity and auditability are paramount.

Hyper-Personalization and User-Centric ERP

Future ERP systems will feature role-based dashboards, intelligent search capabilities, and proactive recommendations, reducing the learning curve and improving productivity. AI-powered personalization will allow ERP platforms to adapt to individual user preferences, roles, and work habits, creating a more intuitive experience.

The importance of user-centric design cannot be overstated, as demonstrated by Edinburgh University's failed Oracle ERP implementation in 2019. The university's new system was designed with financial terminology and structures that required specialized training to use effectively. Tasks that should have taken minutes were taking hours, causing frustration and inefficiency among staff. The lack of intuitive design and inadequate training significantly diminished user confidence in the system, contributing to the project's eventual failure.

By improving accessibility and ease of use, ERP systems will empower employees across all levels of an organization, making data more actionable and decision-making more efficient. The focus must be on creating systems that work for users rather than forcing users to adapt to poorly designed interfaces.

ERP as a Data-Driven Command Center

ERP platforms are becoming increasingly integrated with IoT devices, AI, and big data analytics, transforming them into centralized command centers for real-time decision-making. Businesses will have access to cross-functional insights that allow them to respond to market shifts, customer demands, and operational challenges proactively.

By leveraging ERP as a data-driven decision-making tool, companies can enhance agility, mitigate risks, and optimize performance across all departments. Future ERP systems will no longer be just process automation tools; they will be intelligent business advisors that shape strategy and drive innovation.

Strategic Planning for Future Technological Landscapes

To prepare for the next wave of ERP and digital platform innovations, organizations must adopt a forward-thinking, strategic approach that aligns technological advancements with business goals. Future-proofing digital transformation efforts requires proactive investment, skill development, and a flexible IT infrastructure that can adapt to changing market conditions.

Develop a Long-Term Digital Roadmap

Organizations must craft a long-term digital transformation roadmap that outlines their ERP evolution strategy. This roadmap should consider business growth objectives, emerging technological trends, and regulatory compliance requirements. The failure of projects like the NHS National Programme for IT demonstrates the importance of having a clear, realistic roadmap that accounts for organizational complexity and change management requirements.

By taking a phased approach to ERP modernization, companies can gradually transition to new technologies while minimizing disruption. Pilot programs, proof-of-concept initiatives, and gradual module upgrades can help organizations test new functionalities and ensure alignment with business needs before full-scale deployment.

Invest in Workforce Upskilling and Change Management

As AI, automation, and emerging technologies become more embedded in ERP systems, workforce skills will need to evolve accordingly. Organizations must invest in upskilling employees, ensuring they have the knowledge and expertise to leverage next-generation ERP capabilities.

The Queensland Health failure underscores the importance of change management in ERP implementations. The project suffered from inadequate stakeholder engagement and insufficient communication about the impact of changes on daily operations. Many employees were unprepared for the new system's complexity, contributing to the widespread payroll errors that followed go-live.

Change management strategies will be crucial in facilitating employee adoption and minimizing resistance. Providing hands-on training, interactive learning modules, and AI-assisted user guidance will ensure that employees can effectively navigate and maximize the benefits of new ERP functionalities.

Adopt an Agile and Scalable ERP Approach

To stay competitive in a rapidly evolving technological landscape, businesses must embrace an agile approach to ERP implementation. Traditional, large-scale ERP overhauls are being replaced with incremental, scalable upgrades that allow organizations to integrate new features as they emerge.

The US Air Force's failed implementation demonstrates the dangers of attempting to solve all problems simultaneously. The project's scope expanded continuously over eight years, creating an unmanageable level of complexity that ultimately led to its cancellation. In contrast, successful organizations focus on delivering value incrementally while maintaining system stability.

By prioritizing flexibility and scalability, companies can future-proof their ERP investments, avoiding the pitfalls of rigid legacy systems. Cloud-based, modular ERP solutions offer the scalability needed to accommodate business expansion while keeping IT costs manageable.

Leverage AI-Driven Insights for Continuous Optimization

Organizations that incorporate AI-powered analytics into their ERP strategy will gain a significant advantage in data-driven decision-making. AI can analyze historical performance data, detect inefficiencies, and recommend process optimizations in real-time.

However, organizations must approach AI implementation with realistic expectations. Many ERP vendors promise AI capabilities that are still in development or require significant customization to deliver value. The key is to focus on specific, measurable use cases where AI can demonstrate clear business impact rather than pursuing AI for its own sake.

By continuously monitoring key performance indicators and leveraging AI-generated insights, companies can refine their ERP strategy on an ongoing basis, ensuring that technology investments deliver tangible business value.

Prepare for Regulatory and Security Challenges

As ERP platforms evolve, so do regulatory compliance and cybersecurity risks. Organizations must stay ahead of data privacy laws, industry regulations, and security threats to protect sensitive business information.

Implementing robust cybersecurity protocols, blockchain encryption, and AI-driven threat detection will be essential for securing ERP platforms against cyberattacks. Additionally, businesses must ensure regulatory compliance with evolving data protection laws, such as GDPR, CCPA, and industry-specific regulations.

The Future of ERP Is Intelligent, Modular, and Data-Driven

The future of ERP and digital platforms is being shaped by AI-driven automation, composable architectures, cloud-native infrastructure, and advanced data analytics. Organizations that strategically plan for these technological advancements will unlock new efficiencies, enhance decision-making, and drive sustained business growth.

The lessons from major ERP failures serve as crucial guideposts for this journey. The NHS National Programme for IT, Queensland Health payroll disaster, and US Air Force ECSS failure all share common themes: inadequate stakeholder engagement, poor project governance, insufficient change management, and unrealistic expectations about technology's ability to solve organizational problems.

By adopting scalable, AI-powered ERP systems while learning from past failures, companies can stay ahead of industry disruptions, foster digital innovation, and create agile business models that thrive in an increasingly complex digital landscape. Success requires not just technological sophistication, but organizational maturity, disciplined execution, and unwavering focus on delivering business value.

Chapter 20

Ethics and Corporate Responsibility in Digital Transformation

As organizations embark on digital transformation journeys, ethical considerations and corporate responsibility must remain at the forefront. Digital projects, particularly those involving emerging technologies such as artificial intelligence, data analytics, and enterprise resource planning systems, can introduce complex ethical dilemmas. The spectacular failures of major digital transformation initiatives often stem not just from technical or project management shortcomings, but from fundamental ethical lapses and inadequate attention to corporate responsibility.

The collapse of companies like Revlon following ERP implementation disasters demonstrates how technology failures can have far-reaching consequences beyond immediate operational disruptions. When Revlon's SAP implementation faltered, the cosmetics giant faced not only technical challenges but also broader questions about corporate governance, stakeholder responsibility, and the ethical implications of pursuing digital transformation without adequate safeguards.

Ensuring that digital transformation initiatives align with ethical principles and corporate social responsibility commitments is crucial for building trust, maintaining compliance, and fostering sustainable business practices. However, the pressure to modernize systems and remain competitive often leads organizations to make shortcuts that compromise ethical standards and long-term sustainability.

Navigating Ethical Considerations in Digital Projects

Digital transformation initiatives often involve vast amounts of data collection, automation, and decision-making powered by AI. While these advancements offer numerous benefits, they also present ethical challenges that businesses must address proactively. The failure to consider ethical implications early in the transformation process can lead to devastating consequences that extend far beyond technical problems.

One of the primary concerns in digital projects is data privacy and security. Organizations must ensure that customer and employee data are handled responsibly, complying with regulations such as the General Data Protection Regulation (GDPR) and the California Consumer Privacy Act (CCPA). Transparency in data collection, clear consent mechanisms, and robust cybersecurity measures are necessary to prevent data breaches and misuse.

The Queensland Health payroll disaster illustrates the human cost of inadequate data protection and system security. When the system went live with over 2,000 known defects, it exposed sensitive payroll information for over 80,000 employees. Healthcare workers faced financial hardship when they were not paid or were paid incorrectly, with some employees being overpaid by hundreds of millions of dollars collectively. The subsequent effort to recover overpayments created additional ethical dilemmas, as the government attempted to reclaim money from employees who had been victims of the system's failures.

Additionally, AI-driven decision-making raises concerns about bias, fairness, and accountability. AI systems can inadvertently reinforce societal biases present in training data, leading to discriminatory outcomes in areas such as hiring, lending, and law enforcement. Businesses must implement ethical AI frameworks, conduct bias audits, and ensure human oversight in critical AI-powered processes to mitigate these risks.

Ethical AI governance requires companies to regularly test AI models for unintended consequences and retrain algorithms to eliminate bias and discrimination. Transparency in AI development and deployment, including explainable AI models, will help build public trust and regulatory compliance. The challenge becomes more complex when AI systems are integrated into ERP platforms where their decision-making processes may be obscured within larger business workflows.

Accountability in AI Systems

Accountability in AI systems represents another significant ethical concern. When automated systems make decisions, determining responsibility for errors or unintended consequences becomes complex. Organizations must establish clear lines of accountability, ensuring that AI-driven actions can be traced back to human decision-makers.

The US Air Force's failed Expeditionary Combat Support System provides a cautionary tale about accountability in large-scale digital transformation projects. Despite spending over $5 billion and eight years on the project, there was never clear accountability for the program's direction and outcomes. The Senate investigation found that "it was not clear which Accountable Officer had responsibility for the overall governance and successful completion of the whole project."

This lack of accountability created an environment where problems were concealed rather than addressed. Program managers were reluctant to deliver factual status reports that contained negative information, fearing that honest communication would result in project cancellation. This culture of selective truth-telling prevented effective problem-solving and contributed to the project's ultimate failure.

Ethical AI principles advocate for the "human-in-the-loop" approach, where final decisions involving sensitive or high-risk scenarios remain in the hands of trained professionals rather than being fully automated. This approach ensures that human judgment and ethical considerations remain central to critical business processes, even as AI capabilities become more sophisticated.

Corporate Greed and Vendor Responsibility

The issue of corporate greed in digital projects warrants particular attention. Many organizations rush digital implementations to cut costs and increase short-term profits without considering long-term ethical implications. Some ERP vendors and digital service providers push customers into expensive, restrictive contracts that offer little flexibility, undermining the spirit of true digital transformation.

The Queensland Health disaster reveals troubling aspects of vendor behavior during ERP implementations. The official inquiry found that IBM had acted improperly and corruptly in forming and submitting its tender to the government. Key IBM staff had been provided confidential information by government executives relating to the available budget, and the company used its pre-existing system access from other projects to retrieve internal government documents related to the tender. Additionally, IBM staff improperly accessed the proposals of its competitors.

Such behavior raises fundamental questions about the ethics of vendor relationships in digital transformation projects. The inquiry concluded that had the government been aware of these failures, IBM would have been automatically excluded from the procurement process. This case demonstrates how vendor misconduct can compromise not only project outcomes but also the integrity of public procurement processes.

Companies must ensure that vendor relationships are built on ethical partnerships, focusing on value delivery rather than solely on profit maximization. This requires due diligence not only on technical capabilities but also on vendor ethics, transparency, and commitment to customer success.

Transparency and Stakeholder Communication

Transparency in digital transformation represents another crucial ethical consideration. Stakeholders, including employees, customers, and investors, must be informed about the objectives, risks, and impacts of digital projects. Open communication and ethical leadership play a significant role in ensuring that digital transformations are not merely profit-driven but are also aligned with corporate values and societal well-being.

The NHS National Programme for IT failure demonstrates the consequences of inadequate transparency and stakeholder communication. Despite spending over £10 billion on the program, there was insufficient consultation with key stakeholders, particularly healthcare professionals who would be using the systems daily. Doctors and general practitioners expressed concerns early on that the system didn't meet accessibility or use requirements, but their feedback was largely ignored.

The top-down approach to the NHS program reflected a broader ethical failure in stakeholder engagement. Political leaders and senior administrators made decisions about healthcare IT systems without adequate input from the people who would be most affected by those decisions. This lack of transparency and consultation contributed to widespread resistance and ultimately to the program's failure.

Promoting Corporate Responsibility in Digital Transformations

Corporate responsibility extends beyond profit margins—it encompasses social, environmental, and ethical dimensions of business operations. Digital transformation presents an opportunity for organizations to integrate corporate social responsibility principles into their strategies and leverage technology for the greater good.

Environmental Sustainability

Sustainability represents a key aspect of responsible digital transformation. Businesses must consider the environmental impact of technology, including energy consumption, electronic waste, and carbon footprints associated with cloud computing and data centers. The massive computational requirements of modern AI systems and blockchain technologies create significant environmental concerns that organizations must address.

Investing in green computing, optimizing resource usage, and prioritizing sustainable IT infrastructure can help reduce the environmental toll of digital initiatives. AI-powered data centers and blockchain technologies are increasingly adopting energy-efficient models to mitigate their environmental impact. However, organizations must balance performance requirements with environmental responsibility, recognizing that the most powerful systems are often the most energy-intensive.

The environmental considerations become more complex when organizations are migrating from legacy systems to cloud-based platforms. While cloud computing can offer efficiencies through shared resources and optimized data centers, it can also lead to increased overall consumption if not managed carefully. Organizations must conduct thorough environmental impact assessments as part of their digital transformation planning.

Employee Well-being and Job Security

Responsible digital transformations also focus on employee well-being and job security. Automation and AI adoption can displace jobs, creating workforce anxieties that must be addressed through ethical leadership and responsible planning. Organizations must balance efficiency gains with responsible workforce management by reskilling employees, providing career transition programs, and fostering a culture of lifelong learning.

The human impact of digital transformation failures extends far beyond immediate project stakeholders. When Queensland Health's payroll system failed, over 35,000 healthcare workers experienced payroll errors that created significant personal financial stress. Many employees had to take out loans or seek financial assistance to cover basic living expenses while the system problems were resolved. Some healthcare workers left the profession entirely, contributing to staffing shortages that affected patient care quality.

Ethical leadership involves preparing employees for digital changes rather than treating them as casualties of technological disruption. Companies should promote AI-assisted work models that augment human capabilities rather than replace them outright.

This approach recognizes that successful digital transformation requires human expertise and judgment, even as technology capabilities expand.

Ethical Sourcing and Fair Business Practices

Incorporating ethical sourcing and fair business practices into digital transformation strategies represents another way to uphold corporate responsibility. Organizations must evaluate their supply chains, ensuring that digital tools and technologies are developed and deployed under ethical labor conditions. Ethical procurement policies can help avoid partnerships with vendors that engage in exploitative practices or environmental harm.

The global nature of technology supply chains creates complex ethical challenges. Components for digital infrastructure may be manufactured in countries with questionable labor practices, while software development may rely on workers in regions with inadequate labor protections. Organizations pursuing digital transformation must consider these broader ethical implications rather than focusing solely on cost and technical capabilities.

Governance and Compliance Mechanisms

Governance and compliance mechanisms play a pivotal role in enforcing corporate responsibility in digital projects. Establishing independent ethics committees, conducting regular audits, and integrating ethical guidelines into digital policies can help organizations maintain ethical integrity throughout their transformation journey.

AI ethics boards within organizations can oversee the development and deployment of AI solutions, ensuring alignment with societal values and legal standards. These boards should include diverse perspectives, including ethicists, legal experts, and representatives from affected stakeholder groups. The goal is to create governance structures that can identify and address ethical concerns before they become major problems.

However, governance mechanisms are only effective if they have real authority and influence over project decisions. Too often, ethics committees become token gestures that provide the appearance of ethical oversight without actual power to prevent problematic implementations. Organizations must ensure that ethical considerations carry real weight in project planning and execution decisions.

Bridging the Digital Divide

Furthermore, organizations must consider their role in bridging the digital divide. Digital transformation should not exacerbate existing inequalities but rather create inclusive opportunities for all. Investing in digital literacy programs, supporting underserved communities with technology access, and fostering diversity in tech leadership are steps toward a more equitable digital landscape.

Companies that prioritize inclusion and accessibility in digital initiatives can contribute to broader social good while expanding their market reach.

This includes designing systems that work for users with disabilities, providing multilingual support, and ensuring that digital services are accessible to people with varying levels of technological sophistication.

The NHS program failure, while primarily attributed to poor project management and stakeholder engagement, also reflected broader issues of digital equity. The proposed systems were designed primarily for technically sophisticated users, with insufficient consideration for the diverse technological capabilities of healthcare workers. This design bias contributed to user resistance and implementation difficulties.

Autonomous Decision-Making Systems

AI ethics also extend to autonomous decision-making systems, particularly in areas such as healthcare, finance, and law enforcement. The potential for AI to be used in predictive policing, credit risk assessment, and automated medical diagnoses raises profound ethical questions about bias, accountability, and individual rights.

Ethical AI frameworks must ensure that decision-making remains explainable, auditable, and subject to human review to prevent unintended harm and discrimination. This is particularly important when AI systems are integrated into ERP platforms where their decision-making processes may affect multiple business functions simultaneously.

The challenge becomes more complex when AI systems learn and adapt over time, potentially developing decision-making patterns that weren't explicitly programmed. Organizations must develop monitoring systems that can detect when AI behavior drifts from intended ethical guidelines and implement corrective measures quickly.

Long-term Ethical Considerations

As businesses navigate the complexities of digital transformation, ethical considerations and corporate responsibility should not be afterthoughts but foundational pillars. The failure to address ethical concerns early in the transformation process can lead to consequences that extend far beyond immediate project outcomes.

By prioritizing transparency, fairness, sustainability, and inclusivity, organizations can ensure that their digital projects serve not only business objectives but also the broader society. Ethical AI governance, responsible corporate practices, and sustainability initiatives will define the future of digital transformation.

The lessons from major digital transformation failures demonstrate that ethical lapses often compound technical and organizational problems. When organizations pursue digital transformation without adequate attention to ethical considerations, they create risks that can ultimately undermine project success and organizational reputation.

Embracing ethical digital transformation fosters long-term trust, mitigates risks, and positions businesses as responsible corporate citizens in an increasingly digital world. This approach recognizes that sustainable business success depends not only on technological capability but also on maintaining the trust and support of all stakeholders affected by digital transformation initiatives.

Chapter 21

Preparing for the Next Digital Revolution

The rapid acceleration of digital innovation has fundamentally altered the business landscape, and organizations must act now to position themselves for future transformations. Those who remain complacent risk obsolescence, while those who take proactive measures can ensure long-term success. Digital transformation is no longer a one-time initiative but an ongoing process that demands strategic foresight, adaptability, and continuous investment in technology and human capital.

However, the path forward is marked by both tremendous opportunities and sobering lessons from organizations that have failed to navigate digital transformation successfully. The story of Waste Management's failed SAP implementation serves as a cautionary tale about the dangers of pursuing digital transformation without adequate preparation and realistic expectations.

In 2008, Waste Management, North America's largest waste services company, partnered with SAP to implement a comprehensive ERP system. The project was supposed to deliver $100 million in benefits within 18 months while streamlining operations across the company's complex network of facilities and services. Instead, the implementation became a $100 million disaster that ultimately led to a lengthy legal battle between the two companies.

The Waste Management failure illustrates several critical challenges that organizations must address when preparing for digital transformation. SAP had promised that the company could achieve $106 million to $220 million in annual benefits from a consolidated ERP system that could be implemented in 18 months. However, Waste Management quickly discovered significant gaps between what was promised and what was delivered in the software.

The failure wasn't primarily due to technical inadequacies but rather to fundamental misalignment between vendor promises, organizational expectations, and the reality of digital transformation complexity. Waste Management had failed to verify SAP's claims through proper due diligence and proof-of-concept testing before making the executive decision to proceed with the implementation.

The Foundation of Digital Readiness

To prepare for the next digital revolution, businesses must first acknowledge the pivotal role of technology in shaping modern commerce. Investing in cutting-edge IT solutions is no longer optional but a necessity. Cloud computing, artificial intelligence, and big data analytics have become indispensable tools that enhance operational efficiency, customer engagement, and decision-making.

Cloud-based platforms offer scalability and flexibility, allowing businesses to scale operations up or down as needed without the burden of maintaining costly physical infrastructure. However, organizations must understand that cloud migration requires more than simply moving existing systems to new infrastructure. It demands fundamental changes in how applications are designed, data is managed, and security is implemented.

AI-driven automation, on the other hand, optimizes workflows, reduces human error, and enables hyper-personalization in customer interactions. Yet the promise of AI must be balanced against realistic expectations about implementation complexity and organizational readiness. Many organizations pursuing AI initiatives discover that their data quality, process maturity, and organizational culture are inadequate to support sophisticated AI applications.

Big data analytics equips companies with deep insights into consumer behavior, market trends, and internal operations, enabling leaders to make data-driven decisions with a higher probability of success. However, the value of big data depends entirely on an organization's ability to collect, process, and act on insights in a timely manner. Too many organizations collect vast amounts of data without developing the analytical capabilities necessary to extract actionable insights.

Fostering a Culture of Innovation

Beyond technology, businesses must foster a culture of innovation. Innovation is not confined to research and development teams; it must be embedded in the very DNA of an organization. Employees should be encouraged to think creatively, experiment with new ideas, and challenge conventional methods. Cross-functional collaboration, open communication, and reward systems that incentivize innovative thinking can cultivate an environment where new ideas flourish.

The contrast between innovative cultures and those that resist change is evident in the comparison between successful digital transformations and spectacular failures. MillerCoors' failed attempt to consolidate seven legacy systems into one SAP instance in 2014 illustrates what happens when organizations underestimate the cultural dimensions of digital transformation.

MillerCoors attempted to implement a unified system across multiple breweries and distribution centers, but the project encountered significant resistance from employees who were comfortable with existing systems and processes. The company had invested heavily in technical infrastructure but had failed to invest adequately in change management and cultural transformation. The result was a project that faced continuous delays, cost overruns, and user adoption challenges.

This culture of innovation allows businesses to remain adaptable, even in the face of rapid technological disruption. Organizations that successfully navigate digital transformation treat it as an ongoing journey of continuous improvement rather than a one-time project with a defined endpoint.

Cybersecurity as a Foundation for Digital Transformation

Cybersecurity represents another pressing concern that must be addressed as businesses embark on digital transformation journeys. With increased connectivity comes heightened risk. Data breaches, ransomware attacks, and phishing schemes have become more sophisticated, and businesses that fail to prioritize cybersecurity may suffer devastating consequences.

The Mission Produce ERP implementation failure in 2022 demonstrates how cybersecurity concerns can compound other digital transformation challenges. When the company's new supply chain management system went live, there were not only order processing delays and inventory inaccuracies but also concerns about data security vulnerabilities that had not been adequately addressed during implementation.

Protecting sensitive customer data, intellectual property, and proprietary business information should be a top priority. Organizations must implement robust security protocols, conduct regular vulnerability assessments, and educate employees about cyber threats. A single data breach can not only result in financial loss but also erode customer trust—a resource far more difficult to rebuild than any IT infrastructure.

The challenge becomes more complex as organizations adopt cloud-based systems and integrate with external partners and vendors. Each new connection point represents a potential vulnerability that must be secured and monitored. Organizations must develop comprehensive cybersecurity strategies that address not only technical vulnerabilities but also human factors and process gaps that attackers often exploit.

Digital Literacy and Workforce Development

In addition to cybersecurity, businesses must focus on developing digital literacy across their entire workforce. Digital transformation is not just about adopting new technologies; it is about ensuring that employees at all levels understand and effectively use digital tools. Many businesses fall into the trap of investing in state-of-the-art software without properly training their employees on how to utilize it.

The failure of Edinburgh University's Oracle ERP implementation highlights the importance of user-centric design and comprehensive training. The university's system was designed with financial terminology and structures that required specialized knowledge to use effectively. Tasks that should have taken minutes were taking hours, causing frustration and inefficiency among staff. The lack of intuitive design and inadequate training significantly diminished user confidence in the system.

Without proper training, technology remains an untapped resource. Organizations should prioritize continuous learning through training programs, certifications, and hands-on workshops that empower employees to integrate digital tools into their daily workflows. This democratization of digital skills ensures that transformation initiatives do not remain siloed in IT departments but become an organization-wide movement.

The training challenge becomes more complex as technology capabilities expand rapidly. Organizations must develop learning programs that can adapt quickly to new technologies while building foundational skills that remain relevant across different platforms and applications.

Aligning Digital Initiatives with Business Strategy

A crucial element of preparing for future digital revolutions is aligning digital initiatives with overall business strategy. Many organizations make the mistake of viewing digital transformation as a separate initiative rather than an integral part of their long-term strategic vision. Technology should serve as an enabler of business goals, not an isolated project.

The University of Washington's delayed finance platform migration illustrates the importance of strategic alignment in digital transformation projects. Initially planned for 2022 as part of a $340 million five-year transformation project, the rollout was delayed by a year due to inadequate alignment between technical implementation and business process requirements.

Before implementing new digital tools, business leaders must assess how these technologies align with their mission, objectives, and customer needs. Digital transformation should be tied to measurable outcomes such as increased operational efficiency, improved customer satisfaction, or revenue growth. Without this alignment, businesses risk investing in technologies that do not deliver meaningful returns.

This alignment requires ongoing collaboration between business leaders and IT professionals throughout the transformation process. Too many organizations treat digital transformation as an IT project rather than a business initiative, leading to solutions that may be technically sophisticated but fail to address real business needs.

Strategic Foresight: Anticipating Future Change

While businesses must take immediate action to prepare for digital transformation, long-term success requires the application of strategic foresight—the ability to anticipate and prepare for future industry shifts. Strategic foresight goes beyond trend-watching; it involves structured methodologies such as scenario planning, predictive analytics, and continuous environmental scanning to foresee opportunities and risks.

Organizations that integrate strategic foresight into their decision-making process are better positioned to adapt to unforeseen challenges while seizing emerging opportunities. The contrast between proactive and reactive approaches to digital transformation is evident in how different organizations responded to the COVID-19 pandemic.

Companies that had invested in remote work technologies and digital customer engagement platforms before the pandemic were able to transition seamlessly to new operating models. Organizations like Chipotle, which was migrating to Oracle Cloud ERP while simultaneously implementing new curbside pickup services, demonstrated how strategic foresight could enable rapid adaptation to changing market conditions.

Proactive Adaptation

One of the primary benefits of strategic foresight is proactive adaptation. Instead of reacting to disruptions as they occur, organizations that employ foresight are able to anticipate change and develop contingency plans in advance. For instance, companies that recognized the potential of remote work technologies before the COVID-19 pandemic were able to transition seamlessly, while those that had not considered this possibility struggled to adapt.

The same principle applies to emerging technologies such as blockchain, quantum computing, and the metaverse. Businesses that explore these technologies early can gain a competitive advantage, while those that wait for widespread adoption risk falling behind. However, early adoption must be balanced with realistic assessment of technological maturity and organizational readiness.

Organizations must develop frameworks for evaluating emerging technologies based on their potential business impact, implementation complexity, and strategic alignment. This evaluation process should consider not only technical capabilities but also regulatory, ethical, and competitive implications.

Enhanced Agility

Another key advantage of strategic foresight is enhanced agility. The digital age has ushered in an era of constant flux, where customer expectations, regulatory requirements, and technological capabilities change rapidly. Businesses that embrace foresight cultivate agility, allowing them to pivot quickly in response to shifting market dynamics.

Agility is not just about speed; it is about making informed, strategic decisions that align with long-term goals. Organizations that continuously monitor technological advancements, consumer preferences, and competitive landscapes can refine their strategies in real time, ensuring they remain relevant in an evolving market.

FedEx's successful transformation of its finance and supply-chain systems demonstrates the value of strategic agility in digital transformation. The company didn't simply replace legacy systems but reimagined its entire approach to financial management and supply chain operations. By implementing Oracle Cloud ERP and dozens of other Oracle Cloud applications, FedEx created a platform for continuous innovation rather than a static solution.

Sustainable Competitive Advantage

Strategic foresight also contributes to sustainable competitive advantage. The businesses that endure the longest are those that do not simply follow trends but actively shape them. By leveraging foresight, companies can identify unmet customer needs before their competitors do, allowing them to introduce innovative products and services that set them apart.

For example, the most successful tech companies did not merely respond to consumer demands; they anticipated them. Companies like Apple, Amazon, and Tesla have continuously leveraged foresight to redefine industries, from personal computing to e-commerce to electric vehicles. Their success stems from their ability to think beyond the present and invest in long-term technological advancements.

However, sustainable competitive advantage requires more than just technological innovation. Organizations must also develop business models, organizational capabilities, and customer relationships that are difficult for competitors to replicate. This multidimensional approach to competitive advantage ensures that technological investments translate into lasting business value.

Implementing Strategic Foresight

For organizations seeking to integrate strategic foresight into their business model, several practical steps can be taken. First, leadership teams must prioritize long-term vision over short-term gains. Many organizations fall into the trap of focusing solely on quarterly earnings and immediate ROI, neglecting investments that may yield greater returns in the future. Leaders must create a balance between immediate profitability and long-term sustainability.

Second, businesses should establish dedicated foresight teams or advisory groups responsible for monitoring emerging trends and assessing their potential impact. These teams can conduct scenario planning exercises, exploring multiple future possibilities and preparing strategic responses to each. The use of AI-driven predictive analytics can further enhance foresight capabilities by identifying patterns in consumer behavior, economic trends, and technological advancements.

Finally, businesses must cultivate an organizational mindset that values adaptability and continuous learning. Foresight is not a one-time exercise; it is an ongoing process that requires regular reassessment of assumptions and strategies. Companies should encourage employees at all levels to participate in future-focused thinking, whether through internal innovation hubs, knowledge-sharing platforms, or cross-industry collaborations.

The ability to foresee and respond to change should be embedded into the very fabric of the organization. This requires creating incentive systems that reward long-term thinking, developing communication channels that facilitate rapid information sharing, and establishing decision-making processes that can respond quickly to new insights and opportunities.

Learning from Failure: Building Resilience

The next digital revolution will undoubtedly bring new challenges and opportunities that are difficult to predict. Organizations that have learned from past failures and built resilience into their operations will be better positioned to navigate uncertainty and capitalize on emerging possibilities.

The lessons from major ERP failures provide valuable insights into the types of organizational capabilities that will be essential for future success. Whether examining Waste Management's vendor relationship problems, MillerCoors' change management failures, or Edinburgh University's user experience challenges, common themes emerge around the importance of due diligence, stakeholder engagement, and realistic expectation setting.

Organizations preparing for future digital transformations must develop institutional memory that captures lessons learned from both successes and failures. This includes creating knowledge management systems that document decision-making processes, implementation challenges, and solution strategies that can inform future initiatives.

The Future Belongs to the Prepared

As the next digital revolution unfolds, businesses must recognize that digital transformation is not just about technology—it is about strategy, culture, and foresight. Those who invest in advanced technologies, foster a culture of innovation, prioritize cybersecurity, and align digital initiatives with their business goals will be well-equipped for the future.

However, true success lies in the ability to anticipate what comes next. Strategic foresight enables businesses to navigate uncertainties, seize new opportunities, and build a legacy that extends beyond short-term gains. Organizations that combine technological sophistication with strategic thinking, cultural readiness, and operational excellence will be positioned not just to participate in the next digital revolution but to lead it.

The future belongs to organizations that do not merely adapt to change but actively shape it. By embracing digital transformation with a forward-thinking mindset, businesses can position themselves not just to survive, but to thrive, in the next era of technological evolution. Success will require continuous learning, strategic investment, and unwavering commitment to building organizational capabilities that can evolve with changing technological and market conditions.

Chapter 22

Conclusion: Mastering the Digital Jungle

As we reach the conclusion of this journey through the complexities of the digital jungle, one thing becomes evident: digital transformation is no longer an option—it is an imperative for survival and growth in our current interconnected world. The digital landscape, much like a jungle, is teeming with opportunities, yet fraught with challenges. Businesses and organizations must navigate this terrain with strategic foresight, adaptability, and strong leadership to harness the full potential of digital innovation.

The digital revolution has fundamentally altered the way businesses operate, how customers interact with brands, and how leaders make decisions. From cloud computing and artificial intelligence to data analytics and automation, the tools available for digital transformation are vast and ever-evolving. However, success in this landscape is not merely about adopting technology—it is about rethinking business models, embracing cultural change, and leading with vision.

Throughout this exploration, we have witnessed both remarkable successes and spectacular failures that illuminate the path forward. The wreckage of failed digital transformations—from the NHS National Programme for IT's £10 billion disaster to Queensland Health's payroll catastrophe that affected 80,000 healthcare workers—serves as a sobering reminder that technology alone cannot guarantee success. These failures share common threads: inadequate stakeholder engagement, poor change management, unrealistic expectations, and fundamental misunderstanding of the organizational transformation required to support new technologies.

Key Takeaways and Strategic Insights

Throughout this book, we have explored the many facets of digital transformation, dissecting the strategies and leadership principles necessary for success while learning from the cautionary tales of those who have stumbled along the way. Here are the key takeaways and strategic insights that will help organizations thrive in the digital jungle.

Embracing Change with a Clear Vision

Digital transformation begins with a vision that extends far beyond technology implementation. Companies that embark on this journey without a clear purpose often struggle with misaligned initiatives, wasted resources, and employee resistance. The contrast between successful transformations and failures often comes down to the clarity and authenticity of the driving vision.

Cook County's successful completion of a mammoth ERP project that consolidated eight separate systems into one unified platform demonstrates the power of clear vision combined with persistent execution. Despite facing "tremendous skepticism" and a project timeline that extended far beyond initial expectations, Cook County succeeded because leadership maintained a clear vision of improved service delivery and operational efficiency that resonated with employees at all levels.

In contrast, the US Air Force's failed Expeditionary Combat Support System suffered from a constantly shifting vision that expanded in scope and complexity over its eight-year lifespan. What began as a straightforward system consolidation project evolved into an unwieldy effort to solve every operational challenge simultaneously, creating a level of complexity that ultimately proved unmanageable.

A clear vision serves as the North Star, guiding every decision and investment in the transformation process. It ensures that technology adoption aligns with the broader business strategy rather than becoming an isolated IT project. Leaders must communicate this vision effectively, ensuring that every stakeholder understands the 'why' behind digital transformation and how it will impact the organization's future.

Strategic Digital Leadership as a Driving Force

Leadership is the cornerstone of successful digital transformation. The digital jungle is not a place for passive decision-making—it requires bold leadership that embraces change, fosters innovation, and aligns teams toward a shared goal. Leaders must serve as change agents, championing digital initiatives and cultivating a culture that supports technological advancement.

The Queensland Health payroll disaster illustrates what happens when leadership fails to provide adequate oversight and accountability. Despite warning signs and escalating problems, project leadership continued to push forward with implementation rather than addressing fundamental issues. The official inquiry found that program managers were unable to deliver factual status reports that contained negative information, creating an environment where problems were concealed rather than solved.

Successful digital leaders possess a mix of strategic thinking, adaptability, and emotional intelligence. They must navigate resistance to change, bridge the gap between IT and business strategy, and ensure that digital investments drive measurable value. More than ever, leadership must be data-driven, leveraging insights to make informed decisions and anticipate future trends.

The success of companies like Netflix and Amazon in continuously evolving their digital capabilities demonstrates the importance of leadership that treats digital transformation as an ongoing journey rather than a destination. These organizations have built cultures of experimentation and adaptation that enable them to respond quickly to changing market conditions and emerging technologies.

Harnessing Data and Technology for Competitive Advantage

Data is the lifeblood of the digital age. Organizations that effectively leverage data analytics, artificial intelligence, and automation gain a significant competitive advantage. The ability to collect, analyze, and act on real-time data empowers businesses to optimize decision-making, personalize customer experiences, and drive operational efficiencies.

However, harnessing data is not just about technology—it requires a cultural shift. Businesses must cultivate a data-driven mindset where insights guide strategy rather than intuition. This means investing in the right tools, training employees to interpret and act on data, and establishing governance frameworks to ensure data integrity and security.

The challenge of AI implementation in ERP systems reveals the complexity of translating data into actionable insights. While vendors promise embedded AI capabilities and predictive automation, the reality is that most AI implementations require significant customization and organizational readiness to deliver meaningful value. Organizations must approach AI with realistic expectations while building the foundational data quality and analytical capabilities necessary for success.

FedEx's transformation of its finance and supply-chain systems exemplifies successful data-driven transformation. By implementing Oracle Cloud ERP and dozens of other Oracle Cloud applications, FedEx didn't just replace legacy systems but created a platform for continuous innovation powered by real-time data and analytics.

Overcoming Challenges with Resilience and Agility

The digital jungle is unpredictable. Challenges such as integration complexities, cybersecurity threats, regulatory hurdles, and skill gaps can derail transformation efforts if not managed proactively. Resilient organizations anticipate these challenges and develop strategies to mitigate them before they become major roadblocks.

One of the biggest obstacles in digital transformation is resistance to change. Employees often fear job displacement, increased workloads, or unfamiliar technologies. The failure of Edinburgh University's Oracle ERP implementation demonstrates how user resistance can undermine even technically sound systems. The university's new system required specialized knowledge to use effectively, creating frustration and inefficiency that diminished user confidence and adoption.

Overcoming this resistance requires transparent communication, upskilling initiatives, and change management strategies that make employees active participants in the transformation process rather than passive recipients. Organizations must invest in comprehensive training programs that not only teach technical skills but also help employees understand how digital transformation will benefit their work and career development.

Furthermore, flexibility is key. Businesses must adopt an agile approach, iterating on digital initiatives based on real-time feedback and market shifts. Those who rigidly adhere to outdated strategies risk falling behind as competitors rapidly adapt to new trends. The contrast between Hershey's rushed 30-month ERP implementation disaster and organizations that take measured, iterative approaches illustrates the importance of balancing speed with careful planning and execution.

The COVID-19 pandemic provided a real-world test of organizational agility, with companies like Chipotle successfully implementing new curbside pickup services while simultaneously migrating to Oracle Cloud ERP. This dual transformation demonstrated how agile organizations can turn unexpected challenges into opportunities for accelerated digital adoption.

Building a Sustainable Digital Future

Digital transformation is not a one-time project—it is an ongoing journey. Organizations that succeed in the digital age continuously evolve, updating their strategies and technologies to stay ahead of market trends. Sustainable digital success requires a commitment to continuous learning, innovation, and strategic reinvestment in technology.

The story of Cook County's successful ERP transformation, which took nearly a decade to complete, demonstrates that sustainable digital transformation often requires patience and persistence. Rather than attempting a "big bang" implementation, Cook County took an incremental approach that allowed them to learn from each phase and build support for the broader transformation initiative.

Moreover, as businesses integrate digital solutions, they must also prioritize ethical and sustainable practices. The rise of artificial intelligence, big data, and automation brings ethical considerations around data privacy, security, and job displacement. Companies that balance innovation with responsibility build trust with customers, employees, and stakeholders, ensuring long-term viability in the digital landscape.

The environmental impact of digital transformation also requires careful consideration. As organizations adopt cloud computing, AI systems, and blockchain technologies, they must account for increased energy consumption and electronic waste. Sustainable digital transformation involves making conscious choices about technology deployment that balance performance benefits with environmental responsibility.

Thriving in the Digital Age: The Power of Foresight, Flexibility, and Firm Leadership

The digital landscape presents unparalleled opportunities for those who are prepared, strategic, and forward-thinking. Success in this dynamic environment hinges on three fundamental pillars: foresight, flexibility, and firm leadership. These principles, informed by lessons learned from both successes and failures, provide a framework for navigating the complexities of digital transformation.

Foresight: Anticipating Change and Staying Ahead

Foresight is the ability to anticipate industry trends, technological advancements, and shifts in consumer behavior before they become mainstream. Organizations that cultivate foresight are not merely reactive; they proactively shape their strategies to align with future possibilities.

This requires continuous market research, investment in emerging technologies, and a culture that encourages innovation. Businesses that embrace foresight do not wait for disruption—they create it. Companies like Netflix, Amazon, and Tesla have thrived by predicting where their industries were headed and strategically positioning themselves to lead those changes rather than follow them.

The contrast between proactive and reactive approaches is evident in how different organizations handled major technology transitions. Companies that invested in cloud infrastructure and remote work capabilities before they became necessary were able to adapt seamlessly to changing business conditions, while organizations that waited for external pressure to drive change struggled with rapid transformation requirements.

However, foresight must be balanced with realistic assessment of organizational readiness and market timing. The failure of many organizations to successfully implement AI capabilities despite significant investment demonstrates that technological possibility must be matched with practical implementation capability and genuine business need.

Flexibility: Adapting to an Ever-Changing Digital Landscape

Flexibility is the hallmark of resilient organizations. The digital jungle is constantly evolving, and businesses that cling to rigid structures and outdated processes will struggle to compete. Agility is key—companies must be willing to pivot, iterate, and embrace new ways of working as technology reshapes their industries.

An agile organization fosters a culture of experimentation, where failure is viewed as a learning opportunity rather than a setback. Whether through adopting DevOps methodologies, implementing modular technology architectures, or leveraging real-time data for decision-making, flexibility enables businesses to navigate uncertainty with confidence.

The US Air Force's failed ERP implementation demonstrates what happens when organizations lack the flexibility to adapt their approach as circumstances change. Over eight years, the project scope expanded continuously without corresponding adjustments to governance, resources, or expectations. The inability to pivot or scale back when problems emerged ultimately led to the project's cancellation after consuming over $5 billion.

In contrast, successful organizations like Hearst Communications have demonstrated the value of flexibility in digital transformation. With over 360 distinct businesses operating diverse systems, Hearst took a flexible, phased approach to consolidating their finance and HR systems, allowing them to adapt their strategy based on lessons learned from each implementation phase.

Firm Leadership: Guiding Organizations Through Transformation

Digital transformation is as much about leadership as it is about technology. Strong leaders inspire confidence, align teams around a shared vision, and drive execution with precision. They understand that digital success requires more than investments in software—it demands cultural change, cross-functional collaboration, and a relentless focus on delivering value.

Leadership in the digital age also involves making tough decisions—whether it's sunsetting legacy systems, restructuring teams, or shifting business models. Leaders who are firm in their commitment to transformation ensure that digital initiatives do not stall due to internal resistance or short-term obstacles.

The Queensland Health payroll disaster provides a stark example of leadership failure in digital transformation. Despite clear warning signs and escalating problems, project leadership continued to push forward with implementation rather than addressing fundamental issues. The lack of accountability and transparent communication created an environment where problems festered rather than being resolved.

Effective digital leadership requires the courage to make difficult decisions based on accurate information, even when those decisions may be unpopular or politically challenging. Leaders must create environments where problems can be identified and addressed quickly rather than concealed or ignored.

Lessons from Failure: Building Institutional Wisdom

The numerous failures we have examined throughout this book provide invaluable insights into the common pitfalls that organizations must avoid. Whether examining the NHS National Programme for IT, Queensland Health's payroll disaster, the US Air Force's failed ERP implementation, or

Hershey's Halloween crisis, common themes emerge that transcend specific technologies or industries.

First, successful digital transformation requires genuine stakeholder engagement from the beginning of the process. Top-down mandates without adequate consultation and buy-in from affected users consistently lead to resistance and failure. Organizations must invest time and resources in understanding user needs, addressing concerns, and building support for change.

Second, realistic expectation setting is crucial for maintaining project credibility and momentum. Vendor promises and executive enthusiasm must be balanced with honest assessment of implementation complexity, organizational readiness, and potential risks. Organizations that underestimate the challenges of digital transformation often find themselves struggling with scope creep, budget overruns, and timeline delays that undermine stakeholder confidence.

Third, change management is not optional—it is essential for success. Technical implementation must be accompanied by comprehensive programs to prepare employees for new ways of working, provide adequate training, and address resistance to change. The human dimensions of digital transformation are often more challenging than the technical aspects and require dedicated attention and resources.

Fourth, governance and accountability structures must be clearly defined and consistently enforced. Successful digital transformations require clear decision-making authority, transparent communication channels, and mechanisms for identifying and